Stepping Stones to Achieving your Doctorate

Focusing on your Viva from the Start

Vernon Trafford and Shosh Leshem

Open University Press

Open University Press
McGraw-Hill Education
McGraw-Hill House
Shoppenhangers Road
Maidenhead
Berkshire
England
SL6 2QL

email: enquiries@openup.co.uk
world wide web: www.openup.co.uk

and Two Penn Plaza, New York, NY 10121-2289, USA

First published 2008

Copyright © The authors 2008

A catalogue record of this book is available from the British Library

ISBN-13: 978 0 335 22543 9 (pb)   978 0 335 22542 2 (hb)
ISBN-10: 0 335 22543 6 (pb)   0 335 22542 X (hb)

Library of Congress Cataloguing-in-Publication Data
CIP data applied for

Typeset by RefineCatch Limited, Bungay, Suffolk
Printed and bound by CPI Group (UK) Ltd., Croydon, CR0 4YY

Fictitious names of companies, products, people, characters and/or
data that may be used herein (in case studies or in examples) are not
intended to represent any real individual, company, product or event.

The **McGraw·Hill** Companies

Our book is dedicated to
Fran, Eira, Ansal and Nina
and
Menahem, Elad, Yair and Michal

Contents

List of examples

List of figures

List of tables

List of tasks

Acknowledgements

We have been fortunate in supervising and working with doctoral candidates who have asked questions, shared their difficulties with us and spoken of their experiences. Similarly, supervisors from different countries have explained their respective practices and talked about the ups and downs that they have encountered with their candidates. Then, there are the examiners who have explained their approach(es) to examining. Finally, our international professional colleagues have generously shared their knowledge and experience freely with us. All these discussions have provided us with rich first-hand insights on the doctoral process.

Initially, these comments opened up our understanding of the topic, but, more recently, they confirmed what our research has shown. In this way, they were authenticating our conclusions about the nature of doctorateness and the doctoral viva. Thus, we can view our investigations over the past decade as either a form of action research or insider-based practitioner enquiry.

We have also been fortunate in presenting our ideas at international conferences and one-off workshops through this decade. Participating in such events as the Association of Teaching English as a Foreign Language, the European Association for Learning and Instruction, the European Conference on Educational Research, the Institute of Reflective Practice, the National Postgraduate Committee (UK) and UK Grad has been an important proving ground for our ideas. We have taken heart from these discussions especially through their relevance for candidates, supervisors and examiners too! Our presentations at these events have confirmed just how generic the nature of doctorateness is across disciplines and between countries.

Among the many people who deserve especial mention are Emeritus Professor Peter Woolliams and Emeritus Professor Graham Badley.

Peter has always managed to challenge our thinking from quite surprising perspectives and this has always raised our levels of thinking. Just when we thought that we had understood some new concept or idea, Peter has always suggested another perspective that fits our needs perfectly.

Graham has challenged how our ideas were being presented through the written word. As a result, we have become 'textually critical' of our writing. This has been a refreshing experience. Pointing out the obvious is not always an easy thing to do, but Graham does this elegantly and for that his guidance has been so valuable.

We are grateful to Faber and Faber for permission to use extracts from the works of T.S. Eliot on pages 12 and 229 of this book.

Finally, we extend sincere thanks to Melanie Havelock, our editor at the Open University Press McGraw-Hill, who believed in our book from the start.

We hope that this book justifies the help that you have all given to us. Thank you everyone.

1

Introduction

Welcome to our book.

Before we explain why we wrote the book and what it contains, we would like you to consider the following:

> Assume that you are reading a doctoral thesis that explores a topic in your field of interest.
>
> Initially, you may wonder why the author chose the topic, what it was seeking to discover or prove and its presumed importance to other research in related fields of knowledge. As you read further into the thesis, you would certainly want to know why the research had been designed and conducted in a particular way.
>
> Finally, when you reached the conclusions, you would want to understand how the evidence enabled the author to relate them to the research of others. Here, you would look for arguments that provided coherence to the research and allowed you to accept it as a contribution to the particular field of study.
>
> In passing, you would inevitably note how the thesis had been presented and the appropriateness of the language that was used.

No doubt, you recognised the various implied questions in this text. As readers of research proposals, doctoral theses and master's dissertations, we too have often had similar thoughts. However, these questions have also arisen as we read other forms of research such as research articles and reports. We expect that you have had the same experience during your own reading of research.

As a result, it seems that these questions apply to any piece of research but especially those undertaken in the social sciences. Thus, these questions can be viewed as being generic; they represent critical aspects of research that readers expect authors to address and to answer for their benefit – as readers.

If authors appreciated these expectations and addressed them when they wrote up their research, then they would be meeting the needs of their readers.

As a result, their readers would appreciate exactly what authors had intended their research to achieve. But isn't this what happens when examiners recognise that a doctoral thesis is worthy of a clear pass with no alterations?

Reasons for writing the book

We have certainly benefited in recent years from reading the accumulating number of books and articles on the doctoral process. In their respective ways, they have shed light on processes, procedures, techniques and approaches that have illuminated the roles of candidates undertaking doctoral study, plus their supervisors and examiners. This corpus of literature provides a most helpful foundation of advice and challenge for those who are involved with the doctoral process.

In our respective roles as supervisors and examiners, we are aware of the difficulties that candidates encounter undertaking their doctorate. We have also seen the independent and consolidated joint reports that examiners make on theses. If a thesis gains a pass with no alterations, it is usual for the examiners to offer some words that commend the strengths in that work.

If, however, a thesis is judged not to be worthy of a pass, the problems that have to be rectified are ones that examiners regularly identify as requiring further attention. These problems represent weaknesses in the theses that examiners read and assess. As researchers, we were intrigued why more supervisors and their candidates have not recognised these sources of primary data on the doctoral process. These data are first-hand documentary evidence of good and bad practice in doctoral research as judged by examiners.

This set of circumstances made us curious. We realised that if it was possible to identify the criteria against which theses were evaluated through the questions that examiners asked and the dynamics that occurred in vivas, then these insights could guide candidates throughout the doctoral journey to their viva. This realisation totally changed how we saw our roles as supervisors and examiners.

We have used this perspective on doctoral study as the single theme in this book – just as it has been in our research and workshops over recent years. As you read our book, you will meet occasional references to other chapters. This process of reading is no different from the iterative and parallel processes that we all follow in our own research. We hope that you will find these occasional cross-references helpful to your reading rather than intrusive.

Depending on local regulations at the university that holds them, examiner reports may be viewed as confidential to those taking part in each viva. Many universities annotate these reports and produce anonomised items for consideration by their respective research degree committees, or their equivalent. These items contain aggregate data that show trends, clusters, correlations and critical incidents occurring in doctoral vivas. For researchers – such as supervisors, candidates and ourselves – this evidence explains how scholarly judgements have been reached to determine the outcome of each doctoral viva. Its potential to assist supervisors and candidates alike to produce 'good-quality doctoral theses' is enormous!

We have drawn on these data to explain what examiners expect from two perspectives. First, the reports contain detailed observations on the strengths and weaknesses of theses. These can be analysed to provide a template of criteria that examiners tend to use as they assess theses. Second, we have extrapolated from those analyses to identify the characteristics of doctoral study that candidates can/might/should include in their thesis. If candidates incorporate these characteristics in the text of their doctoral thesis, then they are more likely to meet the expectations of examiners than if they do not.

Thus, our book has been written with the specific intention of improving candidates' capabilities to undertake doctoral research and present theses that are more closely aligned with these expectations. The title for the book reflects this approach to understanding the doctoral process. Starting from the assumption that everyone who registers for a doctorate intends to complete it successfully, the first part of the title suggests that there are sequential stages that you can follow in that quest. The stages are dealt with, cumulatively, in the following chapters.

The distinctive feature of our approach follows in the second part of the title. We suggest that the key to achieving your doctorate is to appreciate that the evidence from how examiners examine doctoral theses represents your starting point. If you understand the criteria that examiners use and the type of questions they ask in doctoral vivas, then you have a template against which your thesis will be judged. But this perspective also provides you with a template against which to compare your work as you progress through your doctoral journey to your viva. Thus, the title of this book combines your doctoral aspirations with the cumulative outcomes of our research.

Purposes of the book

Our book focuses specifically on how doctoral candidates can raise levels of thinking about their topic, their research process and their contribution(s) to knowledge. In particular, our argument aligns itself with what examiners expect to see in *doctorally worthy* theses and which they then explore during the viva. These expectations contain a high degree of generic features that transcend disciplines and this is the foundation of our text.

The text includes extensive references, extracts from theses, examiner reports and cameo accounts of doctoral *experiences*. Its appeal will be in exposing the obvious, which is so often obscured in descriptive accounts of *doing a doctorate.* To help you appreciate these features, we have provided visual models that capture relationships and items of significance. We explain each model so that its significance is easily apparent for you to apply and use.

In particular, our book will emphasise the nature of conceptualisation sought by examiners within theses. The practicality of the book is how it identifies what candidates need to address in order to demonstrate doctorateness. We argue that candidates should *start to prepare for their viva* as they plan, undertake and write up their research. In this way, their text will address those essential characteristics of doctorateness that examiners look for in a *good thesis.*

We provide examples of how candidates, and their supervisors, can audit the draft thesis using a template that has been designed to reflect the profile of examiners' questions. Thus, our book is not about *how to do research* or *how to write a thesis,* rather, it shows how candidates can display doctorateness within their thesis and so convince examiners of its merit before their viva.

Terms used in the book

We have chosen to use the word 'candidate' when we refer to those who are undertaking doctoral study. Our reason for this is because they are seeking an award that is quite unique in the educational process. Unlike school attendance, there is no legal obligation on them to register for a doctorate. The quality of the degree is examined against universal criteria and no marks are given for their work. They are not in competition with others since each doctorate is awarded only to an individual candidate. Finally, the doctoral degree involves every candidate making a contribution to knowledge as the primary outcome from their research.

Doctorates are very personal qualifications. You will have noticed how candidates say *I am half-way through my doctorate* or *I gained my doctorate at . . .* This sense of ownership follows from candidates choosing the topic, doing the research and defending their thesis in a viva. These conditions become even more personal when you receive the award and the title doctor from the university. For any doctoral candidate or doctoral graduand the award is 'theirs'. Thus, the term 'candidate' correctly describes the status of a person who seeks membership with those to whom a university has already granted the title of doctor.

The word 'thesis' is used when we refer to the text that candidates produce as an account of their research. Drawing on the Greek notion of 'believing in', a thesis represents a piece of work in which its author has belief. Their belief would relate to its presumed merit and wider relevance. This view is consistent with the notion of candidates defending their thesis in their viva. The defence therefore represents the candidate explaining and justifying to their examiners their belief in and rationale for their research.

We recognise that sometimes the terms thesis and dissertation are used interchangeably. However, since the meaning of dissertation does not have the scholarly resonance of the Greek meaning of thesis, we have not used it. You will see how these two words capture and reflect significant aspects of 'doing a doctorate' in the chapters that follow.

We have used the word university to signify the awarding institution for your doctorate. In this way, it includes non-university higher education institutions that do not themselves possess degree-awarding powers but enjoy delegated powers from a legal and formal association with a university. It also embraces those few professional bodies whose charters entitle them to award degrees of equal standing to those of a university.

Readership for the book

We have written this book specifically for doctoral candidates. You are our primary readers. You may be just starting your doctoral journey, well down the road to completion or in the final stage of completion. Wherever you are on this continuum, we know that you will find the book helpful as it presents contemporary evidence from the doctoral process. Throughout the text, we address you as the reader quite deliberately to emphasise specific points of argument or concern. Since we, too, have been doctoral candidates we can identify with the concerns that you will be experiencing at this time. Thus, we have tried to make our text accessible and relevant, through examples of practice and questions for you to think about.

Whether you are registered for a PhD or a professional doctorate you will be required to produce a thesis or a portfolio of scholarly materials. If you have to produce a portfolio then its content must be collectively equivalent to the traditional doctoral thesis in academic standards and word count. In both degrees, your thesis would have to display the generic features of doctoral research and scholarship that are outlined in this book.

You might be undertaking your doctorate by published works. In your case, although your thesis will contain substantially fewer words than other types of doctorate, it will still be expected to demonstrate comparable scholarship. For these reasons, the arguments that we advance in this book will assist you to prepare the synthesis of your collected published works and draft a doctoral thesis for defence in your viva.

Supervisors will also find this book helpful. If you are just starting to supervise, then the book will provide you with an array of insights on the doctoral process that should be useful to you and your candidates. If you are an experienced supervisor, we hope that you will find reinforcement of your existing practice(s) from the ideas that are presented. You may also encounter new insights on the doctoral process that can be adapted to your circumstances and for your candidates.

If you are (also) an examiner, then we expect that you are already familiar with some of the approaches that we present here. If you are a new examiner, however, we hope that the frameworks and concepts will provide ideas that can guide your approach to this important scholarly role.

You may be a trainer or developer of doctoral candidates or doctoral supervisors. For you, the chapters should provide rich ideas to explore with participants on your workshops and programmes. Our examples portray activities that occur in the doctoral viva. They also illustrate starting points for discussing the roles of candidates and supervisors, plus examiners, in the doctoral process.

Our experience of teaching and examining at the master's level suggests that this book will also be helpful to students and their supervisors. Master's-level work requires students to understand the processes of research and, normally, to exhibit this within their dissertation. In these respects, Chapters 4 to 10 in particular will have direct applicability for master's students and their supervisors. Although their dissertations will be shorter in length than a doctoral thesis, nonetheless it will need to show that they are familiar with and can apply the essential features of serious research.

Finally, we believe that our book has relevance to doctoral candidates in countries other than the United Kingdom. Our evidence for this view can be found not in their respective educational regulations but in the doctoral process itself. All doctorates are expected to demonstrate clearly written high levels of scholarly research that can make a recognised contribution to knowledge. The criteria that indicate this position are essentially the same in those systems that either use oral examinations of candidates (the viva) or use panels of experts to evaluate the submitted thesis independently of candidates. The finer administrative details of examination systems may differ between country systems, but their respective essential scholarly critical determinants of quality are similar. Our book addresses those determinants of doctoral scholarship.

What the book does not do

We want to explain what you will not find in our book and why these things are not included. This information will prevent you from being disappointed at not finding things that we did not intend to write about anyway!

The focus of our book is on the nature of the doctoral process that examiners expect candidates to display in their thesis. Thus, discussions of the following items are outside our boundary of intent for this book:

- **research methodology or techniques/methods.** Many admirable books already exist on these topics and we do not wish to add to that literature. However, questions will be posed in the following chapters regarding how you have introduced, justified and explained these aspects of the research process in your thesis.
- **specific details of local regulations, customs, traditions and practices regarding the entire doctoral process.** It is your responsibility as a doctoral candidate to be familiar with your university's administrative and procedural framework in which your doctorate is registered and where your thesis will be examined. We have not provided detailed examples of such regulations since they are essentially similar and one example hardly captures the minor variations between university institutional frameworks for doctoral studies. However, the significance of these arrangements is dealt with when it impinges directly on your doctoral study.

Sources of our evidence

We have been fortunate that our respective academic roles have enabled us to witness all aspects of the doctoral process. For 6 years we have collaborated in the design and conduct of workshops for doctoral candidates at different stages of their registration. Doctoral candidates from at least 30 disciplines, in different universities and from over 50 countries have attended these events. This exposure to questions and feedback has been invaluable in providing us with cross-disciplinary understandings of doctoral processes. It has confirmed that the critical components of doctoral processes are generic. Candidates, supervisors or examiners have not challenged our conclusion. This is despite technical variations in how respective examination processes or supervisory systems operate in different countries.

We have also been able to attend, at the time of going to press, over 100 doctoral vivas in different universities. These opportunities have been afforded by being either a candidate, examiner, supervisor in attendance or Chair of the viva. As persons with a particular research interest, this has been a privilege since it has allowed us to observe or participate in processes that would otherwise be denied to external researchers.

Each of these viva experiences is a one-off event, unrepeatable and unique to the dynamics created by those who were present. However, noting the questions that examiners asked shows that patterns do appear in the style and nature of those questions. Candidates and supervisors can learn from these patterns.

Conversations with examiners, candidates, supervisors and Chairs both before and following vivas have provided real-time commentaries on what transpired. These data may suffer from overlays of instant excitement or emotion.

Nonetheless, in most cases they are deep in meaning and significance for candidates and supervisors alike. Examiners, though, tend to offer more detached observations on the dynamics and processes of their viva than candidates or supervisors. Both sets of comments represent insider accounts of the doctoral viva. Cumulatively, they have demystified that process for us – and for those with whom we have collaborated and worked.

We have had access to two sources of documentary evidence. First, draft text and completed theses have allowed us to observe how candidates tackle the task of assembling and writing theses. Correspondence, conversations and discussion groups have combined to create case examples of difficulties, coping strategies and good practices. Second, initial and joint reports show the care and attention that examiners give to assessing the merit of submitted theses. Analysing the language that examiners use and the issues they identify indicates how they perceive and evaluate scholarship. In turn, this indicates the type of criteria that candidates and supervisors can usefully act on.

Supervising and examining over the years has its own regular harvest of experiences. This must be the most challenging and rewarding part of the doctoral process. It has given us the opportunity to witness the ups and the downs that occur; the blockages that suddenly appear; the importance of the apparently trivial protocol or administrative regulation plus the joy of scholarly discovery and personal growth.

Over 1200 candidates and 400 supervisors have participated in workshops and international conferences where our research evidence has been presented and discussed. With over 40 doctoral completions and as many examinerships, this body of 'fieldwork' constitutes a very substantial source of evidence on how examiners assess doctoral theses.

Structure of the book

Reading a thesis and writing a thesis share a common feature of asking questions and looking for the answers. We have adopted a similar approach in how we structured the 12 chapters in this book.

We start the book with Chapter 2, *The end is where we start from*. Here the case is made for candidates to devote serious attention to how their thesis will be examined. The types of question asked by examiners form an agenda of items to be addressed and met by doctoral candidates, first, in their writing and, second, in their viva.

We define and explain the notion of doctorateness in Chapter 3, *What is doctorateness?* This question is answered through evidence that is grounded in examiner questions. The associated concepts and implications of this notion are central to the arguments in the remainder of our book.

We then look at how candidates can view their thesis if they produce an overview of its structure and how it fits together. Our term for this is 'an architecture' and Chapter 4, *Architecture of the doctoral thesis*, is devoted to this topic. We show how this tool helps candidates and supervisors to track progress and modify writing plans.

In Chapter 5, *Exploiting the literature*, we explain ways to engage with the literature and so enhance your text. This approach avoids the mechanical and formulaic 'literature review' in favour of developing theoretical perspectives to show conceptual grasp of the research topic.

The driving force in doctoral work is explored in Chapter 6, *Thinking about research design*. The connections between the components of research are dissected and attention is given to the specific research decisions that candidates have to make. Examiners commend positive features of theoretical understanding and writing.

The choice of words determines how ideas and arguments are presented in theses. Chapter 7, *What's in a word?* illustrates how expressions and vague words cannot build tight or defensible arguments. Using the correct nomenclature of research adds value to theses. Attending to this aspect of the thesis ensures clarity of meaning in communicating ideas to readers – and especially to the examiners.

Emphasis is given to explaining that conceptualisation rather than description is the critical element in drawing conclusions. In Chapter 8, *How to conclude a thesis in one chapter*, distinctions are made between the relative importance of the components that make up this chapter in doctoral theses.

The smallest piece of academic text in a thesis receives full attention in Chapter 9, *The abstract*. This chapter explains what this single page is usually expected to contain – technically, structurally and academically.

It is an obligation on all doctoral candidates to demonstrate that they understand the process of research. In Chapter 10, *The magic circle: putting it all together*, visual models illustrate how interconnectedness between the components of research can be displayed and used by candidates to self-audit their thesis before it is submitted.

In Chapter 11, *Preparing for the viva*, we argue that this is a process which should commence at registration, rather than being left to when the thesis has been submitted. Examples are provided to show how this preparatory process can be woven into the overall doctoral experience.

The rite of passage is confronted in Chapter 12, *The dynamics of the doctoral viva*. The minutiae of what occurs are not described because this chapter focuses on how candidates can become involved themselves in the viva process rather than becoming unwilling victims of that process. Cases of pathos, humour and amusement illustrate the other side of the viva and highlight the developmental roles of examiners.

What can now be asked in your viva that you have not already addressed and answered in your thesis? In the Epilogue, *Arriving back where we started*, we argue that candidates who have followed the arguments of the previous chapters should be able to view their doctoral journey as answering the scholarly questions they had when they started.

A final comment

Together these chapters will present you with a meta-level appreciation of thinking about the process of doctoral research. None of them is concerned with the *how* or the *what* of research. Instead, they focus on the *why* of research. This gives the chapters and this book an emphasis that is different from that of other texts concerned with doctoral study. Our intention is to make you – the reader – think about doctoral research at a conceptual level. This is because conceptualisation is the feature that determines the outcome of vivas.

This book offers a grounding in thinking conceptually about doctoral research. Doing that will strengthen the work of candidates and supervisors as they discuss research design, undertake fieldwork and write up the research. In turn, this will provide a foundation from which candidates can defend their thesis at their viva.

2

The end is where we start from

This chapter will:

- present our approaches to understanding doctoral study;
- explain what examiners look for when they read a thesis;
- identify the key features of doctoral research;
- show how research plans can be informed by the questions in doctoral vivas.

Introduction

We present a pinch of poetry to illustrate how ends and beginnings are closely related. From here we argue that recognising the two stages which examiners use to assess the merits of a thesis shows that the outcomes of a viva are essentially determined by the quality of the written thesis. The implications of this view are explored to identify the practical opportunities for you as your thesis is produced.

We explain how examiners use certain identifiable features to judge the merits of theses. Since these features are critical factors for examiners, their importance should also be recognised and used, by you and your supervisor(s) throughout your doctoral journey. Examples of how examiners assessed two theses plus the transcripts of questions asked in the subsequent vivas illustrate our approach to explaining the doctoral examination process. We show how examiners' questions can be categorised and used by you to plan, compile, write and so help you to achieve your doctorate.

Visualising the doctoral journey

T.S. Eliot was not necessarily thinking about doctoral study when he wrote these lines:

> *What we call the beginning is often the end*
> *And to make an end is to make a beginning.*
> *The end is where we start from.*
> (Eliot, 1974: 208)

Nonetheless, his words contain practical advice on how you might think about undertaking your doctoral study. Think for a moment about your assumptions regarding the end of your research quest. These may well have changed over the time of your research. They will have developed and been modified as you revised your thoughts about the research and your intentions for it. Each end of 'something' will have been the opportunity for you to start a new beginning. This is apparent in the way that completed research can lead into something else for you. Assume that 'the end' are the various criteria used by examiners to judge the merit of the thesis as they read it and create their agenda of questions to ask in the viva. Examiners use those two sets of evidence to decide on the outcome of the viva. In turn, this determines the level of award that they will recommend to your university.

So knowing what these criteria are and the type of questions that will be asked in your doctoral viva provides a practical framework from which to approach and undertake your doctoral research. It also provides a practical template in which to write, present and submit your doctoral research. Knowing about 'the end' is therefore the starting point for your doctoral research. The examination of the thesis should be seen as the end of the doctoral journey. If examiners judge the thesis to be worthy of a doctoral award then what follows is the beginning of another journey. If, however, the thesis requires further attention, revision or submission, then the original journey remains unfinished.

Making the research destination (*the end*) explicit should be the starting point and guide to the subsequent planning and execution (*beginning*) for your doctoral research. In this sense, Eliot's words offer a way for you to visualise your doctoral journey. The words allow us to identify many important relationships between ends and beginnings through:

- clarifying the scholarly purpose of research to show the final destination of the research;
- using judgements of merit for a thesis as criteria of quality throughout the research itself;
- converting measures of quality about 'the end of the research' into explicit

standards of scholarship and presentation that should be displayed in the research;
• auditing progress towards achieving a successful examination of the thesis right from the beginning of the research.

These connections between beginnings and ends lead us to consider how they appear in the examination process itself.

Your examiners are responsible to your university for judging the merit of your thesis. In most universities, they are required to provide an independent report on your thesis some while in advance of the viva. This preliminary report represents the first assessment of your thesis. Examiners will read your text more than once. Pearce (2005: 47–64) explains that this process involves examiners in noting its key points, checking how research questions are used, evaluating the appropriateness of its research assumptions, approach and design plus assessing the claims for originality and knowledge of the field. In addition, they consider how the thesis is presented and how it complies with university regulations for layout, referencing, etc. Only when they have addressed these issues will examiners form an independent judgement on its academic quality and draft their respective initial reports.

The importance of this first reading is emphasised by Tinkler and Jackson (2004: 30) who show that in 74% of cases: 'The viva merely served to confirm the examiner's opinion of the candidate.' Similar findings by Denicolo (2003) suggest that: 'The degree of influence of the viva upon the final outcome is variable' and 'In marginal cases, performance in the viva can be critical.' Received wisdom among supervisors and examiners suggest that in practice the correlation between examiner's judgements before and after the viva maybe closer to 90% – or even higher. Tinkler and Jackson (2004: 123) suggest that the initial report: 'serves to present and justify their preliminary judgement of the thesis. It also identifies points for discussion in the viva – these form the basis for the agenda.'

Pearce (2005: 65) confirms these views by arguing that when the examiners meet before the viva these reports enable them to: 'discover whether or not their preliminary recommendations concur and hence determine the function of the viva'. She then points out that examiners use their reports to: 'confirm an impression or to determine an outcome'. What happens next is that examiners agree upon their: 'key opinions, concerns and differences before then arriving at what they expect the post-viva result to be' (Pearce, 2005: 67). Depending on the administrative regulations of each university, the anticipated outcomes from the doctoral viva may range from 'pass with no alterations', 'pass subject to minor alterations', 'pass subject to major alterations' or 'fail'.

These views show that before your viva, examiners will already have a considered view as to the merit of your thesis. This shows that a candidate's defence of their thesis in the viva is more likely to confirm the initial view of examiners than to change their opinion. Thus, it is critically important for you to ensure that the writing and presentation of your thesis explicitly addresses and meets the scholarly expectations of examiners. This conclusion presents a fundamental issue for you to consider as you write your thesis. You may think that this is not easy if you do not know who your examiners will be. Furthermore, the renowned individuality of examiners may suggest that trying to predict their respective approach to their task would be unproductive!

However, using evidence that now exists on this topic you may be able to map and explain the approach that examiners adopt towards their task. As a result, you can anticipate the implications of examiners' attitudes and action within the doctoral viva and thus incorporate them into how you write your doctoral thesis. In this context we concur totally with Murray's observation that: 'It could be argued that it is never too early to start thinking about your viva' (Murray, 2003: 45). Thus, you will have used the end (*judgements on the merit of a thesis*) as a guide from the start of your doctoral journey (*how you undertake your research and present your research*). This approach to 'doing your doctorate' is explained throughout our book.

What is your research all about?

During your doctoral journey you will certainly be asked the question: *What is your research about?* Your reply would, no doubt, be influenced by who asked that question. You might also think about why they asked the question in the first place. Different answers could well be given to a family member, a friend, an acquaintance, a fellow doctoral candidate, a tutor, a supervisor or an examiner. A simple reply might be to provide the current title of your research. That is a fairly safe response and it allows for further questions if anyone wants to know more about your research.

However, consider what lies behind this question. If it were asked by examiners in your viva, then they could be posing a quite different, and implicit, question: *What is this thesis all about?* This goes beyond seeking the more obvious meanings within the title for your research. This second question focuses instead on the conceptual imperative of the thesis. To provide a satisfactory response you would now require a more considered, and intellectually deeper, reply.

The answer that you should give in your viva would draw on the discussions between you and your supervisor(s). One issue would certainly have received constant attention in these exchanges of views: what concepts are associated with the topic of your research. This would move your thinking beyond explaining your topic simply as: *My research is into the nature of heavy-traffic flow at night on arterial roads in rural Norfolk.* These words state what your research would address on a descriptive level.

However, in the viva, examiners would expect more than this. They would want to hear how the topic fitted into the wider world of scholarship in this field of study. They might also like to hear you explain why you believe that your research is distinctive. They could even anticipate an outline of the contribution to knowledge that you believe would follow from your research. In each of these possible replies, your answer would need to be more abstract than descriptive. Your explanation of the research could be rephrased as: *The effectiveness of time scheduling strategies used by long-distance business transport firms.* This statement now emphasises 'effectiveness' (cost reduction due to journey times at night), 'scheduling strategies' (policy of preferring arterial routes) and 'long-distance business transport firms' (owners of heavy vehicles) to signify the essential components of the research. Although both statements relate to the same general issue, they project different emphases to those who ask the question.

You might, though, prefer to have a mental vision of your research. This type of model is helpful in combining the essential factors of your doctoral research. Holding this in your mind will provide you with an easy way to work through its components – appropriate, of course, to who is asking you the question! Figure 2.1 shows a generic model of how you might see the essential components of your research. You can use it as a frame on which to add as many or as few words as you feel are appropriate for your audience.

Obviously, you would need to modify how you responded in order to reflect where you had reached in your doctoral journey. At the start of your doctoral studies, you might only be able to describe how you are clarifying your gap in

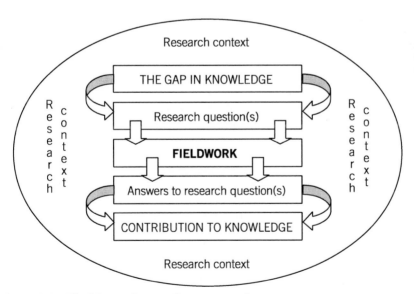

Figure 2.1   The bigger picture of your research.

Source: Leshem and Trafford, 2007

knowledge. Later on, you could describe more fully how you had reached that particular point in your studies. Towards the end, you might describe the whole journey and even the contribution to knowledge that you expected to make. The model offers you considerable versatility in how you use it for this purpose. Once you have submitted your thesis, then the model provides you with a shorthand way of explaining your entire doctoral journey.

The model provides a 'simplified bigger picture' overview of your entire research process. It locates your research as being surrounded by your research context. From that context you would identify a gap in knowledge. This would enable you to devise research questions that incorporate ideas that you draw from your reading and theoretical perspectives on your research topic. These questions would provide you with an explicit set of issues for which you seek answers. The data you plan to collect during your fieldwork would provide you with answers to your research questions. As a result, you would expect to advance your claim of making a modest contribution to knowledge.

The model may appear to be naively simple due to the implied causality between each of the stages. We know that research may not always be as smooth as that. You may have difficulties with either your research planning or its execution somewhere along that route. Nonetheless, allowing for problems in data collection or some type of minor technical difficulties, the sequence of stages in the model will still hold true for you – just as it did for us when we tackled our own doctorates.

Most researchers encounter some problems during their research – even if they choose not to admit it. Your account of such difficulties would acknowledge changes in the context of your specific research environment. You would need to explain this in detail within your thesis. By including such explanations in your text, you are telling your readers about the reality of doing research. This brings the experience itself alive and shows that you too have experienced the 'ups and downs' of undertaking serious and complex research. In particular, you would need to show how successful you were in minimising, or even avoiding, jeopardising your research strategy. Thus, the model constitutes a practical overview of research to be used as you start to visualise your research.

When examiners examine a thesis they are concerned to understand how you 'see' your research topic. This concern would be in their mind as they read the thesis, as well as later when they conduct the viva with you. This concern is irrespective of the various differences in doctoral topic, discipline, focus, research approach and other differences between theses. In their scrutiny of doctoral theses examiners look for one or possible two of the following scholarly features:

- application of conventional research instruments in new fields of investigation;
- combining disparate concepts in new ways to investigate a conventional issue;

- creating new understandings of existing issues;
- design and application of new field instruments in a contemporary setting;
- extending the work of others through a replication of their original methodology;
- identification of new and emerging issues worthy of investigation and explanation;
- originality in using the work of others.

Each feature represents a discrete characteristic of doctoral research. The features are also almost mutually exclusive. The 'almost' acknowledges the common issue of rigour and analysis that are always expected of doctoral research. You will, of course, recognize that each of the features would be testing theory, developing theory or both if multiple methods of research were used.

Task 2.1 will now help you to answer the question that opened this section.

Task 2.1   What is your research *really* all about?

Identify the feature(s) that best describe(s) your research. How and where have you dealt with it in your text?

A thesis will normally exhibit one or perhaps two of these features. If your thesis contained more than two such features then your research risks becoming too diffuse and it would lack a clear methodological focus. Since the seven features are neither aims nor objectives of research, they represent overarching strategic and conceptual considerations that typify doctoral research. In this sense, they also contribute to establishing boundaries for the research itself in how each one tacitly implies the use of a particular methodological approach and fieldwork methods. Thus, these generic features represent unique characteristics that can distinguish one doctoral thesis from another.

So how can they be used? Ideally, readers need to appreciate the distinctiveness of your doctoral study early in the thesis. The appropriate feature(s) should certainly appear in your introductory chapter(s) where the accompanying text would serve to answer the question: *What is this research all about?* By including such text, your examiners would have their question answered before the viva. They would be delighted to have this early indication that your thesis reflects scholarship. Additionally, you could use the feature(s) to delimit the disciplinary and methodological scope of the research. In turn, this would lead into explanations of purpose, aims, and research approach, and so help you to justify a focus for the entire thesis. This will be dealt with later, in Chapter 5.

Explaining the appropriate feature(s) is often implicit in the text of theses. In these cases, an opportunity is therefore missed to inform readers exactly how the thesis should be viewed within the world of scholarship. Including such statements establishes your scholarly credential by association with significant writers or schools of thought in your field of study. Thus, you are helping your readers to locate your work in the wider discipline(s) and their respective context.

Introducing one or two of these features into your thesis can therefore answer a likely question by examiners. So expressing them in a language that is appropriate to your discipline conveys powerful messages to your readers too. Carefully selected use of the feature(s) could occur twice in your thesis: in the early chapter(s) to introduce the uniqueness of your research and in your chapter of conclusions as a form of reinforcement. This latter use serves three purposes. First, it reminds readers of the rationale for your research. Second, it reemphasises the boundaries of the research within which you intend to defend your research. Finally, it tells readers that you have consciously closed the circle between the start of your research and its conclusions. Thus, you could use the feature(s) to frame the real purpose of your research.

Focus of questions

'Being asked to examine a doctoral thesis is one of the greatest honours you can be afforded as an academic' (Pearce, 2005: 1). In these few words, Pearce acknowledges both the importance of the doctoral award itself and the role of examiners in recommending that a university should award a doctorate to a successful candidate. An implication from this observation is that how examiners actually arrive at their recommendation is an established practice of examining. Regrettably, this is not so.

Over a decade ago, Burnham (1994) offered a sad commentary on the process of the doctoral viva in British universities. Starting off by describing what went on as 'a mystery' he proceeded to suggest that what transpired was: 'one of the best kept secrets in British higher education'. He continued by pointing out that: 'Secrecy surrounding the viva both humiliates the examinee and diminishes the credibility of those who examine.' He concluded with this observation: 'Surviving the viva depends fundamentally on preparation and students ability to demystify the examination procedure.' As we will see in Chapter 11, other writers have taken up Burnham's challenge and started to illuminate what happens within the doctoral viva.

The work of Winter et al. (2000) showed that there were 'inconsistencies' across disciplines in the way that examiners examined. This view is confirmed by Denicolo and Boulter (2002), who also endorse the need for candidates to appreciate how examiners approach their task of examining. They conclude that candidates should acknowledge this as they embark on their doctoral journey.

Since it is apparent that questions asked in doctoral vivas are not totally arbitrary, it is reasonable to suppose that they follow certain patterns. This assumption is well-founded, since: 'The flow of questions and their inter-pretation, shows that examiners recognize and commend two significant approaches which the candidate had to the research. First, the examiners explored how the thesis exhibited innovative features of research design that used concepts in a developmental manner. Second, the examiners com-mended the scholarship and interpretations of "realities" that were presented by the candidate' (Trafford and Leshem, 2002a). These approaches represent two distinctively different ways in which examiners' questions can be categor-ized: 'innovation and development' and 'scholarship and interpretations'.

These two categories can be used to create a matrix in which each quadrant emphasises the primary focus for distinctively different questions in the viva. This provides a practical framework for analysing the respective significance of questions in doctoral vivas. Figure 2.2 shows how these quadrants differ in their respective level of conceptualisation:

- **Quadrant A deals with the technology of the thesis** and includes such issues as structure, presentation, content of the thesis and resolving admin-istrative and technical aspects of 'doing' the research. These features repre-sent non-academic considerations as a thesis is prepared for submission and includes structure, presentation, formatting, pagination and compliance with protocols.
- **Quadrant B deals with the theoretical perspectives** and includes such issues as identifying the research paradigms, awareness of the wider litera-ture, theoretical perspectives and the implications of the findings. These features demonstrate understanding of the academic content in which the research is located and on which it depends for its conceptual insights and frameworks.
- **Quadrant C deals with the practice of research** such as the emergence and use of the research questions, choice of topic, access to field data and explanations surrounding the gap in knowledge. These features demon-strate understanding of research as a process and an ability to undertake complex research in a critical and appropriate manner.
- **Quadrant D deals with demonstrating doctorateness** such as establishing conceptual links between findings, synthesising evidence into conceptual conclusions, critiquing the research process, advancing contributions to knowledge and defending doctorateness in the thesis and throughout the viva itself. These features are the critical prerequisites of scholarly merit in doctoral level research.

The features in each of the quadrants are singly and collectively important in the production of a doctoral thesis.

Figure 2.3 shows the distribution between the quadrants of questions that were asked by examiners in one viva. Thirty-six questions were asked and their sequence is shown in brackets following an indication of their respective topic or emphasis. Note how the proportion of questions asked in each of the

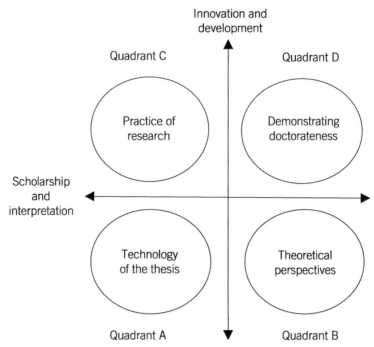

Figure 2.2   Relative significance of questions in a doctoral viva.

quadrants varied quite considerably – 9% in Quadrant A, 17% in B, 21% in C and 53% in D. You will see that four questions (3, 31, 2, 34) addressed single issues, while all other issues were explored by two or more questions. In Quadrant D, most of the issues attracted blocks of four or more questions, showing how the examiners clustered their questions as they explored those issues with the candidate.

Other questions were asked in a continuous sequence in Quadrant D (establishing links and concepts; developing the conceptual framework; contribution to knowledge). During this viva, the theme of synthesising concepts was explored three times by the examiners – early in the viva (11, 12), in the middle (20, 21) and towards the end (31). The final four questions in the viva (33, 34, 35, 36) were all located on the high/high axis in Quadrant D and thereby signified the examiners' attention to doctorateness in the thesis.

The analysis of the questions in this viva show that it is possible to distinguish between the relative focus of examiners' questions. It also shows that the ordering of the questions follows a detectable pattern and that some issues and themes will attract more questions than others. The significance of these findings is that they highlight how a successful viva proceeded in respect of the questions that were asked by examiners. Moreover, it implies that, for this thesis, other aspects of research were not discussed because, apparently, the

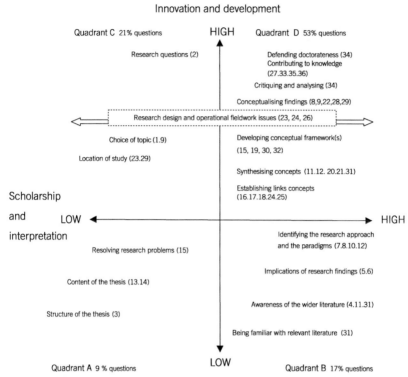

Figure 2.3 Relative location and significance of questions in one doctoral viva examination.

Note: Numbers in brackets refer to the sequence in which examiners asked the questions.

examiners were satisfied with how they had been handled in the thesis. Thus, our understanding of the scholarly process in a doctoral viva can be extended by analysing the questions that examiners ask of the candidate.

Type and use of questions

The quadrants display their respective significance when they are used to illustrate what happens during the doctoral examination process. The preliminary reports and questions asked by examiners provide genuine insights on what they consider to be the critical features of the doctorate (Trafford and Leshem, 2002b). Not surprisingly, the majority of these questions normally follow from the main points that have been raised by examiners in their preliminary reports. Other questions may emerge as supplementary issues for examiners to explore once the candidate had given an answer. Together, opening and supplementary questions will, in turn, address an aspect of the thesis that examiners want to hear the candidate explain, justify or defend.

However, there is consistency across the disciplines as to the types of question that may be asked in a doctoral viva. This suggests that there are generic clusters which can be detected in the sequence of questions put to candidates during doctoral vivas. Each cluster represents a theme that may be explored by any number of questions since examiners will undoubtedly wish to express their own questions in their own way. Nonetheless, these clusters of questions: 'can act as a template for you to check that you have incorporated appropriate answers to them in the text of your thesis' (Trafford and Leshem, 2002b).

The clusters of questions or opening statements that invite a response are shown here, each with their generic question:

- Opening questions – *Why did you chose this topic for your doctorate?*
- Issues of conceptualisation – *How did you arrive at your conceptual framework?*
- Approaches to research design – *How did you design your research?*
- Research methodology – *How would you justify your choice of methodology?*
- Research methods – *Why did you decide to use XYZ as your main instrument(s)?*
- Sampling/data collection – *How did you select your respondents/materials/area?*
- Conceptual conclusions – *How did you arrive at your conceptual conclusions?*
- Fundamentals of research – *How generalisable are your findings and why?*
- Contribution to knowledge – *What is your contribution to knowledge?*
- Being critical or reflective about the research – *We would like you to critique your thesis for us.*
- Postdoctoral issues – *What are you going to do after you gain your doctorate?*
- And finally – *Is there anything else that you could tell us about your thesis which you have not had the opportunity to tell us during the viva?*

These questions can be answered as you undertake and write up your research. If you do that then you will have sorted out the underlying 'research puzzle', which is 'what do you want to explain?' Mason (1996: 14) reminds us that answering this question is the driving force behind all serious research. Her remarks apply equally to your doctoral research.

At the end of this chapter, there are two examples of doctoral examinations: Appendix 2.1: A successful submission and defence; and Appendix 2.2: An unsuccessful submission and defence. These appendices contain the examiners' preliminary reports and provisional recommendations for each thesis. These are followed by their respective (numbered) questions which each examiner asked, as signified by A or B. The final paragraph in each appendix shows the outcome of the viva.

Task 2.2 involves you doing your own research into the significance of the

---

Task 2.2   Interpreting the questions from examiners' reports

Consider the meaning or function of the questions asked in each viva. Then, using the four quadrants that are shown in Figure 2.1, place each question number into what you consider to be its appropriate quadrant. When you have done this task for Example 2.1, repeat it using the evidence of the questions that were asked by examiners in Example 2.2.

---

questions asked by examiners in the two vivas shown in Appendices 2.1 and 2.2. It will illustrate how such questions follow a discernible pattern that focus of different, but equally critical, aspects of doctoral scholarship.

You may find that a few questions could be located in either of two adjacent quadrants due to how you interpret the presenting and underlying meanings that they might contain. Most though are likely to fit clearly into just one quadrant. You will also have noticed that closely related issues were raised by the examiners in a sequence of questions. You will also recognise that the questions asked in Quadrants A, B and C: 'lack criticality in determining the outcome of the viva voce examination' (Trafford and Leshem, 2002a).

However, if the majority of questions are outside Quadrant D then the examiners have focused their attention on what they believe the candidate can cope with. This is especially so if the questions are mainly in Quadrant A where the emphasis is on the technical aspects of producing the thesis. This signifies the examiners' conclusion that the candidate was unable to conceptualise their work and so no questions would be asked about this aspect of research. It is only in Quadrant D that issues, which were high in scholarship and interpretation, plus innovation and development, were direct determinants of the scholarly outcome of the viva.

The four quadrants differ, however, in their respective level of conceptualisation. In this sense, Quadrants A, B and C provide the foundation for Quadrant D. It is the explicit focus on scholarship and conceptualisation, shown in Quadrant D, that examiners look for when they read a thesis. If they find it then the candidate will be judged to have produced a doctoral thesis that can be successfully defended. Thus the practical significance of the quadrants is they provide you with a template against which to audit your thesis and prepare for your viva.

These views of how questions in the viva offer insights about doctorateness are based on four quite practical conclusions:

1 Examiners recognise the merit of a submitted thesis through their initial reading and this determines the agenda of questions that they ask in the viva.
2 'Good' theses will attract proportionally more questions concerning issues of doctorateness than 'poor' theses.
3 'Poor' theses will attract proportionally more questions on the technology, literature and practice of research than 'good' theses.

4 When you successfully defend the scholarship in your thesis this provides a firm foundation on which then to defend your thesis by answering the examiners' questions in the viva.

The significance of these conclusions is that they can help you to organise your thinking about your thesis. This should occur before you commence writing. The conclusions above can also assist you to produce a vision of what your thesis might look like when it is complete. By using the quadrants as templates of what to emphasise in the text, you can now recognise that responding to the question *What is your thesis all about?* should, ideally, be from a conceptual perspective.

Taking such a perspective will help you to avoid becoming too over-descriptive of your research or your topic. By identifying the conceptual 'thread' that runs through a doctoral thesis, you will thus make connections between ideas, see how various theories are linked and show how theoretical perspectives influenced your research design, fieldwork and data analysis. This will result in you achieving cohesion in the arguments that you advance in your writing and later defend in your viva. Thus, you will also have achieved academic depth in your thesis.

Looking back and ahead

In this chapter, we have shown how the questions that examiners intend to ask in doctoral vivas is determined by what they read in your thesis. These questions display patterns of emphasis as they are then posed in the viva itself. Recognising and acting on those patterns can provide insights into what examiners consider to be the determinants of doctorateness in a thesis. Thus, this chapter has argued that you can influence the outcome of your doctoral studies by starting at the end of that journey to visualise and plan how to begin and progress through your doctoral journey.

Chapter 3 introduces the concept of doctorateness and explains how you can use it as a template to undertake the combined tasks of tackling your research and planning your thesis.

Appendix 2.1 A successful submission and defence

Ian, an organisational psychologist chose to investigate a phenomenon that was outside his normal field of experience. The title of his thesis was: *The influence of organisational culture, personality traits and social support on mental well-being among secondary school adolescents.* He had two examiners – A had expertise in the theory of culture and research methodology, B had expertise in educational practice and psychology. Both examiners had answered 'yes' to the four closed questions in their preliminary report to the examining university:

1 Does the thesis represent a significant contribution to knowledge of the subject by:
   a discovery of new facts;
   b the exercise of independent critical powers?
2 Does the thesis provide evidence of originality?
3 Is the thesis satisfactory regards presentation and succinctness?
4 Is the abstract of the thesis submitted appropriate?

Independent report by Examiner A

This study demonstrates a high level of capability in practitioner and qualitative/quantitative research. The research question is clear and appropriate for a PhD. The thesis makes appropriate use of extant literature interleafed with a review of the primary evidence. The critical discourse is excellent and integrates many of the components of the argument. The candidate did not include some recent research that might have informed the discussion, but this may have been deliberately excluded.

Provisional recommendation

I recommend the award of a PhD, subject to a satisfactory performance of the candidate at the viva voce and also subject to a few specific additions and improvements that the viva voce is likely to reveal.

Independent report by Examiner B

The candidate has produced a well-structured thesis that progresses logically and convincingly through reviewing the behavioural context of schooling and definitions of well-being. The setting and interrogation of appropriate methodological issues was especially searching. The integrity of his work is substantiated by the explanations that are constantly provided. He clearly understands this field of practice and structures the investigation critically and logically with a systematic self-critical approach throughout the thesis. He makes appropriate links between theory and practice which are then supported by reflection on the internal argument. There is a comprehensive mastery of this field of research through intelligent referencing, logical conclusions, no bias and continual testing of personal ideas. The thesis was accessible and written in an engaging style. I enjoyed working through it step by step and share the conclusions.

Provisional recommendation

PhD to be awarded.

The two reports indicate that the examiners were equally impressed by the quality of the thesis which they had read. In a 20-minute discussion before the viva they agreed to base their respective questions on the main points contained in their respective reports. Examiners A and B asked the following questions in the viva:

Examiner A		Before we start, my colleague and I want you to know how much we really enjoyed reading your thesis. It raises some fascinating issues and we look forward to discussing them with you.
A	1	Please tell us what led you to choose this topic. What really excited you about it?
A	2	How did you know that your topic had not been studied previously; was it because of what you had read in the academic or the professional literature? How long did it take you to discover that the topic had not been investigated previously?
A	3	Did your professional knowledge of 'psychological well-being' allow you to anticipate your results or were you totally detached as you undertook your enquiry?
A	4	You have spent lots of time in schools recently, meeting staff and pupils and collecting your research data. So, what do you now consider to be the main determinants of school culture?
B	5	Your professional background and employment has been as an organisational psychologist in industry rather than in education. So, I would like to hear how easy you found your research journey to be in the quite different social context and the unfamiliar organisational operations of a school.
B	6	How did gender issues influence culture in the school?
B	7	What led you to choose your models of organisational culture?

B	8	What other models of culture did you consider?
A	9	How did you decide on the variables that would be included in your conceptual framework?
A	10	Were you 'theory testing' or 'developing theory' in your research?
A	11	Why did you include the achievement variable in your research design?
B	12	Tell us how you managed to achieve a 100% response rate from your respondents – who, as adolescents in schools, are not known for complying with such requests!
B	13	[A highly specific and technical question was asked on the selection and operation of a statistical issue.]
A	14	Did the finding about DDDDD surprise you and how did you explain it?
A	15	Have you heard about the RRRR theory? [The candidate indicated that he had not heard of this theory, so Examiner A outlined its primary components.] OK? Well, let me put my question another way – if you *had* heard of the RRRR theory, how might you have used it in your research? [Laughter all round before the candidate responded to the revised question.]
A	16	Please explain how you arrived at, and distinguished between, your factual and conceptual conclusions. How did you move along from discussing your many pages of very detailed findings to these quite precise conclusions?
B	17	How might your conclusions influence public policy or professional practice, and who do you think might be interested in your results?
B	18	How do your conclusions relate to other conceptual models that explain well-being, either in your own professional field or in education settings?
A	19	How could your findings be transferred to other corporate cultures?
A	20	What correlations did you draw between the concepts in your thesis?
B	21	If you were to follow up on your research or encourage others to build on it, which specific aspects of it do you believe deserve further investigation?
A/B	22	[A 5-minute conversation then took place between the two examiners and the candidate. It dealt with the width of the investigation and the many variables and concepts that comprised the conceptual framework were discussed. The exchange of opinions rather than questions gave the discussion its direction.]

A   23   We would like to hear you summarise for us any criticisms of your research that you or anyone else might make.

B   24   Are there any aspects of your research that you would like to tell us about that we have not discussed?

When the viva closed after 54 minutes, the candidate was asked to leave the room. It took the examiners 3 minutes to agree that each of their questions had been successfully defended and that the text of the thesis required no alterations. The candidate was invited back into the room and congratulated on gaining his doctorate.

Appendix 2.2 An unsuccessful submission and defence

Pamela, a hospital manager, chose to investigate for her doctorate a topic that related to her own work. The title of her thesis was: *The effectiveness of rehabilitation programmes for patients after suffering thrombosis*. One of her examiners (A) was a specialist in thrombosis and the other (B) was a health educator. At this university, examiners were required to answer five questions and then to provide a preliminary report followed by a recommendation as shown here.

Responses by Examiners A and B to these questions were:

1 Does the thesis represent a level of scholarship which makes a contribution to knowledge?   No/No
2 Does the thesis show that the candidate has a sound understanding and appropriate working knowledge of research?   No/No
3 Does the thesis display a critical stance towards the sources that have been used and the concepts that have been developed?   No/No
4 Does the thesis contain a clearly expressed purpose and provide conclusions that relate to that purpose?   Maybe/Partially
5 Does the presentation of the thesis comply with the university regulations?   No/Yes

Independent report by Examiner A

The thesis is weak in a number of significant areas. The title hardly describes the content of the thesis. I read 167 pages before learning what the research question was and there were only 279 pages! Unless I missed it, there was no explicit theoretical focus for the work despite 140 pages being devoted to 'literature reviews'. The majority of the references were 'old' and unrelated to the hypotheses that were *based upon my extensive reading* (page 168). Most of the text was descriptive with unchallenged theories, regular use of value-laden terms instead of objectively supported views, with only an occasional explanation of 'why' a particular approach/method/stance was chosen. The methodology was stated rather than justified. Issues of access to patients and their related ethical considerations were touched on but not fully explained. As a result, there was an obvious lack of scholarship and rigour in this work.

Recommendation

The thesis has clearly not achieved the pass level. I reserve my recommendation until after the viva.

Independent report by Examiner B

I have major concerns about this piece of work. The abstract describes a different thesis to what has been submitted. There is little critical analysis in the badly presented literature review chapters. The majority of sources are so dated that their findings have been superseded by recent research and the primary journals in this area were underused. The choice of a quantitative methodology was not explained and justified even though it was quite appropriate. Why were the sample sizes 'restricted to just 12 patients' and 'only surveyed' during the second period of their treatments? This and the way that the tests were undertaken must be explored and explained. I need to be convinced that the conclusions are as significant as is claimed since they do not prove anything that it not already generally known on this topic.

Recommendation

I am concerned about its appropriateness for the award of PhD.

Before the viva started, the examiners agreed that the thesis was not particularly good and they took 50 minutes to decide what questions needed to be asked.

Examiner B		Thank you for submitting your thesis for us to read. We have a number of questions that we would like to ask and I'll invite my colleague to open the viva.
A	1	Why did you select rehabilitation as your topic and why then focus on thrombosis as the context for your study?
A	2	Can you talk us through your selection and use of the literature that you included in the four chapters of literature review?
A	3	Why didn't you include more recent authors in your review since there are only 15 citations from the last decade of published research in those chapters?
A	4	I was surprised to see what your hypotheses were when I reached them. Given what I had read in your selections of sources, how did you arrive at the four that you used?
B	5	Can we now look at the methods that you used. They were fairly standard modes of collecting data from patients. What other methods did you consider using and why, for instance, didn't you include a behavioural approach? Something such as focus groups could have provided you with a quite different angle on effectiveness through the discursive voices of patients.
B	6	How did you pilot your survey and the mini-questionnaires – and isn't the mini-ness simply the number of questions

that it contains rather than a particular category of survey instrument?

A	7	Why did you choose 12 patients as your regular sample size? Also, why did you only survey them during their second period of treatment?
A	8	How did you gain agreement from patients to take part in your research?
A	9	What levels of clearance did you require before you could start on your research?
B	10	We know that pulmonary embolism can be treated through anticoagulants and that most programmes combine medical and non-medical aftercare. So how did you isolate the respective values for the medical and non-medical consequences of treatment in your patient–respondents?
B	11	What did you see as difference between your methodology and your methods, since you appeared to use the terms interchangeably?
B	12	If you had conducted your enquiry without any surveys but instead you had spoken at considerable length with patients over time when they visited the outpatients' clinic how might your findings have given you a different set of conclusions?
A	13	After all the reading that you clearly did, what sort of new insights did you have on your topic?
A	14	What was the conceptual focus for your research?
B	15	So if you did not have an explicit conceptual focus, how did you design your research?
B	16	Let's look again at the methods of collecting data which you used. Were there any problems that arose during or between your surveys? If so, what were they and how did you handle them?
B	17	I would have found it helpful if you had told me in your thesis how you administered the third questionnaire since that one is then presented in your thesis as containing the most crucial data that you collected.
B	18	How did you account for the relationships between gender, age, occupation and ethnicity in assembling your populations and then allowing for these variables in your data analysis?
B	19	Why, then, were there equal numbers of self-employed patients in groups three and four?
A	20	I would like to raise a question about diet. You mentioned this on page 197. How did diet come into your investigation since it was not a topic that appeared in your literature chapters?

A	21	How did you choose the software systems that were used in your data analysis?
A	22	Why did you prefer T-tests over other equally appropriate tests?
A	23	How did you classify the data between 'the primary and secondary variables?'
A	24	How would you explain the links between patient recovery times and the programme itself?
A	25	How reliable are your findings?
B	26	Since the nature of care and treatment for suffers of thrombosis have altered greatly in recent years, how relevant are the works of the past to the treatments of the present?
B	27	Are there other ways in which your patients might have recovered apart from the programme that you were monitoring?
B	28	Can you explain why your abstract does not comply with the layout that the university requires and, it also seems to me, not to record what your thesis actually contains?
B	29	Can you outline to us what the contribution to effective medical care practice might be from your research and how that might be incorporated into care programmes generally?

When the viva closed after 67 minutes, the candidate was asked to leave the room. The examiners agreed that she had not provided satisfactory answers to the questions. They also agreed that the answers that she had given were, in the main, superficial. They further agreed that she had shown a fundamental lack of understanding of the research process both in her thesis and in her viva. They had serious doubts over how the data had been collected, analysed and then interpreted. They concluded that the research lacked both rigour and conceptualisation. These deficiencies were evident throughout the entire thesis and they were unrecognised by her during the viva. They agreed that the conclusions in the thesis were not justified by the evidence that had been presented and that no contribution to knowledge had occurred. The candidate was invited back into the room. She was then told by the external examiner that her thesis had not reached the necessary standard for an award and thus it had failed.

3

What is doctorateness?

This chapter will:

- illustrate the distinctiveness of the doctoral degree;
- explain the notion of doctorateness;
- present the practical features of doctorateness;
- indicate the characteristics that examiners look for as they read a thesis.

Introduction

Unlike other degrees that British universities award, doctorates endow their recipients with a title. This accolade is not easily earned. The entry criteria, mode of study, academic demands and process of assessment combine together into a framework that is very demanding on those who seek a doctoral degree. Recognising this obvious set of differences allows us to identify additional characteristics that influence how the assessment process operates and what criteria are used by those who undertake this task.

Each university possesses its own institutional framework document in which it lays out regulatory procedures that apply to its degrees. For the doctorate, the mechanics of registration, induction, training, progression, supervision and examination plus associated roles for supervisors, examiners and candidates will be detailed in these documents. However, there are generic features of 'the doctorate' that transcend the individual university and its procedures. These are features of received wisdom, which examiners often refer to as the 'gold standard' of the doctorate. When met, they constitute doctorateness, which is what examiners look for in theses.

To achieve your doctorate it is necessary for you to go beyond these facts. They represent the knowledge that you need to possess about the degree which you seek. A far more challenging level of thinking is for you to understand the scholarly nature of the degree. To do this, it is necessary to appreciate the connection between doing research, writing a doctoral thesis and defending that thesis in your doctoral viva. This chapter shows how examiners view these three features of doing a doctorate as being interdependent. The practical significance of this view is emphasised in this chapter.

Doctorates are different

It is relatively easy to view bachelor's, master's and doctoral degrees as following a hierarchy of awards. This would emphasise differences in the levels between these classifications of degrees, as well as their respective associated notions of depth of academic study. However, these awards differ more importantly in how each deals with knowledge. The Quality Assurance Agency for Higher Education (QAA) (2007) states that doctorates should only be awarded to students who have demonstrated:

- the creation and interpretation of new knowledge, through original research or other advanced scholarship, of a quality to satisfy peer review, extend the forefront of the discipline and merit publication;
- a systematic acquisition and understanding of a substantial body of knowledge that is at the forefront of an academic discipline or area of professional practice;
- the general ability to conceptualise, design and implement a project for the generation of new knowledge, applications or understanding at the forefront of the discipline and to adjust the project design in the light of unforeseen problems;
- a detailed understanding of applicable techniques for research and advanced academic enquiry (QAA, 2007).

These criteria constitute the template against which examiners would therefore assess the merit of a doctoral thesis that a candidate had submitted for the award of a doctoral degree.

In a bachelor's degree, students acquire knowledge from lectures, tutorials and their reading. The extent and depth of learning are then tested by combinations of essays, assignments, examinations and, in some cases, a small investigatory project. Here, the acquisition of knowledge represents a foundation for subsequent postgraduate study. Then, in a master's degree, learning becomes more specialised and substantial assignments are normally followed by a research-based dissertation in which knowledge is applied to a specific topic or area.

The distinguishing features of the first two degree levels are, first, acquisition and, second, application of knowledge (Trafford and Woolliams, 2002: 59–72). In the final level, the doctorate degree exists to create and extend knowledge through purposeful research as the QAA criteria indicate. The quality and merit of this degree are usually assessed through a single piece of work, the doctoral thesis. Doctoral candidates report on their original research to demonstrate how they have made a scholarly contribution to knowledge. Then, in their viva, candidates defend their thesis and the research that they have undertaken.

Just deciding to register for doctoral study implies your personal commitment to research and scholarship of a high level. Consider some of the questions that you may well have been asked by people who knew that you were undertaking doctoral study:

'Why do you want to register for your doctorate in this university?'
'How are you getting on with your doctorate?'
'When do you expect to complete your doctorate?'
'What are you going to do when you have finished your doctorate?'

You will have noticed that tutors, supervisors, colleagues, friends and examiners often use the words 'your doctorate' in these types of question. These two words capture why the doctorate is a unique academic degree more clearly than any definition or lengthy explanation. They combine 'the personal' and 'the academic' in one phrase. They emphasise your ownership of your research and thereby acknowledge the nature of the award that you seek. Thus, the words 'your doctorate' accentuate the difference between other degrees and the doctorate.

The difference is doctorateness

You will already know that studying for your doctorate extends over many years and involves prolonged high-quality research. You will write thousands of words on your research and these will be bound into a thesis which you then have to defend before two or more eminent examiners. So the doctorate could be described as being different from other academic degrees due to the length of study, level of scholarship, size of the finished output and method of examination. These are fairly obvious features of difference.

Have you thought about what makes this degree special? Is there a common factor that is present in all doctorates? Is there a special 'something' about these degrees that can be recognised by those who examine them or those who already possess a doctorate? The answer to these questions is that the distinctive difference between it and other degrees is the nature of doctorateness itself. Maybe you have heard holders of a doctorate saying: 'I may not understand their topic and may never read their thesis, but I know that what they had to do to get their doctorate will have been similar to what I had to do.' This rather intuitive observation suggests that there is a recognisable 'something' that differentiates the doctorate from other degrees.

No doubt you have already thought about such differences and you will already have identified a number of features. You may well have recognised that no single one is predominant. As you looked further you would then have realised that they were all interdependent. You could have concluded that doctorateness combines the two issues of research process and research technique into a single notion. As a result, like others who have also thought about their own doctorate, you will appreciate that the notion of doctorateness is pluralist. It combines both 'doing and achieving' a doctorate.

In the previous chapter, Figure 2.2 portrayed how examiners' questions focus on four interrelated quadrants of a thesis: Technology of the thesis (A), Theoretical perspectives (B), Practice of research (C) and Demonstrating doctorateness (D). Then, Figure 2.3 showed how 36 questions in one viva could be mapped against those four quadrants. Doctorateness is achieved when you display high levels of capability in these four areas. If this is apparent in your thesis, then examiners – and others too, of course – will recognise it. They will see evidence that shows your doctoral thesis to be a sophisticated, conceptually coherent and complex piece of research. It will have met exacting standards of intellectual rigour and scholarship. They will also see that your thesis has been well-presented.

Figure 3.1 shows a typical distribution of questions between the four quadrants in two vivas whose outcomes would have been 'clear pass' and 'clear fail'. Model A represents a viva in which the candidate would have gained a doctorate due to the high quality of the research and its defence. Note the high proportion of questions that would have concentrated on doctorateness (Quadrant D) and the general discussion that would have replaced the normal questioning process. Model B represents a viva in which the examiners would have been unable to ask many questions in Quadrant D (doctorateness) due to the candidate's apparent lack of conceptual grasp. Instead, their questions would have concentrated on the low-risk technology issues of the thesis (Quadrant A) plus the relatively 'lower' levels of Quadrants B and C. The models highlight how the emphasis of examiners' questions would have distinguished the 'good' viva from the 'poor' one.

We can now see that to be successful you have to make sure that many different issues receive due attention. This is quite a challenge for someone who may not previously have tackled such a large and time-consuming piece of work. The task can be made slightly easier by breaking down the bigger picture into its component practical pieces. Doing this allows you to see exactly what examiners say they look for at the practical level of a thesis.

As we show throughout this book, examiners ask questions in your viva that invite you to explain the research that you have completed and accounted for in your thesis. Obviously, they cannot achieve this through a single question!

Model A: 'good' Viva

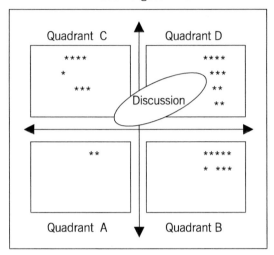

Model B: 'poor' viva

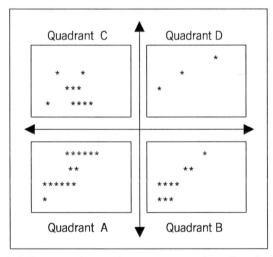

Figure 3.1 Modelling emphasis of questions in a 'good' and a 'poor' viva.

Therefore, vivas contain numerous questions as examiners focus on different aspects of your research. Their questions inevitably follow certain patterns that reflect their thinking and experience. But those patterns are discernible through the sequence of their questions.

Certain critical elements of doctoral research interest examiners. Their questions may address these elements directly or indirectly, but all these elements will be explored at sometime during each viva. Figure 3.2 shows the 12 most

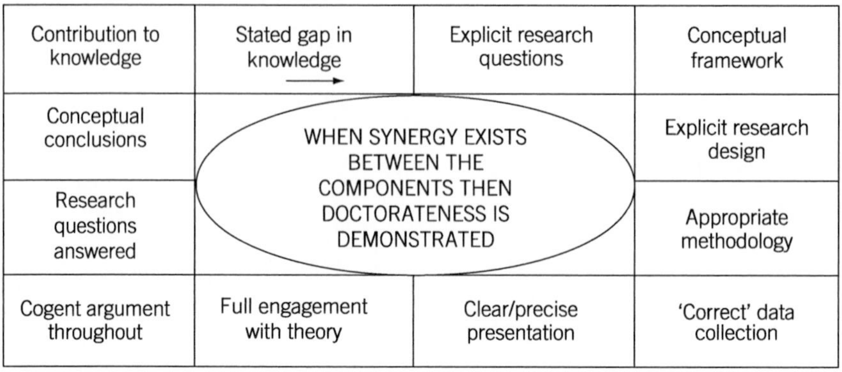

Contribution to knowledge	Stated gap in knowledge	Explicit research questions	Conceptual framework
Conceptual conclusions	WHEN SYNERGY EXISTS BETWEEN THE COMPONENTS THEN DOCTORATENESS IS DEMONSTRATED		Explicit research design
Research questions answered			Appropriate methodology
Cogent argument throughout	Full engagement with theory	Clear/precise presentation	'Correct' data collection

Figure 3.2   Components of doctorateness.

frequently occurring issues of interest to examiners as indicated by their questions. They are portrayed as being connected when the model is viewed in a clockwise manner. Each box represents an essential element of research activity that has to be accounted for and explained in the text of your thesis. While these elements are recognised stages and activities in most post-graduate research, they are inescapable prerequisites at the doctoral level of research.

When all 12 elements are appropriately displayed in your thesis, two con-sequences follow for your readers. First, they will acknowledge that synergy has been achieved between the account of the research that you have under-taken and the text that you have written. Second, they will recognise how your presentation of argument and structure makes the thesis coherent as a piece of scholarly research. If examiners can draw these two conclusions then they would also conclude that your thesis demonstrates doctorateness.

The initial reports that examiners provide contain their judgements on the presence or absence of academic quality in theses. Two examples of examiner reports show how they have applied similar criteria to arrive at conclusions about theses of contrasting academic merit. Example 3.1 is brief and to the point. It acknowledges the merit of the thesis and commends the candidate's scholarship. In contrast, Example 3.2 is extracted from a lengthy and detailed examiner's report explaining why the thesis lacks academic merit. These examiners made informed judgements by relating their reading of the respec-tive theses to a common template of academic standards. It is this underlying factor in the two examples that is explored as we look at the components of doctorateness.

Example 3.1 An examiner's report on a
                 'good' thesis

This is a good thesis. It reports on some new and exciting results in an important yet surprisingly under-investigated area. The use of similar reagents in the purification of contaminated water is widespread and this makes the contribution all the more valuable. Not an easy study to undertake but it is clear that a satisfactory methodology has been followed which is not only rewarding from the researcher's point of view but a valuable educational process too.

The thesis has also been written in a clear, easily understandable style. The layout is good and the aims of the work, the state of the current art and the conclusions are all clearly drawn. Throughout, the work is well-referenced and I am unaware of any serious omissions. The tables and figures are clearly drawn and serve the text well.

Overall, from all important viewpoints, this is a satisfactory thesis; well-written, well-presented and based on good scientific method and approach.

I believe the degree of PhD should be awarded.

Example 3.2 An examiner's report on a
                 'poor' thesis

This thesis does not meet the university's criteria for the award of a PhD. There are major omissions and errors in most areas of the research and how it is presented.

1   The work is substantially under-theorised. Many cited works are incorrectly referenced both in the text and the reference list. The chapters concerned with the literature are wholly inadequate at the doctoral level and might not be acceptable either in master's research. The discourse is bereft of critical understanding, deals discursively with relevant issues and fails to problemitise the topic being studied. There are no signals to show how the research was conducted and so theory is disconnected from how the research was designed. This omission has quite a profound result. The research is not framed in a paradigm that contextualises or seeks to justify particular data-gathering methods and there is no effective technical discussion of the research as an intellectually defensible process.

2   There is complete confusion in the descriptive elements of the research. Sampling procedures are unclear, the piloting process was also unclear and there seemed to be a skewing of the outcomes that were due to deliberate action or ignorance. The boundaries for the study were not explained either.

3   Research data are not separated from discussions of those data. Often the discussion of the data seems to deviate from a disinterested perspective to the researcher interposing questions whose origins are not explained. Pages of text are devoted to describing the minutest of details which then are not referred to in any subsequent analysis.

4   The conclusions of this research are, at best, a function of how the sample was drawn. They are hardly new and add nothing to knowledge. Apart from that, they are questionable due to the poorly handled methodology and the absence of a clear statement of intent for the research.

5   The presentation is poor throughout. It needs to be fully proofread to correct numerous typographical and grammatical errors. A standard use of headings, point sizes and the use of indentations would improve the appearance of the text.

This thesis requires a lot of work doing to it just to get it up to an acceptable standard for submission. The basic idea for the research has some merit, but, in its present form, it is a clear fail.

Demonstrating doctorateness

Let's now explore the significance of the 12 elements of doctorateness that are shown in Figure 3.2.

The boxes in the following subsections show the types of question that examiners would ask at your viva in respect of each element (Trafford and Leshem, 2002a). These questions are generic and seem to be predictable since they address the fundamental aspects of research, and they are not discipline specific. Examiners tend to use such questions to open up the topic before then asking supplementary questions that focus more precisely on aspects of the topic or methodology. You too can follow this line of questioning by interrogating your actual or proposed text, as suggested in Task 3.1.

As we have already noted, examiners will read your account of how you handled these 12 elements in your thesis as they prepare to draft their initial independent report. At the viva they may ask questions about the elements – despite being satisfied with your textual account. The reason for this is that

---

> **Task 3.1** Locating doctorateness in your thesis
>
> As you read through the questions and their accompanying commentaries, check where and how you have handled these issues in your thesis – or where they will be handled. Use your conclusions to compile an agenda of items to discuss with your supervisor(s).

their questions are intended to see how you explain that particular element. Your answers should therefore provide an accurate response to the question as well as demonstrating understanding of the underlying concerns within those questions.

Following each box are some ways in which you might handle the questions and how they link into your thesis.

Stated gap in knowledge

> How did you identify the gap in knowledge which your research investigated?
>
> Why do you believe that the gap existed?
>
> Why had the gap in knowledge not been investigated by other researchers before you?

Consider addressing this type of question early in your thesis – possibly in Chapter 1. You could explain how you recognised a possible gap in knowledge due to:

- changes in contemporary knowledge, emergent understanding about the topic, how the topic is viewed in the contemporary context, alterations to legislation or evolving technology;
- literature that contained philosophical or technical disputes about the topic, showed an absence of research into/publications on the topic or no recently published research into the topic;
- familiarity with practice where your hunch, assumption, observations or direct knowledge suggested a lack of satisfactory explanations about something where there was a need to know.

You can establish the legitimacy of this gap by using citations from the literature, published reports or other sources, as appropriate. You can then use this text to frame your research question(s) (Andrews, 2003). Later, in the final chapter, you can remind readers of your original research destination as you explain how the outcomes from your research can be viewed as making a contribution to knowledge.

Explicit research questions

How did you create your research questions; where did they really come from?

Why did you decide on those questions rather than something else to investigate?

Once you had settled on those questions how did you use them?

The purpose of research questions is to clarify exactly what you will address in your research. You may include them in an early chapter as you explain the scope and nature of your research. They should convey the immediacy and significance of the gap in knowledge to which your investigation is directed. Alternatively, they could emerge after you have investigated the research context so that their link is clearly situated. Research questions should be expressed so that their meaning is explicit. They should be capable of being investigated within the time, resources and methodologies that are available to you. By making these conditions explicit in your text, your readers will recognise that evidence generated from your research will allow you to answer the research questions. However, if you use a staged or action-research approach then the question(s) might emerge from exploratory investigations and so appear later in your thesis. In these instances, research questions would normally appear after each exploratory stage to guide your investigations in the subsequent stage(s).

It is necessary that you express your research intentions – both as an aid to planning exactly what you are going to do and so that your readers appreciate those intentions (Robson, 2002: 80). Doctoral candidates usually include a statement of purpose for their research in their theses. These purposes are often presented in one of three ways. In worked Example 3.3, induction to a new company illustrates the three possible alternative statements of aim/focus, objectives and research questions. Any reference to boundaries has been excluded from the statements.

Example 3.3 Aims, objectives and research questions

Aim/focus   This research will focus on the strategic use of induction as a way to introduce newly appointed staff to the culture and operational procedures of the company.

Objective 1   The research will identify how three small-to-medium sized companies (SMEs) use induction as a way of

> introducing newly appointed staff to their respective organisational culture and operational procedures.
>
> **1A** It will assess the nature and extent of informal induction that occurs by colleagues for newly appointed staff in three SMEs.
>
> **1B** It will explain how formal company-wide induction events are designed and presented and related to wider corporate staff development policies.
>
> **1C** It will evaluate the perceived value of induction by newly appointed staff, plus their respective immediate managers and working colleagues, in the three SMEs.
>
> **2** It will evaluate the relative efficacy of induction programmes as endorsing prevailing cultural and work norms among newly appointed staff in the three SMEs.
>
> **Research question(s)**
>
> What are the strategic considerations that three small-to-medium sized companies have towards the use of formal induction events and how effective are they considered to be by their respective providers, recipients and co-colleagues?

Research questions have an advantage over the other ways of expressing your research intentions; researchers have to provide an answer to the question(s) and so demonstrate closure to their research quest! Having a focus, an aim or an objective can provide you with a broad statement that captures your general intentions. However, such phrases are likely to be more open ended than a question and so lack the specificity of a closure. As a consequence, examiners may suggest that you could have collected more data or continued your investigation, thereby opening a discussion about the clarity of your research intentions, specificity and boundaries.

Conceptual framework

> How did you devise your conceptual framework?
>
> Why did your framework combine those specific concepts instead of X, Y or Z?
>
> How did your conceptual framework help you to design your research?
>
> I understand the concept of internal marketing. You do, too, but you could have interrogated that concept more strongly and more critically too before placing it at the centre of your research.

Conceptual frameworks provide a theoretical overview of your intended research and order within that process (Leshem and Trafford, 2007). Whether your research approach is deductive or inductive, you will have interrogated the literature to discover what others have written on or around your topic. Their ideas will have given you theoretical perspectives that can guide your thinking about exactly what it is that you will investigate. Those ideas will influence your choice of research approach and methodology, too. If you devise hypotheses to test, then their wording will reflect certain theoretical assumptions. However, if your research concludes with propositions for others to test, then they too will contain theoretical assumptions.

Numerous alternative terms are used to account for the functions that are served by a conceptual framework – bridging theory and practice, concept mapping, focal theory, picture of the theoretical territory, theoretical scaffolding. As Bell (2005: 102) observes: 'The label is not important, but the process of establishing a map or framework of how the research will be conducted and analysed is.' All research contains assumptions and those assumptions are themselves theoretically founded. At the doctoral level of research, it is important that your assumptions are, first, explicit and, second, soundly located in theories that are explained and located in a framework. Your conceptual framework might appear after those chapters(s) that present your theoretical perspectives or later in the thesis if it is used to draw together your theoretical findings.

Explicit research design

> Your research design sections were well-thought through and justified in a convincing manner.
>
> What assumptions did you have about how your research should be designed?
>
> What practical/methodological considerations influenced your choice of research design and how were they resolved?
>
> Why do you believe that your research strategy 'did not need to be'/'needed to be' revised later in your research?

When others read your thesis, they will expect to see an account of how you planned your research. In this sense, they want to understand the strategy for your research. Think of this strategy as building a theory of your own to show how your research was planned and undertaken. It is usual for this to appear in a chapter before your account of the methodology and methods. The reader will look for a detailed account of how the theoretical perspectives that you had developed from reading the literature influenced your choice of an investigatory strategy. This would include explaining the role of your conceptual framework in determining your choice of research paradigm.

Readers would expect evidence of internal cohesion between your theoretical perspectives on the topic and the practical implications of how you proposed to investigate that topic. These explanations should provide a robust base for your research. As a result, there should be no doubts in your readers' minds over the choices that you considered and the rationale for the decisions that you made. Such a foundation becomes critical if your research involved staged phases which required you to adopt and justify a combination of different methodologies.

Appropriate methodology

Throughout your thesis I could follow exactly what you were proposing and how you were going to do it. I had no worries that it would work as you had described. And it did.

Please explain your methodology to us.

What choices of research approach did you consider as you planned your research?

How would you justify your choice of methodology?

Can you outline how your reading of theory on this topic influenced your choice of methodology and the methods used in your fieldwork?

Readers should understand exactly why you chose your research approach after reading your chapter(s) on research design. They should then be able to follow your explanation of how you assembled the methodology as a bridge between your theory (research strategy) and your research practice (tactics or methods). Whether you adopted methodologies that were single or multiple, linear or iterative, inductive or deductive, you need to justify that choice. Readers may not be too concerned which of these alternatives you chose, but they deserve to know how you made that choice. This will require you to show your understanding of the philosophical as well as the practical implications of your choice. The argument that you provide has also to show how you balanced two potentially contrasting considerations. These are the contextual matters of access to data, ethical aspects, time, resources, etc. all of which have to be balanced against the technical suitability of various possible data collection techniques. Thus, the choice of research methodology obliges you to think longitudinally from theoretical perspectives onto research methods. Allowing readers to 'see' your thinking process will convince them that you are acting like a researcher rather than simply following a do-it-yourself research kit!

'Correct' data collection

How do your research methods relate to your conceptual framework?

Why did you choose to use those methods (A or B or C) of data collection?

What difficulties did you have in your data collection process and why do you think they occurred?

How did you avoid straying outside the boundaries that you had set for your research?

Now that your research is finished, and with hindsight, do you think that there were other ways to assess the data that you needed?

Following your account of the research methodology, you would then describe the methods (*means*) that you chose to collect that data necessary to achieve the purpose(s) (*ends*) of your research. This chapter will be quite technical because these methods are themselves data collection techniques. It should contain very detailed accounts of the methods that would be used to collect the data required. You should also acknowledge any limitations in these method(s) and how you dealt with it/them. Having explained and justified your selection of research methods you would then present an account of how you collected your data. This is the fieldwork component of your thesis.

Depending on the nature of your research, you might spend your time in a laboratory, in an archive/library, thinking and reflecting or personally interacting with your respondents. Each of these is a different way in which 'fieldwork' could occur. A detailed account of your time in the field must be included in your thesis. You should mention any critical incidents that occurred, too.

Examiners enjoy hearing about the reality of research in the field. This includes their knowing about smooth-running research as well as the difficulties that arise. In the latter case, an account of how you handled them will provide insights into your capability as a researcher coping with real-world situations in the field. You should also satisfy yourself that your chapters on these methods/techniques and your fieldwork present a convincing case that shows your choices to have been appropriate. If you achieve that then your data collection processes will be seen as being correct.

Clear and precise presentation

Why did you decide to have so many/few chapters for the text?

Please explain how you decided on the order of the chapters in your thesis.

[Examiners do not normally ask questions about an attractively produced and presented thesis since this is what they expect to receive. If they do remark on it then they would be likely to say 'Thank you.']

Your entire thesis should project clarity in the text and ease of reading. The use of suitably expressed and reasonably brief headings will act as helpful signposts through parts, chapters, sections and the thesis itself. Think of the first impressions that you want your thesis to give to anyone who opens it. Presentation is a critical yet simple determinant of quality for a thesis. Care and time has to be taken in checking and rechecking the text, plus ensuring consistency of formatting, grammar, cross-checking the appearance of sources in the text and the reference list.

But, as everyone knows, a poorly presented piece of writing also conveys a lack of concern for its readers. This is particularly true of examiners if they receive a badly presented thesis. Compliance with all the protocols – referencing, format, pagination, font and point styles, etc. – is not a difficult thing to do. Time invested in this relatively minor activity pays off as you produce a well-presented thesis. Ignorance of or non-compliance with the protocols conveys its own poor impression!

Engagement with theory

> You provided a sound foundation for your research from the literature. You did a good job of summarising, critically analysing and then focusing on the key segments of the topic. Here you showed real understanding of the ideas in your field.
>
> Your literature sources are extensive. That was good, but you also showed how it all built up over the years to create the schools of thought that we now have. That was even better.
>
> Why did you only cite literature from the past decade when much was written in the previous three decades on this topic? Some of it established real breakthroughs in understanding, too!
>
> Although you have cited all the expected sources on the topic, they appear more as a list than as a discussion. Why was that?

Doctoral candidates are expected by everyone to be well-versed in theories. The association between theory and doctoral degrees is long established in the mind of the public. It is also firmly established in the attitude that examiners have towards doctoral theses. They expect to see that you have a sound familiarity with the main schools of thought that relate to your topic. From that position, they want to see that you were able to relate authors and their ideas one to another to build an argument. This is more than simply listing the ideas that authors have produced. Instead, it requires you to make connections between their respective ideas. The strength of these connections will show the depth of your understanding. Engagement is illustrated when you use theory in a confident manner as a tool to explain, analyse and interpret your research. When you achieve that, then you are also demonstrating engaged scholarship through your use of abstractions to advance an argument.

Coherent argument

> Please tell us how your theoretical perspectives helped you to frame the research issues, develop conceptual frameworks and design your research.
>
> You chose to use the idea of 'flow' to describe how ideas are developed and then works by introducing the concept as an overarching theory and a practical technique. This was a clever way to combine theory and practice and it was a strong part of your argument. Well done.

An intellectual argument involves selecting ideas and presenting them for a particular purpose. In your doctorate, you have to do the same. The ideas that you handle will be drawn from the writings of others, plus commentaries on those writings. You will inevitably have to read widely to assemble breadth and depth of ideas. You will need to distil that quantity of reading to arrive at the essential beliefs and perspectives which you then use. Choosing the ideas that you find most relevant to your research involves a form of sifting and choice. You have to explain why you preferred to work within one perspective on your topic rather than another.

Assembling an intellectual argument implies discovering and then using a form of reasoning that is plausible to someone else. As you do this in your doctorate you will be displaying scholarship. Boyer captures this task through these words: 'The work of the scholar means stepping back from one's own investigation, looking for connections, building bridges between theory and practice, and communicating one's knowledge effectively' (Boyer, 1990: 16). Readers may not always agree with your view on an issue. However, you need to ensure that they understand why you hold such a view. Your justification for that position should be explicit and fully explained. When you have done that, readers should be able to respect your position despite not agreeing with it. The strength of arguments in your thesis will depend on how you engage with the literature to advance those arguments.

Research questions answered

> Were you surprised by the conclusions that could be drawn from your data?
>
> Please talk us through how you analysed your data and so arrived at answering your questions.
>
> Why did you not include any secondary findings?
>
> The single large statement did cover everything that you looked at. When you

> then arrived at your conclusions, almost anything you discovered answered the question. With hindsight, would it have been better to have had an umbrella question followed by a series of related sub-questions?
>
> Are you convinced that you have answered your research questions?

If a research question represents the intention or purpose of your research, then answering that question is an inescapable obligation on you. The answer(s) to these questions should appear in appropriate places within staged research and in your conclusions chapter. It should not be overlooked since the answer is itself a conclusion! Examiners prefer to see a clear and unambiguous statement regarding the answer. This obliges you to be clear about the answer that you provide. If the evidence that your research has generated is open to interpretation, then you may have to provide a conditional answer to your research question. You may prefer to answer the question(s) quite directly and formally by stating your answer(s) immediately following a restatement of the questions themselves. Alternatively, you could provide a brief contextual setting for the questions and the answers which you provide. If you use this latter form of writing, then you run the risk of repeating earlier text that either interprets or discusses your findings. Examiners prefer not to read something more than once. Thus, you can be quite direct in telling examiners and other readers what the answer(s) are to your research questions.

Conceptual conclusions

> How do your conclusions fit into the ideas of (X, Y, Z) when your methodology and findings were quite different from those they used in their research?
>
> How did you use your conceptual framework to shape the conclusions that you are now proposing?
>
> Your claims for generalisability can be challenged.
>
> In setting out to develop theory, what difficulties did you have in reaching this position of now being able to extend ABC's well-established views?

Making a contribution to knowledge implies either developing (*inductive research*) or testing (*deductive research*) theory. Either way, you are dealing with theory at a sophisticated level of thinking. As a consequence, you need to recognise how your evidence allows you to add to, modify or refute extant theory. Examiners expect to see how you have aligned your conclusions with this extant theory. They will look for statements in your conclusions chapter that were clearly conceptual in their implication. These statements would be abstract and theoretical rather than descriptive or factual. Through these words you would be making your claim for a contribution to knowledge.

Clearly, you would align such statements with what you wrote in the opening chapters of your thesis regarding the gap in knowledge to which your research was directed. Examiners and other readers would then see that you had achieved what you had set out to do. In this way, you would have closed the virtuous circle of your research. They should also recognise that you could only have achieved this if your theoretical perspectives, research design, research methodology and research methods were appropriate, coherent and integrated. Thus, in meeting the expectations of readers through answering the questions in this box, you will also have confirmed the scholarly and methodological merit of your research.

Contribution to knowledge

Why do you feel that your findings justify the claims that you are advancing that they are a contribution to knowledge?

Who else, apart from ourselves and your supervisors, is aware of your claim?

How are you now going to disseminate your findings and share the discoveries with others?

Your claim to having made a contribution to knowledge can really only appear in the conclusions chapter. Text that appears before that chapter provides a basis for your claim. Thus, you should consider whether there are any conditionalities which need to be stated before you then make your claim. A highly experienced international doctoral supervisor and examiner believes that candidates should express their claim as being 'a modest contribution to knowledge, that is reasonable and can be defended' (Woolliams, 2005).

None of the questions that appear in the 12 boxes is particularly complex. Individually and collectively, they represent the building blocks of any serious research. Each question should be relatively easy for a doctoral researcher to answer. But many candidates do not address these questions as they write their thesis, inspite, no doubt, of having handled them intuitively as they progressed through their research. This results in them writing a thesis that contains numerous implicit assumptions about these questions and their research implications. When examiners read the thesis they would recognise these oversights, note them as agenda items for the viva and then explore them through questions to the candidate. In these cases, examiners' questions will expose those elements as serious omissions from the thesis. These candidates will be required to correct the errors and resubmit their thesis.

Reflecting on doctorateness

You will recognise that the focus of the boxes appear in most texts that deal with research methodology. In this sense, you may not be surprised at their appearance in a model of doctorateness. Their significance now is that if they are all present in both the doctoral research process and the thesis, then they create an additional value to that research. Just consider any sequence of three items; the centre item depends on its 'predecessor', and influences its 'successor'. The simple test holds true for all 12 items just as it does for any three.

The interconnectedness between the 12 research-related items implies that each one depends on all the other items in order to produce 'high-quality research'. This shows that, as a doctoral candidate, you are handling a network of issues – all of which have equivalent importance. Doctorateness, as with other high-quality research projects, requires more than a simple summation of the components that comprise the research process to appreciate exactly what it involves. If there is dependency between these separate components, then it is the nature of their interdependencies that will determine their collective and overall effectiveness.

Figure 3.2 is just a model of the pieces that, together, specifically characterise doctoral research. They provide a relatively simple way of portraying what examiners look for in a thesis. They also offer you a potential check list that can be used to audit your research and thesis. When all 12 components are present and interrelated then your research will exhibit high quality, rigour and scholarship. If the components are not apparent, then the research cannot display high quality, rigour or scholarship. Thus, the model has an orienting significance (Hutton, 1972: 18–20) since it gives a practical significance to the notion of doctorateness.

The importance of the model can be easily tested by you in Task 3.2. Recalling the preconditions for a doctoral award, examiners require all 12 elements to be self-evident. If one element is absent from the thesis, then they would not be satisfied that the candidate had grasped the nature of doctoral research. They might well approve of the way that the candidate had dealt with the other 11 elements, but refer the thesis for further work – on the missing element that your coin or finger obscured! Think of doctorateness as a

---

Task 3.2 Testing the 12 components for doctorateness

Select any one of the 12 elements in Figure 3.2. Place a coin or your finger over it so that it is obscured. Only 11 elements can now be seen. Next, ask yourself – if a doctoral thesis displayed these 11 elements would examiners award it a pass?

jigsaw puzzle that can only be fully appreciated when all the pieces are present and fitted together.

Doctorateness therefore results from specific critical research features being present in your thesis. These features should form a mutually interdependent network system of parts that have practical relationships within the thesis. Inherent in this model is the notion of synergy – the whole may be greater than the sum of its parts (von Bertalanffy, 1969). You have a responsibility to ensure that your thesis conveys synergy to your readers as they progress through the pages and chapters and meet the ideas that you have advanced. Thus, doctorateness becomes truly apparent when your examiners and other readers can recognise synergy within your thesis.

Looking back and ahead

Doctorateness has been explained in two ways. First, it is a research vision or strategy that channels your actions as you plan and undertake your research. This represents the 'doing of the research aspect of doctorateness.' Second, it is the underlying purpose of the doctorate that guides your actions, reading and thinking as they are transformed into text. This represents the 'conversion of research activity into the thesis' and it includes the presentation protocols. As you progress through these activities and exploit their interrelationship, this signals your appreciation of doctorateness. You are now thinking like a researcher. Your thoughts should now echo those of your examiners! Both are important and need equal priority by you as you seek doctorateness.

Chapter 4 illustrates how this approach can be devised and used.

4

Architecture of the doctoral thesis

This chapter will:

- explain how a visual strategy assists in undertaking doctoral research;
- outline the importance of structural considerations for a thesis;
- present the advantages and disadvantages of different structures;
- indicate how an architecture can be produced;
- show how candidates and supervisors can use an architecture.

Introduction

If you want to discover more about a doctoral thesis than reading what its title says, a good way to start would be to look at the contents pages. This has assumed that you did not rush to the abstract to gain an overview of the entire thesis! In the contents pages, chapter titles usually convey discrete themes in the thesis with pagination showing the relative length of chapters and sections. Lists of tables, figures, diagrams and appendices illustrate significant points of emphasis that support those chapters. Finally, looking through the reference list would provide an appreciation of the possible scholarship in the thesis. However, your impressions would be based on looking at the finished work. Your search would not really show how the candidate planned for and undertook the research and writing that resulted in the bound thesis.

Contents pages are really just the public face of a thesis. They show how you chose to present the outline content of your thesis to readers. An architecture is more than the lists shown in contents pages and it serves three functions. First, it is the map of how ideas about research relate to each other. Second, it indicates the anticipated relative size of written components of text. Third, it serves as a plan against which you can assess progress as you tackle the task of producing your thesis.

Writing your doctoral thesis may well place considerable demands on you. The act of writing itself could be less demanding if you approach this task with an overview of how the thesis might look when it is finished. This chapter outlines how producing and using an architecture can assist you to devise and then use such an overview for your thesis.

Creating a visual strategy

Let us assume that you are registered for your doctorate, or MPhil/PhD. Ahead of you lies 'doing the research' and 'writing your thesis'. The research and the writing will be easier if you have a plan of action before you start. Our choice to use the term 'architecture' as a metaphor for this activity is deliberate. As with the conventional uses of the word, architecture is used here to represent a blueprint of the possible structure and shape of your thesis.

The term 'architecture' also conveys the respective size and shape of work you have yet to undertake. Furthermore, it acknowledges such features as context, construction, materials, relative size and form. There is a parallel between these functions of an architecture and the functions of researching for, and then writing, a thesis. They share the common notions of a vision, a proposed outcome and a plan against which you can monitor your progress.

Unless you intend to embark on your doctoral research with no plan of action and no expectations of how your thesis might look when you finish writing it then you need to consider 'how to do it'. Producing such a strategy will involve your designing an architecture. In Chapter 2, we explored how you might answer the question *What is your thesis all about?* Providing a single sentence response should capture the 'what' essence of your proposed research. Your architecture then expands this reply converting it into the 'how' aspect of that research within a relatively small document. Most doctoral architectures are between three and five pages in length.

Significance of structure

Before we explore the nature of an architecture, we need to think about the significance of structure for your thesis. You may not have a free choice on this matter. It is essential that you check the regulations of your university to clarify whether:

- the layout and structure of a doctoral thesis is specified;
- candidates have a choice in the layout and structure of their doctoral theses;
- approval has to be sought for any aspect of the structural form of your thesis;
- procedures exist to ratify proposals of the structure of theses;
- structural form of theses is a matter entirely for negotiation between each candidate and their supervisor(s).

These are administrative protocols and you need to respect them. Normally these items would be explained in your university's research degrees handbook or its equivalent. If you are in doubt about any of these items then seek advice from your supervisor(s) so that you understand exactly what is expected of you.

Structure is the vehicle through which you present ideas in your thesis. It determines a particular sequence for your ideas to appear in the text and, therefore, how you intend them to be encountered by your readers. Think of your completed thesis as presenting the story of your research to your readers. You have to decide how that story will be told and how it is presented. Each of these issues involves making decisions about your preferred style and form of your thesis.

Deciding on a structure has strategic consequences for you. You have to balance the choices that exist about structure and decide on the one that you intend to use. Then you can start writing and producing chapters. You might wish to make minor changes to a chapter during the drafting stage. This is quite normal for anyone who is writing a substantial piece of work. Such alterations are minor in that they do not interfere with your original plans for the overall layout and structure of your thesis. This happens anyway in writing and it hardly represents a major disaster, so do not be dismayed if it happens to you.

When you have produced a number of chapters, it may be too late to adopt another structure with a radically different focus for your thesis. Occasionally, some candidates will discover that they have the wrong structure. They recognise that it is not right for the doctoral story that is unfolding from their reading or research. This would be an awful realisation for such candidates to face and their options are not very attractive! First, they could continue with their original structure knowing that it was not ideal for their thesis. Here, they would have a constant doubt about how the thesis would look when it is finally written. This is not a happy position to be in since it could easily undermine academic and self-confidence of any candidate.

The second alternative, of course, would be to revise their structure and then to rewrite existing chapters. In these cases, those candidates had not invested time to thinking about the possible final shape and emphases in their thesis. Had they done that then they would have had to convert those worthy ideas into an architecture that portrayed 'what my thesis might look like when it is finished'. Doing this would have saved them time and many worries about the structure of their thesis.

The importance of textual structure is because it:

- provides a visual overview of the entire thesis;
- displays intended relationships between ideas and arguments within the text;
- offers readers and authors a clear signaled journey through the text of the thesis;
- explicitly acknowledges appropriate protocols;
- displays authors' attention to the needs and expectations of readers.

Thus, appreciating the significance of structure will help you to present your text so that readers will find it interesting and easy to read.

You have to choose a structure for your thesis. Your options are to group your chapters into parts, each with a thematic title, or to have your chapters in an ungrouped numeric and sequential order. Each approach has merits and limitations and these are outlined in Table 4.1.

Table 4.1 Advantages and disadvantages of parts and chapters

Chapters grouped into parts

ADVANTAGES	POTENTIAL DISADVANTAGES
1 Thematic grouping of chapters	1 Contents page may appear to contain 'lots of items'
2 Opportunity to guide the reader through the group of chapters	2 Use of different fonts or bold text to distinguish between 'levels' in the structure
3 Allows for thematic development of the text	3 A tendency to add small chapters with an unclear focus in their text
4 Permits you to draw themes to a close and then provide a textual link to the next chapter	4 Introduction of artificial distinctions between chapters to make them fit into their respective part
5 Easy to add, alter or delete chapters	
6 Facilitates introducing interdisciplinary text in chapters under the part's theme	
7 Opportunity to include chapters of very unequal length	

Chapters not grouped into parts

ADVANTAGES	POTENTIAL DISADVANTAGES
1 A clean and 'uncluttered' look to the structure of the thesis	1 Either very few chapters of considerable length or many chapters that appear to have no explicit linkages between them
2 Each chapter can be quite self-contained	2 A few very large chapters may each have a word count that are the size of a single master's dissertation chapter and so become too diffuse
3 Closer and explicit link to research questions and research statements may be possible	3 Readers can lose their train of thought in very large chapters
4 A more traditional way of presenting the text	4 Too many chapters may lack an explicit cohesion and thematic development

A doctoral thesis is a scholarly piece of writing. *Your* external examiners will view it as such and so *you* should view it similarly. Thus, we suggest that you should not write it as a report where every paragraph is numbered sequentially or with subdivisions of the text where each one receives an ever-increasing series of numbers. Such a format is an inappropriate way to present a doctoral thesis and it is not very user friendly for readers either.

You need to think carefully about the relative size of chapters. This applies whether you adopt parts with chapters or only chapters as your preferred structure. For instance, how would you structure the length of the chapters that introduce and then conclude your thesis? How do you explain their relative size if measured in either words or pages? What is your rationale for their respective length? You should be able to provide your supervisor(s) with a reasoned explanation for your choices.

Although it is unlikely that examiners would question you on these issues, you should be able to justify your decision, just in case! Examiners apart, you should still be able to explain to anyone who asked *why have you chosen that structure for your thesis?* Once you can answer that question confidently, and convincingly too, then you have started to think like the researcher who gives genuine attention to helping their readers to move smoothly through the text.

Producing an architecture

Once your architecture has been drafted, be prepared to revise it as you progress through your doctoral journey. Always view it as 'work in progress' that portrays how you thought your research and thesis might look. Try not to use it as a commitment to a previously determined format that cannot be changed. Thus, the function of architectures are to provide shape and order for your ideas through the considered sequencing and naming of chapters and sections.

Like research itself, producing your architecture involves you in making decisions. The value of this deliberative process is that having considered the options and made your choices, you will understand the implications that follow from your choice. This will then give you confidence in explaining why you chose a particular structure for your thesis if you are asked that question by your supervisor(s) or examiners. This view corresponds with the ideas of Davis (2007). She saw architectures as achieving a very practical way to create visual 'fit' between a candidate's views of how their thesis might be presented and the regulations that may prescribe the shape of that structure. However, as a result of producing her own architecture she believed that: 'I have told a better research story as a result.'

In order to produce the first draft of your architecture you will need answers to the following practical questions:

1 Will the structure of your thesis be based on parts and chapters or just chapters?
2 What scholarly contributions will each part/chapter make to the thesis?
3 What could be the titles of each part and/or chapter?
4 What could be the titles of each section in each chapter?
5 What might be the relative word count of the parts/chapters?
6 How many diagrams, figures, tables or other non-text items do you anticipate including and where will each one first appear?
7 How many appendices do you anticipate including and in which chapter will each one first appear?

Some of the answers will require you to be creative, while others are relatively technical in comparison.

Question 1 is a basic issue that should be resolved first since it influences your answers to questions 2 and 3. Assuming that you chose to have parts, questions 2 and 3 need to be considered together. Whichever basic structure you prefer to use, it is still important for you to explain the contributions of parts and/or chapters to the thesis. You will need to be creative in how you devise titles for parts or chapters and the sections of chapters. Ideally, titles should be succinct yet convey the complexity of argument and the many meanings that you hope to include in the text. It may take more than one attempt before you and your supervisor are satisfied with the choice of words. Be prepared later to change them if circumstances alter and you feel that it is necessary to revise a title for a part, chapter or section.

It may not be easy either to estimate answers to the technical issues of word counts and exact locations of tables, etc. However, you can reasonably assume that chapters will not all contain the same number of words. It is usual for prologue and introduction to be considerably shorter than other chapters due to their preliminary function in the thesis. Similarly, chapters that deal with interpretations, analysis or discussion are usually longer than a chapter of conclusions (see Chapter 8).

Having a notional idea of the relative word count for chapters will give you an overall view of balance between the size of chapters in your thesis. You may see that one chapter is unduly large or small. If this is a problem for you or your supervisor(s), you may wish to adjust their respective provisional word counts. The aggregate word count for chapters indicates a total for your thesis. Then you have to see how that figure compares with any recommended maximum that is stipulated by your university. Thus, it is essential to have some feel for how substantial each chapter might be before you start to plan and draft it.

Using the architecture

The idea of producing an architecture is not the same as compiling the contents pages.

Many candidates are unfamiliar with this idea. Example 4.1 is an attachment to a letter sent by a supervisor to his candidates soon after they have registered for their doctorate. It explains the purposes of producing an architecture.

Example 4.1 Letter from a supervisor to a candidate: producing an architecture

Think about the architecture of the thesis as a visual strategy to guide your writing. Before you start assembling an architecture, please write down IN ONE SENTENCE what you would say if asked: **What is your thesis all about?**

Be conceptual rather than descriptive in your answer – then you have a benchmark that can be returned to as you produce your architecture. It can also be used in C1 of your thesis! Do revisit it fairly regularly to see if it needs to be amended or if you are unknowingly departing away from your initial ideas. You may need to pause in your writing to rethink exactly how you want the thesis to progress.

You will tackle some very practical issues as you decide what the architecture should contain. Your answers will not always be clear or certain since undertaking the research and then drafting text will cause you to rethink. You may alter your first views and the answers. However, considering these issues before you start will help you to envisage how your thesis might look. The following questions will help you to address these issues:

- What will be the continuous thread/theme/issue that runs through your thesis?
- Where does that thread/theme/issue originate?
- What will your readers' valued memories be after reading your thesis?
- What structure will your thesis have?
- Will it have parts/chapters or just chapters and what sort of sections will be used?
- What are the provisional titles of its parts/chapters/sections?

- What are the expected contributions that each part/chapter will make to your thesis?
- Can you express those contributions briefly in just a few lines?
- What might be the relative word count of the parts/chapters or sections?
- How many appendices might be included and in which chapter might each one appear for the first time in the thesis?

Don't forget, your answers are the start and not the end of your thinking about the structure of your thesis.

Once you have produced an architecture, and we have discussed it, then you would have a workable vision of the shape and format for your thesis. You will find that it might amount to three pages in length. Any component in your architecture can be changed by you, since circumstances may change and, anyway, you may consider a more appropriate title or word balance next week! But without such a strategy, it is difficult to weave a thesis together that possesses genuine coherence. The drafted text that you produce to account for the aims, etc. of parts can be reused in the introductions to those parts within the text of the thesis itself. Nothing need be wasted.

Once you have sorted out your architecture, do please let me have it. I'll offer some questions and comments before then using it as my template against which to read the chapters as you produce them.

The questions that it poses are ones that you should be able to answer. So, why not use Task 4.1 to clarify in your own mind the basic issues about the structure for your thesis?

Task 4.1   Clarifying the rationale for the structure of your thesis

Use the 10 questions that appear in Example 4.1 to provide answers that accurately account for the proposed/actual structure of your thesis.

The response that one of the candidates provided to this suggestion appears as Example 4.2. This single page was the first time that he had produced anything like this. It deals with many of the points in his supervisor's letter but he had combined his views to many of the questions into a single response. As a result, his handling of the final question gave a rather superficial account of his structure.

Example 4.2 A candidate's letter to his supervisor: notes on my architecture

What is my thesis all about?
'An insider's, practitioner's view of his role based on "knowing in action" as opposed to the prescribed job description he has to fulfil for performance management.' It reflects the daily jobs and pressures undertaken with formal job descriptions against which staff are assessed for performance management. The result of this difference of 'knowing in action' and job description produces role tension that has to be reconciled.

What is the continuous thread/theme/issue that runs through my thesis?
This is the insider's view of his role. Knowing in action; practitioner's view of events as social constructivism; insider's perception of their role; role definition of practitioner's vs management role definition; increased professional expertise. The main themes are: power and resolution of uncertainty, power being resource based and the ability of the department/individual to reduce uncertainty and the 'knowing in action' that occurs in my daily professional life.

What will your readers' valued memories be after reading my thesis?
The importance of professional judgement and how these judgements are reached, also the importance of personal values, which is only mentioned briefly in the job description. Another memory will be the rich descriptions of everyday decisions that staff face and how one person resolves them. It is this involvement, and perhaps identification, through the text that will bring the reader into the reality of the practitioner.

What might be the structure of my thesis?
There are five parts whose anticipated relative word counts are shown:

1 *context of the field setting and role of the head of year and research question (3,000)*
2 *conceptual framework (the glue that binds concepts together) illustrating the conceptual framework and related theories (7,000)*
3 *research methodology, paradigms, methodology and why I chose the particular methods from my 'insider perspective' (8,000)*
4 *process of analysis; reasons for the choices made and the timeline (20,000)*
5 *analysis of data, which will describe the conceptual conclusions and my intellectual journey (22,000).*

> *My five appendices will contain: swamplog; vignettes; job description and work-profiling system. This will allow me to balance the word count in Part 4/5 and still maintain the focus that is required within the recommended maximum word limit.*

The supervisor provided some feedback on the initial architecture that he received. His letter appears as Example 4.3. You will see that he has offered positive suggestions how the first version of the architecture might be improved. He has also indicated how he would use the improved version as a map of the thesis. This sequence of examples illustrates how candidate and supervisor can each gain practical benefits from having an architecture for the thesis.

Example 4.3 A supervisor's response to a candidate's draft architecture

Thanks for your letter and the first draft of your architecture.

Since there does not seem to be a single form in which candidates prepare their architecture, the shape and content of it becomes rather personal. This is OK as long as the text provides an explanation and understanding of the vision and shape for the thesis. I can just about see both of those in your text. You could perhaps have expanded the explanation for the parts etc. to give some appreciation of what they would contribute to the thesis as opposed to what they would contain. Maybe you could attend to this when you revise it.

My only real comment is that Parts 4 and 5 suggest an extensive overlap of content. I am sure that was not your intention, but they could be read in that way. If you called Part 5 'Discussion and conclusions' then this would distinguish very clearly that it was not about analysis. That would remain in Part 4. OK? You could then make the discussion chapter more substantial than the conclusions chapter. This would signal to readers exactly what the part contributed to the thesis and how it was different in focus than Part 4. Any views?

We had been worried about your growing word count. You seem to have sorted that out and got in under 60K. Well done, but now you have to monitor how much you produce to make sure that chapter sizes do not overrun.

It would be helpful to both of us if you could now expand the final paragraph to show the chapters that will appear in each of the five parts. If you could also think about the sections, too, then this would be better still. You have to choose titles for your chapters and they will have sections so why not start with provisional ideas now. They can always be changed later. Once this is done then you will have a far better view of the structure and we will have something to talk about, too.

Thanks for this. When you have revised it let me have a copy to use as my map of your thesis.

Example 4.4 shows a more detailed draft of how a candidate outlined his architecture for Part 1 of his thesis. It indicates the approximate length of the text in words and pages. Comments from his supervisor identify issues for attention that would expand the architecture and so help the candidate to visualise the scope of his research. This advice throughout the architecture therefore reviewed this overview of prospective work. The ensuing discussion clarified how each chapter fitted into the whole, thereby avoiding a piecemeal drafting of chapters one by one, which would then have needed to be linked together.

Example 4.4 Architecture for a Part 1

PART I: INTRODUCTION
[The size of this part will be around 15 pages (~5,000 words)]

Chapter 1: Aims of the research

- Aims, focus and research questions.
- Gap in knowledge.
- Research boundaries.

  My boundaries are as follows:
  1 serial founders;
  2 of high-tech start-up firms;
  3 in this country;
  4 during years 1993–2005.

  #### Notes
  1 Serial founders are people who found more than one venture.
  2 High-tech start-up firms definition is as used commonly in the industry.
  3 Time boundary starts at year 1993, in which the professional

VC firms have started operating and thus initiating the blooming of the high-tech industry.
4 I'll try to handle famous serial founders, who are recognised as successful ones. These people are very busy and their time is precious. I believe it will not be easy persuading them to participate in the research.

Comments from the supervisor
These are most helpful explanations to the part. As you move into further reading and then the writing, you will need to devise/adopt/ seek tight definitions of these terms. This would then allow you to explain your findings later. Or, you can offer quite loose definitions to start with and refine them as you progress into your research. I have no strong views on the merit of either of these two approaches – so over to you!

Chapter 2: Context of the research
Context (background) overview.

Comments from the supervisor
What happens in this field, in the world, in your country? Explanations please.

Serial start-up founders – what is your initial personal paradigm of the phenomenon?

Why is this topic important? And to whom? This question will open up your reason for undertaking the research and allow you to show that the gap in knowledge represents a sociological gap as well as a feature of professional ignorance. Thus, your findings could have multiple outcomes and potential uses. OK?

Candidates who seek their doctorate by published works have to produce a critique of their scholarship in a shorter thesis than the traditional PhD. Being restricted to 10,000 or 15,000 words obliges them to plan the shape of their thesis to gain maximum benefit from each word. Example 4.5 illustrates how a candidate explained one of her chapters in her architecture. She allocated 4,000 words for this three-section chapter. The final section in each of her main chapters had the same title – Critique of papers – where she justified the level of her scholarship. Two comments from her supervisor enquired where she was going to locate some essential doctoral characteristics in her thesis. Although they emerged from the evaluation of her draft architecture, they contain another significance. These questions clearly emphasise the similarity between different routes to a doctorate where an architecture can be of assistance to candidates and their supervisor(s).

Example 4.5 Architecture from a PhD by published works

Chapter 4: Supporting families in practice

○ Organisational structures for supporting families.

○ Who knows best – the professionals or the families?

○ Critique of papers.

About 4K words.

Comment by supervisor
Including 'Critique of the papers' as a final section in each chapter neatly introduces this feature into the overall structure of critical reflection on the body of your work. Does this proposed structure imply that you would have advanced a conceptualisation of your work – in general terms – through the introduction? If so, could the introduction become Chapter 1? If not, then where would you expect to provide this conceptualisation of your work?

Another comment by the supervisor
Where in your thesis would you expect to tell readers about your accumulating realisation that a gap in knowledge existed in your professional area of writing and that NOW you can claim to have contributed to knowledge in that area? Being able to visualise where that appears in your thesis will then help you to structure your arguments around those two critical factors of any doctoral thesis by published works.

The four examples show how candidates and supervisors can each benefit from the production of an architecture. For candidates, it can represent a useful stage in their appreciation of the doctoral process by reducing that to a manageable document. Producing such a document is itself a process of learning in which your supervisor(s) can play a guiding role.

A well-designed architecture will:

• visualise what the thesis could look like when it is finished;
• provide the sequence and titles of major components of your text;

- indicate the respective word count of parts and chapters and (possibly) sections;
- show how any proposed change to the proposed structure or word count would affect other components of your thesis;
- enable you to check that the development and flow of ideas is coherently presented in the sequence of sections and chapters;
- provide a template that can be used to self-audit your progress with writing;
- be a basis to identify issues for discussion between you and your supervisor(s).

You can then, of course, use the architecture to compile your pages of contents when you commence writing your thesis. Because you will have already determined the shape for your thesis, converting it into the contents pages should be a relatively simple exercise. This is an added bonus for you that follows from having an architecture.

Looking back and ahead

This chapter has explained how producing an architecture for your thesis offers many benefits for you as you visualise how to write your thesis. We have shown how your supervisor(s) can also benefit from being involved in using your architecture, too.

Chapter 5 explores how your theoretical perspectives emerge from exploiting the literature and extracting meanings from it that can guide your research.

5

Exploiting the literature

This chapter will:

- present a working explanation of 'the literature';
- illustrate what is entailed in engaging with the literature;
- detail the stages in exploiting the literature;
- explain the significance of theoretical perspectives for research;
- show the functions and origins of conceptual frameworks.

Introduction

'Doing a literature search' is an integral part of any serious research. However, when we read research accounts it is not always apparent what the author was searching for. Neither is it always clear what that search found. Doctoral examiners are very clear what they expect this activity to serve. Their perspective allows us to suggest a more accurate title and explicit purpose for this task.

Doctoral research is founded on scholarship and this, in turn, depends on candidates being intimately engaged and conversant, with certain theories. This chapter shows how you can use those theories to demonstrate expected levels of scholarship. In this chapter, we offer a model of using the literature that provides you with a justification for your research. From this position, it also constitutes a central factor in successfully defending your research.

The title of this chapter captures some important beliefs about the literature. It represents a resource that is waiting for you to access and use. While there may be protocols that limit access or determine its use, the literature comes alive when you open a book, read and then think. The literature waits for you to reap the benefits that it contains.

What is meant by 'the literature'?

In academe, 'the literature' has become a collective noun that holds meanings for its diverse users. In contemporary academic parlance 'the literature' is used to describe:

- a physical corpus of published works on a specific topic;
- the extended body of writing that relates to a specific corpus of published works;
- the accumulated knowledge that resides within the corpus;
- work in progress that, when finished, will add to the corpus of knowledge.

These four applications of the term may have slightly different points of significance between and within disciplines. However, the meaning of their end use is the same: 'the literature' describes a specific body of knowledge (the corpus) that is recognised by its respective users.

In many disciplines, the corpus would also include those physical artefacts to which others would refer as exemplifying understanding of particular concepts and practices. The skeleton of an extinct species represents knowledge. It could be an accepted part of the corpus for archaeology, biology, biomedical sciences, environmental sciences, geography and history among others. In each discipline, the significance of the skeleton would be explained differently by their respective 'literatures' through their own lexicon and paradigms. Thus, literature is a term that may be corpus specific or represent a body of writing that transcends disciplines.

Another set of implied meanings is associated with the term. These originate in a behavioural relationship and perspective. Users of the literature may feel a loose sense of identity with others who access the same literature, such as:

- a shared interest in similar bodies of knowledge;
- a mutual recognition of the philosophical and methodological values that lie within that corpus and which distinguish it from another corpus;
- a sense of what is deemed to be included in, or excluded from, the corpus;
- an expertise in handling and manipulating the corpus with the purpose of advancing knowledge;
- a lexicon of terminologies that may be quite specific to that corpus;
- an ability to demarcate between those who understand the corpus and those who do not.

These users therefore exhibit attributes that correspond with the notions of small social systems (Parsons and Shills, 1951) in which members identify themselves as belonging to a group either formally or informally.

Examiners will be familiar with the corpus from which your ideas have been drawn. They will also possess a sense of collectivist identity towards the literature that you both use. If your research is located within a very specialised field, you will then share with them a specialised lexicon. It will contain technical terms with meanings and use that neither you nor your examiners would question. This forms an immediate bond of speaking and writing in which you and they are fluent. Non-members of the specialism would lack that fluency. Thus, the corpus is a professional and scholarly link between you and your examiners that is usually unspoken, but implicitly acknowledged through a mutual use of the lexicon.

Evidence for this link can be seen in examiner reports and questions in vivas, as Example 5.1 shows. The first three extracts are from examiner reports. They all recognise and respect a candidate's handling of literature. These examiners openly acknowledge a shared expertise between themselves and the candidate.

Example 5.1 Examiners' comments on effective use of the corpus

Examiner A   How the literature was handled was excellent. It showed real immersion in the complexities of this subject.

Examiner B   I particularly enjoyed seeing how such wide reading was drawn together through the extensive use of just one article. That it was by the premier writer in our area is not a surprise. But it was used in a masterly way.

Examiner C   The candidate was surgeon-like in how she cut through the volumes of writings on feminism today to expose common concerns towards women musicians. This showed high-order thinking and analysis. It also followed being able to disentangle important concepts from the description that surrounds that topic.

Example 5.2 shows how three examiners posed probing questions to candidates about how they had used their literature. These questions seek expansion on the text that had appeared in their candidate's respective thesis. These candidates were able to respond confidently to those questions because they were totally conversant with and had absorbed the full import of their corpus.

Example 5.2 Examiners' comments on inappropriate use of the corpus

Examiner D   I understand why you limited your reading to the 19th century, but why did you exclude writers from the early 20th century?

> **Examiner E** How would you rank the importance of James Lewis's work on your research?
>
> **Examiner F** Would you agree that most of the writers of merit in our field produced their best work during their early careers?

We have argued here that the literature has an importance that is more than being just a collection of books, journals, reports and artefacts for you to access. A literature starts to have a recognisable identity when someone explains the nature of its corpus, its extent and its accessibility. We will each have our own literature that we have defined as being special to us. Your own relationship to and use of this literature will have grown over the years. It will continue to expand as you progress through your doctorate, too.

Knowing the literature has both an intellectual and methodological benefit for you. It provides new insights on issues through the synthesising of ideas and the reworking of theories or research evidence. It will also acquaint you with the methodological approaches and experiences of others from which you can learn. The result of this, as Hart (2001: 2) proposes, is that: 'An analytical reading of the literature is an essential prerequisite for all research.' This position follows from his earlier observations that reviewing the literature: 'ensures the researchability of your topic before "proper" research commences. . . . It is the progressive narrowing of the topic, through the literature review, that makes most research a practical consideration' (Hart, 1998: 13).

Our respective literatures always overlap with the literatures of others. The uniqueness of your doctoral research and thesis might be due to the composition of the literature that you have chosen to access and combine in your own way for use. If this is what you believe makes your doctorate different, then it needs to be stated very clearly in the thesis so that your examiners can identify with your claim. Task 5.1 invites you to consider this issue.

> **Task 5.1**   What is distinctive about your list of references?
>
> Consider the array of references that you have assembled or will assemble. What is distinctive about that listing which differentiates it from other more run-of-the-mill handling of your topic? How have you exploited that difference as a discrete strength of your thesis and where has it been explained in your thesis?

As any of us embark on another piece of research, we have to consider which literatures to access and which sources to cite. You will have faced similar choices when starting your doctoral research. Once you have recognised and included those 'essential and always quoted works' then you enter a different territory of the corpus. This is when you follow references or footnotes into less familiar fields of writing. You may be reading around the subject but, in practice, you are extending the boundaries of your corpus. However, a deeper reason for doing it may be to discover from the literature another way to make the familiar different.

Example 5.3 shows how four candidates adopted different approaches to accessing the literature.

Example 5.3 Deciding what to read

Candidate A   I knew the primary sources, of course. I had great fun extending it, though, into unfamiliar fields of reading where I had to discover how important authors were whose names I had not heard of a year previously. I used citation indices to judge their standing, though just looking in the references told me all I needed to know. Experts may know that I had included some secondary sources but my examiners did not complain so it must have been OK.

Candidate B   I tracked the writings of Williams through the years and looked for his name in books and articles over the same period. This focused attention on him and those who wrote serious works about him. Later, I widened my reading to include less critical writers and commentators. For my research, they were necessary to know about but not so important to me because they were marginal.

Candidate C   My problem was that too much had been written around my topic. I started by reading everything and then had to get my notes into some order of importance. I used the references in the most recent major text as a filter to eliminate things that I had read by mistake. It worked but took a long time.

Candidate D   There were only four refereed articles and two professional commentaries on my topic. I knew their ideas thoroughly. I relied on major associated works that dealt with the theories that I used conceptually. They were strictly secondary sources but I had to use them to compensate for the lack of literature on my topic. I created my web of ideas between a small and a more substantial primary literature.

Candidate A ensured that he accessed suitably reputable sources when reading outside his particular primary texts by establishing their credential before including them in his text. Candidate B focused her attention on identifiable primary sources. Secondary and other supporting texts were used to provide background commentaries on primary sources. Candidate C only appreciated the extent and relevance of his reading when he was well into his research. Being more discriminating earlier would have avoided the time-consuming task he created for himself. Candidate D confronted a lack of substantial primary sources by privileging those in adjacent fields of study. He extended his reading beyond the immediacy of his topic to include what he referred to as 'major sources' from related disciplines. These examples show the need to make strategic decisions regarding how deep and broad your reading will be.

When you write about 'your literature' the reworking of your original ideas will give a different perspective on the familiar. Suddenly, your readers will be interested in how you have repackaged ideas so that your new perspective is original. But to do that means that you have already assimilated the primary literature. Only then can you add to it from other literatures and so create your new perspectives on the familiar.

You cannot escape from dealing with 'the literature' in your thesis. Viewing it as a tool that helps you in your research may not challenge you to be innovative in reading. However, seeing the literature as something to exploit for your own ends, introduces excitement into research and reading. This may come about through stumbling around among books and journals and suddenly finding one line that produces an 'aha' or 'bingo' reaction from you. Alternatively, you may prefer to read in an orderly way and arrive at new insights following careful thought and reflection. Either way, you have used the corpus quite deliberately to serve your ends. This will show in how you then write and defend your research.

Engaging with the literature

Supervisors constantly exhort their candidates to *'engage with the literature'*. You too may have overheard or received such a request. Examiners devote considerable attention in discovering how far candidates have achieved this. Think about the meanings in this combination of words. The notion contains overtones of proximity between you and the written word. It also includes the sense of interacting with ideas. If the word 'your' is included in this exhortation then *'engage with your literature'* hints at personal choice and, possibly, even ownership through your use of it. These various interpretations of the phrase are associations with what happens when you become close to the literature.

It is quite appropriate to go further with these analogies. Becoming close friends with your significant sources will reveal meanings and nuances that may not initially be obvious to you. Knowing these friends well will usually mean that you read the entire book; read parts of it again; read it anywhere and dip in and out of it to retrieve a good idea or two (Pennac, 2006). Thus, these friends – the literature – will provide you with the original insight or interpretation that a less intimate relationship with your sources may not.

Researchers – you – reveal scholarly depth when successfully engaging with the literature that appears in their thesis. Conversely, the absence of engagement with the literature indicates that although those researchers may have searched and reviewed the literature their understanding of its significance is not explicit. Furthermore, those researchers will have approached this task as essentially a technical exercise. This format usually just lists sources, often in blocks of names and their dates, with little accompanying explanatory text. They will have measured their success by noting how many publications, how recent the respective dates were and how many lines of quotations they were able to include in their text. Bulk use of the literature in this form is always recognised for what it represents – the absence of scholarship.

The purpose of engaging with the literature demonstrates that you have:

1 a comprehensive coverage of the field being studied and have a secure command of that literature;
2 shown breadth of contextual understanding of the discipline(s) that are appropriate to your study;
3 successfully critiqued the various established positions and traditions in those disciplines;
4 engaged critically with other significant work in your field;
5 drawn on literature with a focus that is different from the main viewpoint(s) in your research and explained the relevance of that literature;
6 maintained a balance between delineating an area of debate and advocating a particular approach.

Your demonstration of engaging with the literature will be apparent in three categories of chapter. First, it will appear in those chapters that contain the theoretical perspectives on your research topic. It is those chapters, in particular, where you can relate traditions of thinking to their respective chronological development in your discipline(s). Second, engagement with the literature should also be obvious to readers of your chapters that underpin the theoretical approaches, arguments and justifications for your research design and methodology. Finally, as you analyse, interpret or discuss your findings, you will draw on theoretical perspectives in these processes. This will continue in your conclusions chapter as your claims for contributing to knowledge are associated with extant theoretical positions. Thus, your constant engagement with, rather than detachment from, the literature should be apparent throughout your thesis (Rugg and Petrie, 2004: 103).

In your discipline, you should have no problem in distinguishing between the three main types of source on which to draw for ideas. First, primary sources are those pieces of original work that are considered to have made major epistemological contributions to the corpus. Their merit is that within their respective discipline they brought about a paradigm shift in understanding. They have, therefore, added significantly to knowledge.

The application and dissemination of their ideas by others will also have extended that shift in ways that others see the world (Kuhn, 1996). Others regularly cite them and it is essential for you to engage with these ideas and reflect on their significance within your thesis. They are the academic sources that examiners always look for in doctoral text. You need to appreciate how publications involve external and independent peer review of the articles that will feature as your primary sources. Then you ought also to compare their respective citation scores that indicate professional scholarly standing and the time lag between submission and publication of articles (Dunleavy, 2003: 228). This information constitutes their academic standing, as measured by those indicators.

Second, secondary sources do not usually contain significant original work. They cite and critique the primary, and even other secondary, sources in their respective fields. They are a valuable starting place to find informed interpretations that provide new ways to understand the work of primary source writers or to apply their ideas. They develop new understandings through association with and extension of primary sources. Thus, they represent a valuable second row of sources for inclusion in your thesis, due to their integrative and applied contributions to your discipline.

Third, supporting sources will not normally contain original work. They are not usually research based since their readership is more diffuse than in either primary or secondary sources. Their authors may not judiciously cite the primary sources and they frequently accept the writings of others in an uncritical manner. These authors may be well-informed about the discipline, but they do not seek to extend the boundaries of knowledge in that discipline. However, supporting sources serve another purpose that candidates sometimes overlook.

Monthly professional journals often contain invited articles by primary source authors. Through these relatively short pieces, those significant authors disseminate their research in an applied format. Articles of this type are a particular genre of scholarship. They originate from respectable research and so their arguments and implications are well-informed. Their applied emphasis provides another dimension to the author's original exposition of their ideas and findings. These types of journal have shorter publishing timescales than international peer-reviewed publications. As a consequence, these sources are often more contemporary in their publication date and content. So it is worth investing time perusing professional journals for the theoretical nuggets that sometimes are there.

Just as you are deciding which journals and books to access, so, too, are your examiners. Their discipline and subject interests will have developed over the years and they will also be familiar with the literature that you access. Realising that should help you to see the literature as a reservoir of ideas to select from and combine in your own way. Being selective, explaining the connections between texts and proposing different ways of interpreting the writings in your area introduces you into the literary equation. But, to do that you have to understand and engage with the literature. Task 5.2 invites you to consider how you handle this process.

Task 5.2 Choosing sources to read

How would you describe your system of identifying and selecting sources to read? Are you satisfied that it helps you to keep up to date in your topic and related topics? Do you intend to describe it in your thesis?

Being engaged starts with you knowing your literature. This occurs when you have accumulated a sound understanding of the primary and secondary sources on your topic. Only then will you have the intellectual confidence to select and exclude sources as you seek to build an argument in your text. To do that, though, you need to use the literature as a vehicle through which to advance arguments that others will recognise and accept. As you build that position you are creating the textual foundation for your thesis through exploiting the literature quite deliberately for your own purposes.

Stages in exploiting the literature

There are four distinct stages for you to exhibit in your text before your readers will recognise and accept your theory-based arguments. They are apparent when you *summarise, synthesise* and *analyse* the sources. These initial stages follow a sequence that becomes progressively more insightful as each one builds on your conclusions from the previous stage. When you have completed the analysis stage, you are then able to use your sources to *authorise* the position that you hold towards your research. This allows you to locate your research alongside extant work in the corpus and so substantiate your belief in the need for your research.

Furthermore, progressing through the four stages will also have clarified your presumptions about gaps in the literature and any methodological considerations regarding the investigation itself. Avoid over-claiming for your academic positioning. Be reasonable in where you align your work within the hierarchy of sources and work in the corpus. Suggesting that your findings will be modest is easier to defend than stating that it will gain instant international regard and prizes!

There are aspects of writing where examiners appreciate seeing how candidates view the merit of their own work compared with that of their professional peers. Do meet that expectation, but avoid providing a hostage to fortune in your viva by an unjustified positioning for your work. So use the literature to establish the potential scholarly provenance for your doctoral work. As Murray wisely advises: 'Claim some success without claiming too much' (Murray, 2002: 234). Doing that is far easier to write and it will be more enjoyable for you to defend.

To undertake these four intellectual processes successfully you have to engage totally with the sources, as shown in Table 5.1. Using these stages to give tangible shape to your engagement with the literature provides legitimacy to your theoretical perspectives. It shows that you are exploiting the literature as a positive tool in your research.

Table 5.1 Using texts to substantiate your research

Summary of sources.
This stage provides an overview of the past. It involves searching the literature (the *corpus*) to identify sources that relate to your topic and methodology. The key works of key contributors on the topic are cited and extracts from their writings are quoted. This shows readers that you are familiar with both historical antecedents and individual contributors in your field of study. In their first draft of 'literature' chapters, many candidates present the sources in this stage through exhaustive lists of sources. This is not engagement since it is little more than a list of sources with no accompanying explanation of relationships between those sources.

Synthesis of sources.
This stage clusters the sources as you identify the different schools of thought that are inherent in the corpus. This mapping of sources will explain their temporal relationship one to another by identifying trends in meanings and significances in their respective works. Your thesis would contain explanations of these features by tracing the importance of how these clusters of themes developed chronologically. Alternatively, you might prefer to follow the chronological writings of individual authors over a given period. Your synthesis of these respective sources introduces a higher level of meaning in the corpus than would have been apparent in the previous stage. In this stage, you are now engaging directly with the literature in order to synthesise your sources.

Analysis of sources.
This stage involves critical evaluation of the sources. It requires a detailed consideration of the sources for consistency or flaws in their arguments and the consequences on the conclusions that were advanced. It also tests the relevance of the theoretical perspectives that informed the source when it was written or produced. This historiographic perspective introduces a filter that determines the temporal and contextual appropriateness of earlier sources to the contemporary context of your doctoral research. It prevents you from adopting theoretical perspectives based on circumstances that no longer exist. You can still cite the sources for their contribution to the development of the discipline, but you should acknowledge their limited explanatory power.

Authorizing your text.
This final stage emphasises the relationship between the sources and your own research. Having summarised, synthesised and analysed the sources, you can draw conclusions about the sources and your research. You can now locate your work within the traditions of your discipline and its significant extant literature. State this relationship unambiguously by using such opening words to that sentence as: *'It supports . . .,' 'It confirms . . .,' 'It develops . . .,' 'It differs from . . .'* or you could assert ownership of your work through the more personal: *'My work extends/departs from the work of . . .'.*

To illustrate how sources are sometimes introduced to the text, a series of versions that a candidate produced have been converted into a fictional account. It has been set outside any discipline so that the messages contained in the three versions are generic and undistorted by discipline-related factors. We have adopted the colours of the rainbow as the names for seven authors, and dates of their hypothetical publications are shown. You will no doubt arrive at your own impressions about the scholarly information that the versions A, B and C convey to you as a reader of this 'research'.

Version A Providing a list of sources

Original work in this field of study was produced during the latter part of the 20th century (Red, 1997a, b, c; Orange, 1973; Yellow, 1998a, b; Green, 1976; Blue, 1962; Indigo, 1975; Violet, 1960).

Unless the candidate explained the significance of these sources then it will be little more than a listing of seven persons who each produced seminal work on the topic. These sources would have been important at the time when they were written, but readers were denied any insights from the candidate on the significance of the authors or their respective publications. Also, the random ordering of the sources obscured any immediate significance being made of the respective dates.

Version B Connecting the text with its chronological context

*Violet (**1960**) argued that standing on bridges across motorways to watch traffic on the road below should be charged for. Indigo (**1975**) showed the inhalation of exhaust fumes by watchers to be a health hazard. Orange (**1973**) confirmed this finding from similar studies in America. Blue (**1962**) made connections between bridges on motorways and watchers who were relaxing during breaks from driving. Red (**1997a, b, c**) argued that pricing the private use of private time was unconstitutional. Yellow (**1998a, b**) emphasised the legal aspects of health and safety residing in bridge owners. Green (**1976**) surveyed all bridges over motorways in the north of England and concluded that the incidence of traffic watching from them was infinitesimal.*

Despite the addition of some descriptive text around each source, there is still no engagement between the sources. The relationship of one source or author to another is lost within the random date sequence in which they have been presented. The candidate rather cleverly implies that work by Orange confirmed work by Indigo that appeared 2 years later! The reordering of the sources into a chronological sequence would, instantly, reveal the relative temporal relationship between these respective publications: *Violet, 1960; Blue, 1962; Orange, 1973; Indigo, 1975; Green, 1976; Red, 1997a, b, c; Yellow, 1998a, b.* Having such information sets the 48-year period into three distinct phases of authorship that readers had to work out for themselves from the original list.

Version C Introducing engagement within a chronological text

*Violet (**1960**) was the first to propose charging for standing on bridges above motorways to watch the traffic below. This was redefined when Blue (**1962**) showed high correlations between watchers relaxing from driving and motorway bridges. A decade later, attention emphasised health aspects when Orange (**1973**) compared studies on exhaust fume inhalation by traffic watchers standing on motorway bridges in America and UK. Repeat studies by Indigo (**1975**) confirmed Orange's findings. However, Green (**1976**) surveyed all UK motorway bridges and concluded that the incidence of traffic watching was infinitesimal. National concerns over health then ceased. Two decades later, attention on this issue remerged through legal considerations of usage. This was pioneered by Red (**1997a, b, c**) arguing that pricing the use of private time was unconstitutional. This macro-view was complemented by Yellow (**1998a, b**) focusing on the health and safety responsibilities of all bridge owners for users of their bridges irrespective of their intended use.*

In this version, readers can now follow the development of thinking and writing on this topic through the chronology of authors and their respective publication dates. None of the changes that have been made is radical; nor would they have taken very long to draft. The linking text provides a brief contextualisation for the items. Highlighting the dates through a slight reordering of the text and including 23 additional words has converted arid prose into a readable account of events. The text flows as it takes readers through a sequence that had three distinct dated phases during which these sources were published in the early 1960s, mid-1980s and late 1990s. The text now finally demonstrates some engagement by the author with these eight publications. Thus, this piece of fiction shows that engaging with the literature is to be in control of its use and so improve the comprehension by readers of what is written.

Developing theoretical perspectives

As we saw in Chapter 2, examiners expect your research and thesis to combine high levels of scholarship and interpretation with innovation and development, as shown in Figure 2.3. Quadrant B, theoretical perspectives, represents sets of criteria that examiners will look for in your thesis. They will be curious to discover how you presented your arguments and interpreted your evidence. How you search the literature and engage with it will determine how you attended to these features of doctoral research. Viewing the literature as the source of theoretical meanings can therefore explain how you developed theoretical perspectives on your research topic.

Taking such a view gives a clear and primary purpose to searching and reviewing the literature; to generate theoretical perspectives on your research topic. Rudestam and Newton (1992: 46) point out that: 'The research design clarifies the relationship between the proposed study and previous work conducted on the study. The reader will need to be convinced that not only is the proposed study distinctive and different from previous research, but that it is worthwhile doing. This is the place where the student's critical abilities as a scholar are tested and evident.' These perspectives then guide how your research is designed, analysed and the type of conclusions that you propose, as shown in Figure 5.1.

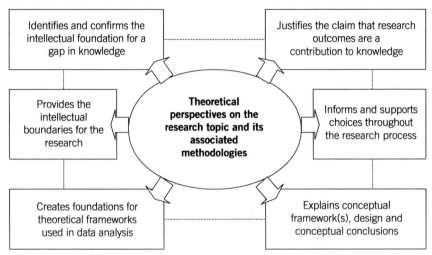

Figure 5.1 Practical influences of theoretical perspectives.

The model in Figure 5.1 illustrates how your theoretical perspectives have two dimensions. First, they will influence how you define or clarify your research topic. Second, they will then influence how you choose your methodological approach and associated methods of data collection. Making the connection between these two central features of your research immediately shows your grasp of serious research processes. Hart stresses this point succinctly: 'Searching the literature will help you to design the methodology for your project by identifying the key issues and data collection techniques best suited to your topic' (Hart, 2001: 3).

Your theoretical perspectives will combine theories on your topic and methodologies through:

- making explicit the gap in the corpus (the literature) to which your research is directed;
- delimiting your research by stating what is included and excluded from your investigation with theoretically justified reasons for those choices;
- developing conceptual positions (paradigms) as frameworks in which to design your research;

- creating the conceptual framework(s) that determine how your research is designed, analysed and then concluded;
- giving theoretical authority to the decisions that you have to make throughout the duration of your research process;
- justifying the conceptualisation of your conclusions as contributing to knowledge within the specific parameters of a stated gap in knowledge.

Each of these consequences should have followed from searching and reviewing your literature. A review of a research literature as Hart (1998: 44) argues: 'is about evaluating the logical coherence of theories, methodologies and findings in a context of informed scholarship'. By explaining how you handled these research processes, you allow readers to understand the practical rationale behind your entire research process. Another benefit accompanies this explanation. The quality of your text will have been raised from descriptive accounts of *What I did* or *How I did it* to the more scholarly explanations of *Why I did it this way*.

Answering the final question provides explanations that involve scholarly and interpretive arguments about your research decisions. Doing that places your textual explanations about the theoretical perspectives firmly at the high end of the scholarship and interpretation axis in Figure 2.1. But, in doing that, also accounts for how those theoretical perspectives constitute the foundation for your research design and the conduct of your research. This will include accounting for the distinctiveness and relevance of those approaches to your research field and topic. These explanations locate your text at the high end of the innovation and development axis in Figure 2.1. Thus, what you write in your thesis about the implications of theoretical perspectives on your research provides the basis for you to demonstrate doctorateness.

Lewin pointed out that the test of a good theory would be that it had actual or practical potential through this phrase: 'there is nothing so practical as a good theory' (Lewin, 1952: 169). Conversely, a bad theory would be one that had no such potential. When he wrote those words, Lewin was making positive connections between theoretical and applied psychology. We have just seen how your (*good*) theoretical perspectives can be (*so*) practical when they directly influence other components in your research. The implication of Lewin's words is that you should tell your readers throughout your thesis of the practical uses that have followed from your theoretical perspectives.

This interpretation of scholarly merit through your theoretical perspectives should therefore correspond with Hutton's view that: 'The highest test of a theory is to show that it, and no other, can logically specify the outcome from empirical observation' (Hutton, 1972: 20). Its ability in this sense is being: 'useful in generating research or offering models to guide it. This is the heuristic function' (Hutton, 1972: 19). These observations on theory are reflected by van der Ven in his observation that: 'Good theory is practical precisely because it advances knowledge in a scientific discipline, guides research toward crucial questions and enlightens the profession' (van der Ven, 1989). If you can assure yourself that these criteria are met in your research, then you have constructed a defensible foundation for that research.

Similar conclusions have been reached by Holbrook et al. (2007), from analysing 1,310 examiners' reports on 501 candidates whose doctoral theses were recently submitted in five Australian universities. Their research explained how examiners dealt with three distinct features of reviewing the literature:

- **coverage** – how thoroughly candidates engaged with their literature in order to formulate appropriate research questions;
- **types of errors** – what type of errors in citation, inclusion and exclusion of sources (noted, though, as being primarily straightforward mistakes in presentation rather then understanding);
- **nature and use of literature** – how candidates used the literature to support significance and contribution, enhance and support interpretation of the findings and underpin argument.

Their findings showed that examiners identified the following as key factors in the candidate's use of literature:

- a working understanding of appropriate bodies of literature;
- a critical appraisal of the body of literature;
- a connection between the literature and the findings;
- a disciplinary perspective on the conclusions.

Holbrook et al. make the telling point that: 'The review of literature, so central to scholarly work and disciplined inquiry, is expected of the PhD student.'

Their findings, although based on an examination system that operates differently from that of universities in Europe or the United Kingdom, arrived at conclusions that are generic of examiner systems for doctoral degrees. The reason for this is that the major criteria against which examiners assess a doctoral thesis are determined by criteria which themselves are generic. The implication of this is that, as we have constantly observed, these criteria transcend disciplines and national systems of higher education. Minor local regulatory items that specifically concern protocols for presentation, layout and referencing though significant are not themselves generic determinants of doctorateness.

Example 5.4 shows comments of three examiners of UK theses that were complimentary towards the work of candidates. Examiner A exemplifies scholarly collegiality in his respect for the candidate's work while commending it, despite him not personally agreeing with it. Examiner B approves how the qualities in the literature review extended into other parts of the thesis. Examiner C picks up the links between the evaluation of the literature (review), analysis and presentation of results all of which were considered to have been impressive.

Example 5.4 Examiners' views about the effective inclusion of theoretical components

Examiner A The presentation of the thesis is of a high standard and shows an appropriate level of scholarship throughout the argument. I found myself disagreeing with the argument regularly, but in a such way that I considered to reflect very well indeed on the thesis. These were basic intellectual differences and not matters that I considered to be objections to the argument of the study itself.

Examiner B The thesis included a thorough critical literature review so that the subsequent experiments are clearly justified and then described. The discussion of findings displays an appropriate level of scholarship.

Examiner C The analysis and critical thought, in Chapters 4 and 5, is of a high standard, with the morass in the literature evaluated effectively. The theoretical analysis and presentation of results are particularly impressive. The thesis is well-written.

Example 5.5 shows less complimentary comments by examiners of three different theses. Examiner D points out the lacunae between the literature review and other components in the thesis where the candidate ought to have explained those linkages. Examiner E points to an overall inadequate handling of the theoretical component in this thesis, concluding that a lack of understanding about the role and purpose of a literature search, review and engagement may explain these weaknesses. Examiner F points to a lack of integration between the theoretical perspectives and other components that resulted in an unbalanced handling of theory in the thesis.

These two sets of examples emphasise the importance that examiners place on how candidates handle theoretical perspectives in doctoral theses. They recognise and commend the attention that candidates devote to this feature when it is handled well. They also recognise when candidates have mishandled it and their comments indicate why they have reached that conclusion. Thus, you should provide a comprehensive account of how your theoretical perspectives were used in your research and the thesis as a prerequisite feature in displaying doctorateness.

Example 5.5 Examiners' views about inappropriate handling of theoretical components

Examiner D   The literature review emphasises that non-economic factors have a substantial influence, but these are not included in the formal modelling. If they are not included, then this should have been fully explained and so should the consequence of it on the interpretation of findings and the conclusions from the research.

Examiner E   The survey of literature on the social consequences of population migration has weaknesses. Some are due to insufficient engagement with the ideas in that literature, some suggest a lack of understanding on points of detail others follow from shallow sourcing of materials. As a result, the bridge between the survey and the methods of documentary analysis is unstable due to a lack of understanding how literature and methodology are linked.

Examiner F   I thought that the key term – entrepreneurship – was under-analysed especially considering the amount of conceptual and evaluative weight it carried all the way through the thesis and especially in the theoretical chapters.

When you embarked on your doctorate, you would have anticipated having to cope with large quantities of reading, thinking and writing. These features typify successfully engaging with the literature, interpreting the theories that you encounter and then providing a written account of your work in your thesis. This process has a fascinating temporal dimension. It entails you are combining the past, the present and the future in order to create something new – your contribution to knowledge. The literature that you access is already part of the history in your discipline. Your engagement with it continues in real time, as you deliberate on how to incorporate the ideas from that literature into your research. Applying those ideas will then guide your research and the subsequent interpretations of findings that have yet to happen.

Developing a theoretical perspective links your reading, thinking and writing into a coherent whole. It provides you with academic authority as you explain how and why you have combined selected theories to provide a perspective on your topic and research methodology. This approach to your writing then avoids your making assertions that lack a substantial justification of argument. Instead, it makes it possible for you to write: *This is what I found out . . ., This is what it means . . ., This is why it is being used here . . .* and *This is how I am using it.* These words are positive introductions to the explanations that follow as you tell readers how your theoretical perspectives were incorporated into your research.

Developing your conceptual frameworks

'Theory informs our thinking, which in turn assists us in making research decisions and sense of the world around us' (May, 1993: 20). By linking theory and research May reminds us that fieldwork is a process of collecting data that have a specific explanatory purpose. It enables us to create and develop theory regarding certain phenomena that previously had no satisfactory explanations. Alternatively, it may prove or refute theories that we had created as the assumptions within the hypotheses that we tested. In both of these cases, inductive or deductive approaches used theoretical perspectives to guide their respective design and the subsequent conduct of investigations. May also places the obligation on you to explain your research decision making at the centre of this process so that the rationale for it is explicit.

Whatever research approach you adopt you will use theory to make sense of the topic before you are satisfied that it can be investigated. Then, theory will be integral to how you 'see' the topic – your paradigm. It is here that you will be evolving conceptual perspectives, or conceptual frameworks, on the topic. Miles and Huberman (1984: 33) define a conceptual framework as: 'the current version of the researcher's map of the territory being investigated'. Their definition accommodates purpose (boundaries) with flexibility (evolution) and coherence of the research (plan/analysis/conclusion). However, for Weaver-Hart (1988), conceptual frameworks are: 'a structure for organising and supporting ideas; a mechanism for systematically arranging abstractions; sometimes revolutionary or original, and usually rigid'. Thus, the conceptual framework provides a theoretical overview of your proposed research and order within the research process.

These ideas echo Kuhn's notion of paradigmatic thinking. He argues that paradigms portray how we see the world through perceptions, understandings and interpretations. In turn, these are the prompts for us to take action. For Kuhn: 'Acquisition of a paradigm of the more esoteric type of research it permits is a sign of maturity in the development of any given scientific field' (Kuhn, 1996: 11). Kuhn's notion that a paradigm shift explains changes in how 'something' is perceived influenced Covey (1989: 30) who observed that: 'whether they are instantaneous or developmental paradigm shifts move us away from one way of seeing the world to another'. The paradigm is therefore a way to model possible patterns and relationships which Barker (1992: 32) suggests: 'establishes or defines boundaries'. Paradigms and conceptual frameworks therefore display certain similar dimensional characteristics and roles which you can make explicit in how you write about this aspect of your research.

These perspectives have direct practical significance in your research. As Berger and Patchner (1988: 156–159) have argued: 'reviewing the literature leads to a delineation of the conceptual or theoretical framework of the study'. They pose three questions that you should be able to answer:

1 'Has the conceptual or theoretical base for the study been clearly described and are they related to the research problem?'
2 'Is there a theory underlying a research question?'
3 'Is there a clear and explicit connection between the theory, earlier findings and purpose of the present study?'

These questions emphasise how conceptual frameworks can give coherence to your research.

The practical relevance of conceptual frameworks to your field of study is made when Bryman argues that: 'A concept provides a set of general signposts for researchers in their contact with a field of study. While the concept may become increasingly defined, it does not become reified such that it loses contact with the real world' (Bryman, 1988: 68). Further emphasis on the practicality of this notion is found in the observation of Cohen et al. (2000: 13) that: 'Concepts enable us to impose some sort of meaning on the world; through them reality is given sense, order and coherence. They are the means by which we are able to come to terms with our experience.'

Robson combines these perspectives by saying that: 'Developing a conceptual framework forces you to be explicit about what you think you are doing. It also helps you to be selective; to decide which are the important features; which relationships are likely to be of importance or meaning; and hence, what data you are going to collect and analyse' (1993: 150–151).

Addressing the need for researchers to explain the components of their conceptual frameworks, Blaxter et al. (1996: 36–37) concluded that: 'Defining the key concepts and contexts of your research project should also assist you in focusing your work . . . They define the territory for your research, indicate the literature that you need to consult and suggest the methods and theories you might apply.' The importance of these views for you is, as Mullins and Kiley (2002) conclude, because experienced examiners: 'look for internal linkages and cohesion within doctoral theses'. Burton and Steane (2005: 53) support this view by arguing that researchers should: 'clarify the intellectual thinking on which the(ir) study is based'. Thus, the conceptual framework occupies an important and central place in your doctoral thesis.

Figure 5.2 shows the three origins of conceptual frameworks. It illustrates how the interactions between reading, reflection and the assumptions that come from experience, each generate concepts. Together these concepts combine to form the conceptual framework(s) used in your research. Conceptual frameworks do not exist independently of the individuals who create them. Someone has to create them. Thus, devising their own conceptual framework(s) is an inescapable task for doctoral candidates.

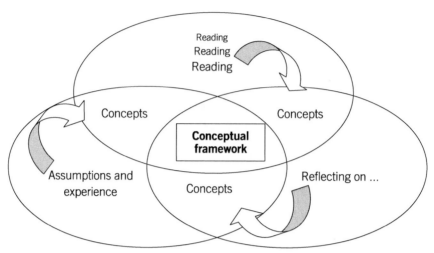

Figure 5.2   Sources for conceptual frameworks.

These various authors present a case for your conceptual framework to fulfil three roles:

1 providing a theoretical clarification of what you intend to investigate;
2 enabling your readers to be clear what the research seeks to achieve;
3 explaining how these roles will be achieved.

Examiners are also very interested in how candidates deal with conceptualising their research. For that reason, these components are imperatives as you to explain your text and the origins of your conceptual framework to anticipate the question.

Table 5.2 shows the contributions that conceptual frameworks make to the research process and the criteria that have to be satisfied for them to make that contribution. Achieving integration between conceptual perspectives and research design, along the lines above, is straightforward for those who grasp the contribution that theory makes to research. However, others have difficulties as shown in Table 5.3. For those who misunderstand the role of conceptualisation, their problems are compounded as they move into the later stages of their research process. Thus, conceptual frameworks are theoretical anchors for your research; modelling relationships before the research and commences then giving conceptual focus to conclusions.

For examiners, your conceptual framework is a mirror on how you think about your research. It reflects an image of your conceptual grasp and higher thinking about the research process. Hills and Gibson (1992) emphasise this point by arguing that: 'One's ability to make flexible, purposeful use of a variety of conceptual frameworks seems to be contingent on possession of a conceptual framework for thinking about conceptual frameworks.' This view

Table 5.2 Contributions of conceptual frameworks to the research process

Conceptual frameworks assist researchers because they:
- reduce theoretical data into statements or models;
- model relationships between theories;
- provide theoretical bases to design and interpret research;
- create theoretical links between extant research, current theories, research design, interpretations of findings and conceptual conclusions;

Thus, conceptual frameworks introduce explicitness and order within and between the processes of research.

The critical test of conceptual frameworks is when they demonstrate:
- unity between appropriate theories;
- direction to research design and accompanying fieldwork;
- capacity to give meaning to the interpretation of research evidence;
- coherence between empirical observations and conceptual conclusions;

Thus, conceptual frameworks provide a self-audit facility for researchers to ensure appropriately grounded conceptual conclusions.

Table 5.3 Candidates' comprehension of conceptualising research

Understandings of conceptualisation	Misunderstandings of conceptualisation	Consequences for candidates and research
Clarifying the research issue(s)	Omitting paradigm(s) which locate and critique the research issues	Focus on research methods at the expense of concepts, focus on 'what' how' and 'when' rather than 'why'
Identifying concepts from a 'survey of the literature'	Not visualising linkages between various concepts in the research	A framework was not devised or its function appreciated, resulting in uncoordinated research strategies
Designing research and explaining methodology and the methods	Overlooking strategic and guiding roles for conceptual frameworks	Lack of explicit or cohesive relationships throughout the research resulting in unreliable fieldwork

Source: Leshem and Trafford, 2007

places an obligation on doctoral candidates to raise their level of thinking from content to meta-levels of conceptualisation. Thus, the practicality of conceptual frameworks is their capacity to introduce order in candidates' thinking process about the conceptual background and context of their research (Leshem and Trafford, 2007).

Looking back and ahead

This chapter has proposed that you have a corpus of knowledge that is specific to you. We have argued that this corpus is the foundation from which to generate the theoretical perspectives that you need to develop on your topic and methodology. These perspectives represent the conceptual foundations for you to devise your research design and, later, give conceptual focus to your conclusions.

Chapter 6 explores how your theoretical perspectives directly influence the design of your research.

6

Thinking about research design

This chapter will:

- explain the functions of the research design chapter in a thesis;
- simplify a potentially complex process by identifying the core components that examiners expect to see in this chapter;
- illustrate how the research design chapter is an integrating component of the thesis;
- provide guidelines on auditing the research design chapter for scholarly consistency.

Introduction

All research is designed. Some design may be little more than a fleeting thought about *how shall I do it?* A more serious approach would involve you deliberating on how you can achieve the purpose of your research. Then, you might ponder on the connections between the 'what' and the 'how' of the research. This would focus your thoughts on the methodological approach(es) that could help you to achieve the intentions of the research. Somewhere in this process of thinking you would consider the three elements of constraints, practicality and time.

At the doctoral level of study, the act of designing research involves a critical thinking process to determine how that research is to be undertaken. In turn, this stage of your doctoral work provides a philosophical and technical foundation from which to defend your thesis in the viva. Thus, research design explains how you devised a strategy to undertake the investigation that is presented in your thesis.

Your research design chapter integrates the methodological components of doctorateness which together 'guide and focus your research' (Hussey and Hussey, 1997: 114–115). It explains how you have used your research question(s) as a tool to focus your choice of research methods (Andrews, 2003). It shows how your reading (the literature) provides a conceptualisation of your topic which in turn influences how you: 'investigate[d] appropriate options for research design' (Walliman, 2005: 224). This then allows you to explain how your fieldwork was planned and conducted (Creswell, 1998: 18). Thus, research design enables you to 'connect research questions (purpose) to the data (collection process)' (Punch, 2000: 52).

This chapter will explain how research design should be located at the centre of your doctoral research process. It will show how examiners home in on research design with questions that explore your understanding of research as a process. It will also illustrate how the internal cohesion of the research emanates from your research design chapter. Finally, it will explain how examiners judge if you are thinking like a researcher *within a system of ideas or way of understanding* (Perkins, 2006: 42) as they read your research design chapter(s).

Functions of research design

Research design represents a series of decisions that comprise the strategy explaining how you will conduct your research. This strategy sets out how you propose to undertake your research. It combines a vision that extends to the conclusion of your research plus the means whereby it will be achieved. It will clearly reflect the conceptual frameworks or focal theories which will guide your research. The design will show what type of data you will seek, the sources from which you will seek them and how you intend to access and collect those data. A well-argued research design chapter therefore enables others to appreciate your research strategy. The absence of an explicit research design will call into question the conduct of any serious research investigation.

As researchers, perhaps we should all thank Kipling (2004: 58) for helping us to clarify our research design. He may not have been thinking specifically about research when he wrote:

> I keep six honest serving-men
> (They taught me all I knew);
> Their names are What and Why and When
> And How and Where and Who.
> (The Elephant's Child)

However, collectively the words form a practical template to help interrogate any issue. Examiners also know about this template, so you can anticipate questions in your viva that open with one of Kipling's names!

You will recognise that the six words *what, why, when, how, where* and *who*, introduce open-ended questions. Compared to closed questions that permit only 'yes' or 'No' responses: 'The chief advantage of the open question is the freedom it gives to the respondents' (Oppenheim, 1992: 112). Posing this type of question is easy, but providing appropriate answers requires careful thought. Before respondents answer, they need to balance some associated questions: 'how much to say,' 'how much information to give' and 'how to express the information as an answer'. In this way examiners gain insights into how you made the decisions that shaped your research design.

These words provide six direct routes into understanding your research design as you answer the questions shown in Task 6.1. The connection

---

Task 6.1   Applying the Kipling questions to your research design

What is it that you want to discover?
Why do you want to investigate it?
When is the investigation to be conducted and over what period?
How do you intend to investigate the topic?
Where is the topic located and where is it to be investigated?
Who are the respondents from whom data are to be collected?

---

between research strategy, research design and the development of theory, was aptly captured by Whetten (1989) in these words: 'The theory-development process and criteria for judging theoretical contributions need to be broadly understood and accepted.' When you use the Kipling questions you are identifying the strategic direction for theory development in your research. However, you will see that each question opens up another layer of questions. These initial questions are a starting point as they oblige you to be explicit about fundamental components of research. Examiners often then ask follow-up questions that explore your answer to these opening questions on research design. Such questions highlight your choices as you discuss their respective merits and limitations. However, accounting for these options and your decisions generates valuable text for this chapter.

Examiners are always interested to hear other researchers explain how their research was designed and Example 6.1 shows the type of broad questions that they ask. The three questions in the example are open-ended and may be used to invite candidates to talk expansively about their topic. They could each be a prelude to further questions on this topic or, alternatively, be a token question that examiners ask about research design. This latter situation occurs when examiners are satisfied that you have provided a thorough textual account of your research design.

Example 6.1 An examiner's questions regarding choice of research design

How did you decide on your research design?

Can you talk us through the stages that were involved in designing your research?

We would have expected to see more of a postmodern emphasis in your research. Why did you choose a quite traditional way to plan your research?

Example 6.2 An examiner's sequential questions about faulty research

Can you help us to understand the links between your literature and your research design, please?

But how did you use the ideas that you found in those texts?

I see that you had five hypotheses. They contain fundamentally different variables and I think that makes a total of 12. How did you expect to test so many broad issues in your fieldwork?

Can you show us where you have dealt with your research boundaries in the thesis? It seems to me that the potential scope of your research was actually unlimited. Am I right?

In your earlier chapters you wrote about power. Chapter 4 concluded with you saying, on page 78, that 'The use of power is a significant way in which individuals seek to influence others in social settings.' It seems that none of the methods that you used collected data about how power was used or seen to be used. Why was that?

Were your potential respondents limited to just the three care homes? Did you test the suitability of your questions before the survey was distributed?

If a thesis includes an unsatisfactory research design then examiners will combine open-ended and closed questions to explore this situation. Their questions will expose that candidate's understanding of research and, if necessary, check simple facts. Example 6.2 shows how a series of questions displays the concerns that an examiner had about a faulty research design chapter. (See also Example 2.2, questions 5–12, 16–19.)

These questions convey a sense of unease that one examiner felt about this candidate's familiarity with research design. Each question probes for information that, apparently, was missing from the text. Receiving unsatisfactory responses convinced both examiners that this candidate lacked scholarly understanding about the design and conduct of doctoral research.

As Hughes (1976: 55) points out theory and evidence (data) are in effect two different languages. He argues that 'translation' between the two is seldom easy. Examiners are consistently evaluating the extent to which candidates are confident and successful in moving between the languages of theory and data. In the earlier example, the examiners were not persuaded that the candidate exhibited that 'translation' capability either in the text of the thesis or in its defence during the viva.

You will recognise that research design has a range of functions. It encompasses both a strategic view of the research and the techniques that you intend to use to collect data. Viewed in this way, the ends and the means of the research that you write about elsewhere in your thesis are linked directly to your research design chapter. Thus, the research design chapter has two primary functions: first, it sets out the investigatory strategy for your research, so that, second, you can successfully defend how you approached and undertook your research in your viva.

Decisions are followed by more decisions

The practical significance of your research design is that it involves a series of linked decisions. Figure 6.1 portrays the sequence of these decisions. A decision on how to proceed with one item inevitably leads into the next but lower order item. The sequence also shows a descending order of relative importance for the four components owing to their respective strategic significance. In your viva, examiners may appear to be less interested in *what* you investigated than *how* you did it. This is especially apparent when they invite you to explain your research design. What examiners really want to hear is your account of how you dealt with the decisions that determined your research strategy. Unless there are errors in your fieldwork, they may only ask you a symbolic question or two about that part of your thesis.

Let us now explore your four major choices as shown in Figure 6.1.

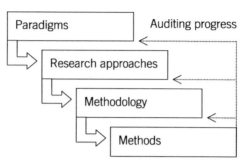

Figure 6.1   Levels of thinking about research.

The first major choice

This choice concerns the paradigms. You have to decide on the paradigm through which you 'see' your research topic. This will then determine the paradigm in which your research will be located. Most candidates refer to and explain their research paradigm or research approach. This may be because much has been written about the methodological debates that revolve around this issue (Bryman, 1998; Sardar, 2000; Fuller, 2006). The primary text is, of course, Kuhn (1996). He explained how paradigms represent ways of seeing the world through a 'definition of the field' (19), the idea that 'shared paradigms result in commitment to the same rules and standards for scientific practice' (11) and how understandings can change quite radically when there is a 'paradigm shift' (109). These views on knowing and how we see the world directly influence how we choose to perceive the research topic and the research approach as our paradigms (Burrell and Morgan, 1979: 1).

Let us assume that you intend to 'explore' the nature of induction provided by the company for recently appointed staff at your place of work and that you are free to decide how you would investigate the topic. Right away, you would have to clarify how you 'saw' staff induction. Example 6.3 presents four paradigms in which you might 'see' this research topic. They range from deductive to inductive in the assumptions that you might hold about each paradigm and their probable methodological investigatory approaches. Note how the economic paradigm has explicit numeric assumptions about induction leading naturally into a hypothesis-testing deductive research approach. This form of research would provide reliable and generalisable outcomes that accord with the practical implications of the economic paradigm.

Example 6.3 Four paradigms of induction

ECONOMIC PARADIGM

The full economic value to the organisation of a new appointee is realised only when that person can operate at an optimum level of performance.

Assumptions within the paradigm
Induction is a means whereby the period of suboptimal operation for newly appointed staff can be shortened, thereby increasing the rate of return and productivity of those new staff.

Investigatory approaches
Deductive, econometric modelling, surveying respondents, reliable, generalisable.

DEVELOPMENTAL PARADIGM

The professional value of new appointees should be nurtured and supported so that they are able to contribute to the collective profes-sionalism in the organisation.

Assumptions within the paradigm
Induction is the development through which new staff become familiar with the existing professional ethic, thereby sharing the expectations and norms of their colleagues.

Investigatory approaches
Deductive/inductive, multi-disciplinary, multiple methodologies.

SOCIAL PARADIGM

Socialisation is designed to inculcate new staff with the 'ways of doing things round here' so that they fit in, avoid making unconscious blunders and quickly feel that they 'belong' in the organisation.

Assumptions within the paradigm
Induction acquaints new staff with the history, culture, procedures, norms and values of their new company – extolling virtues at the expense of possible shortcomings.

Investigatory approaches
Inductive, observational, multiple methods, cameo cases, high in validity.

MICROPOLITICAL PARADIGM
The informal acclimatisation to the work ethic that prevails as a counterculture starts when existing colleagues trust new staff and explain to them 'how it really is' to work in the organisation.

Assumptions within the paradigm
The informal network of values and norms determines how organisations actually work and operate and how individuals really relate one to another.

Investigatory approaches
Inductive, naturalistic, participative, high in validity, negotiated entry to data.

At the other extreme, the micropolitical paradigm locates views about induction within the nature of collegiality and trust that exist in the membership of small workgroups. To access those personal beliefs and values you could well have to become a member of such a workgroup so that you were accepted as an equal. Only then might respondents be willing to divulge their opinions to you about their experiences of company induction policies and practices. Your methodological approach in this paradigm would be inductive with outcomes that were high in validity, low in reliability and therefore not generalisable.

Example 6.3 illustrates the necessity of clarifying how you 'see' your research topic. Once you have determined that view, then you can proceed to define the topic within its respective paradigm. By making assumptions about your paradigm explicit as you commence your doctoral research, it is then possible to align the choice of investigatory approach with your paradigm. This form of reasoning strengthens your defence of that choice both in the thesis as well as in your viva. Task 6.2 invites you now to apply these uses of paradigms to your own research.

Task 6.2   How did you choose your paradigms?

What is the paradigm for your research topic and how did you arrive at it?
What were the assumptions that you had regarding the topic that led you to choose the paradigm for your research approach?
How explicit is this reasoning in the text of your research design chapter?

Doctoral candidates use the terms of deductive (*quantitative*) and inductive (*qualitative*) approaches to describe their research. Both words reflect the respective anti-positivistic and positivistic paradigms in epistemological debates

(Burrell and Morgan, 1979: 5). They also embrace philosophical, conceptual, methodological and practical implications that follow from the choice of paradigm for your research topic and research approach. But these are also characteristics of scholarship that you will display in your research and the text of your thesis. Thus, by making your paradigms explicit you will be raising the level of your thinking, your research, the quality of your writing and your capability to defend your research.

This raises a fundamental philosophical question for you to resolve: do you intend your research to test theory or develop and construct theory? If it is the former, then you would choose a deductive approach. If it is the latter, then you would choose an inductive approach. Alternatively, you might decide to use a mixed and staged approach in order to benefit from the methodological advantages of combining deductive and inductive approaches. All these choices have practical consequences, as Salmon (1992: 81) points out: 'research methodologies are never just about "methods": any methodology incorporates a philosophy which should extend, not merely across practical investigative choices, relations with subjects or ways of analysing data, but right into the complex ways in which the (research) project is defined and communicated through its write-up.'

In the disciplines related to the natural sciences, the scientific method is the accepted way to undertake research. If your doctorate is located in the science-related disciplines, you may not need to make a decision: your research design will take a deductive approach towards inquiry and epistemological issues. In the social sciences, you are faced with a choice of paradigms – the testing of theory through deductive approaches, the development of theory through inductive approaches or a combination of deductive and inductive approaches. Your choice of research paradigm should be determined by its appropriateness to the nature of your investigation.

Either way, examiners will be curious to know how you arrived at your paradigm that describes your research topic. They would welcome seeing text that even states quite explicitly 'as a result of choosing this paradigm my research will test theory' or 'will develop and construct theory'. In many doctoral theses, such a simple statement is missing from the text even though candidates have carefully explained other components of their research. You could remove any doubt from examiners' minds on this matter by making your paradigmic position quite explicit by including it in a single sentence within this chapter.

Being able to explain why your research is 'qualitative' or 'quantitative' exposes your philosophical assumptions about the nature of the human world and the type of data to be collected (Bryman, 1988). As a result, the paradigm adopted for your research approach will depend on the assumptions that you hold towards ontology, epistemology, human nature and methodology (Burrell and Morgan, 1979: 3). Making these assumptions explicit provides the framework in which to design your research. Your choice of research paradigm therefore also has strategic importance because it determines the choices that you have to make in the subsequent levels (see Chapter 3).

The second major choice

The second choice facing you concerns the research approach for your investigation. This choice could follow from the paradigm in which you have decided to undertake your research. If it is deductive, then you will have to choose an appropriate methodology and methods to test your hypotheses. In the deductive approach to research methodology, the underlying assumption is that there will be order and regularity between variables. It depends on using methodologies that incorporate numeric analyses of data to arrive at conclusions that are high in reliability and so can be generalised.

If you decide to use an inductive approach to research then the underlying assumptions are different. Your research data may contain contradictions: human respondents have to provide data and then meanings have to be sought from the data that are available. An inductive approach to research uses various forms of interpretative analysis of meaning-making to arrive at non-generalisable conclusions. Furthermore, it may not always be possible to collect either the volume or type of data that was originally intended. In your thesis, you should acknowledge these constraints and explain how they were handled.

Rather than opting for an approach that is solely deductive or inductive, you might combine both approaches and conduct your research as a staged process. Figure 6.2 shows a four-stage research design involving sequential fieldwork. Each stage generated evidence that related directly to a common set of research questions and the conclusions from each stage fed evidence into the subsequent stage. The assumptions behind this form of research were due to data being located in different forms and held by different respondents who were in different locations. Thus, access to those data

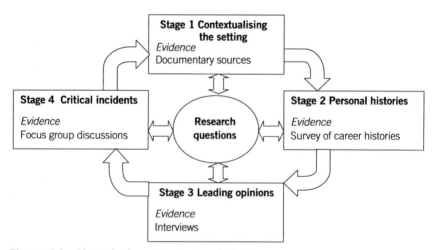

Figure 6.2   Plan of a four-stage research design.

required a combination of methodological approaches, since neither an inductive nor a deductive approach alone would have enabled the research questions to be answered.

The third major choice

This third choice involves the research methodology that you will adopt. Depending on your research approach, you will normally have to decide between methodologies that are deductive, inductive or a combination of the two.

The fourth major choice

This is the stage at which you decide on the methods that you will use to collect data. These choices will be determined by the methodological approach you chose to adopt. Resorting to Kipling, you will need to state:

- **which** data you need to collect;
- **why** those data are significant to your research;
- **where** the data are held;
- **how** they are held;
- **who/what** holds them;
- **how** many data are to be collected;
- **how** the data are to be accessed;
- **how** you intend to analyse the data.

When you have answered these questions, then you need to check that, in total, they combine to provide evidence that allows you to answer your research questions. Thinking through the answers to these questions you will no doubt have to make choices between alternative methods of data collection. It is important that you make the reasons for your choices explicit to provide a textual justification for how your fieldwork was undertaken.

The array of methods and instruments for collecting data is large and complex. From an oversimplified perspective, deductive methodologies are normally exemplified by structured data collection techniques. These methods embody certainty, sampling and collection of data within tightly specified parameters. In contrast, inductive methods of data collection are influenced by philosophical traditions, each with its respective schools and disciplines of thought. Inductive methods tend to be less structured than deductive methods, more open to modification and adaptable to contextual circumstances. Both types of methods share a common characteristic. The chosen method(s) should allow the candidate – you! – to access and collect data in the most effective and appropriate manner.

If, later, it becomes necessary to alter the method(s) then you must explain that change of research plan in your thesis. Your explanation can incorporate the earlier rationale to show how the changed circumstances required a different method to collect data. So, ensure that you can justify each of your choices in the research design process and that you have fully explained them all in this chapter. Usually, changes in your research context would be responsible for such a situation (see Figure 2.1).

These four decisions are critical because they prescribe methodological boundaries to your research. They provide direction to your research and guide you in one direction rather than another. During your viva, your examiners will explore *why* you arrived at the decisions and then *how* that influenced the direction of your research. They will place greater importance on your answers to these questions than to any questions about *what* you did or even *how* you did it. The emphasis of these questions is that they want to receive interpretative rather than descriptive responses from you.

Ethical considerations

If your research involves human subjects then you will require ethical approval from the appropriate body. This must be attended to before you commence that research. Contact with human participants normally means your observation of them, your participation with them in some way, the administration of any substances to them or any procedures that involves the use of human tissues. It also refers to the collection and storage of data that relate to those human subjects. These protocols include any potential invasion of an individual's presumed or actual privacy. Similar protocols apply to research with other living creatures.

Your university will have regulations for approving the ethical dimensions of your research. Depending on your professional discipline, you may also have to seek approval for your research from national or international bodies. Your supervisors and the university will advise you on how to comply with these specific procedures. Ethical considerations are an integral component of designing your research since they may show that it is not feasible to collect some data in the way that you had intended. If that happened, you would then have to rethink your methodology and methods. Thus, gaining ethical approval to undertake your research is a critical part of designing and planning the fieldwork of your research.

Appendix 6.1 illustrates how a candidate provided her readers with details of ethical aspects that were inherent in her research and how they were handled. Linking research design processes with ethical considerations removed any questions that examiners might have had about ethics in her research. Thus, she had shown how ethical considerations were integral to her research design process.

Linking back to earlier chapters

It is important that your readers can see how the research design chapter links to other parts of your thesis. This is a self-evident observation, but it has a very practical side. The chapters in a thesis should relate one to another to create a coherent and integrated piece of writing. Readers always appreciate attention to this matter because it saves them time working it out themselves. Including a single sentence in your chapter to state the obvious would, of course, show your understanding of this fundamental element of research design.

As we explained in Chapter 1, you might have included a brief overview in an opening chapter that told readers how your thesis was structured. While this is helpful, it is likely to be just a few lines of description for each part or chapter. A more detailed explanation may sometimes be quite justified for certain chapters. The research design chapter is such a case since you should indicate, briefly, how it acts as a research gearbox through its links to other chapters.

You will obviously have to decide how to structure and present your chapters. Inevitably you will be guided, or even constrained, by your disciplinary traditions, the regulations of your university, your supervisor's preferences – or even all of these! Once you have accommodated these viewpoints, you should have an agreed way to structure your chapters. So, let's consider how this chapter relates to other parts in your thesis.

The structure and shape of theses vary. Therefore, it would be inappropriate to indicate a number or title for a chapter where the following items might appear. Instead, broad contexts refer to where your research design chapter derives its purpose. It draws on research components that will have appeared earlier in your thesis:

1 Your research statement and research question(s) could be restated in the introduction to this chapter. This would remind readers of your research quest. Later in the chapter, you can then show how your research design focused the research around these elements.

2 Earlier in your thesis you will have generated theoretical perspectives on the research topic. These could be hypotheses to test, the conceptual framework(s) that map the critical features of your focal theory or assumptions about the nature of the field that you will investigate. It is important that you explain how each of these perspectives influenced the design of your research.

3 Assuming that your conceptual framework appears in the text before the research design chapter, then its link to and significance for that chapter must be explained. Your conceptual framework illustrates the relationship between stated theories that provide an abstraction of the topic to be investigated. Thus, it is important that your readers understand how you

converted that abstraction into the practical actions of planning and collecting data to illuminate your topic.

In Appendix 6.2, we show how a candidate explained these features of her research in considerable detail. In this account, we have provided linking commentaries that highlight the critical points that are made by the candidate. The conceptual framework referred to in Appendix 6.2 appears in Figure 6.3. You will recognise the six components as common features of any teaching–learning situation and the cultural variable reflects the particular focus of this research. Her account shows how the conceptual framework determined her choice of research methods due to the interactive nature of its six components. Thus, the theoretical perspectives in the conceptual framework had practical application in how she designed and conducted her fieldwork.

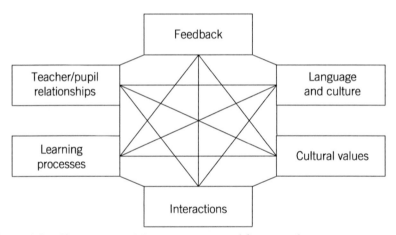

Figure 6.3 Classroom activity as a conceptual framework.

Consider the metaphor of research design as scaffolding for a doctoral thesis. If the framework and links between its components are not planned and coordinated, then it will not bear the weight that is placed on it. It is similar with your research design chapter. Inadequately designed research will fall apart when put to the test in the field – research boundaries would be vaguely defined, sampling frames would be inadequately specified and defined, imprecise data would be collected and, consequently, findings would not fully relate to the research questions. Given these errors, any analysis, discussion or interpretation would only compound the initial inadequacies. As with a collapsing scaffold, poorly planned research design is academically dangerous, methodologically faulty and to be avoided. It certainly cannot be defended successfully in a doctoral viva!

Auditing your research design

It is worth auditing your fieldwork plan. This exercise will show if the plan will deliver data and findings that accord with your research design and methodological approach. Undertaking such an audit should confirm the coherence of the research design and this would be reassuring for you to know. If you conclude that your research plan is not coherent then modifications can be made to 'correct' the research plan and its associated research design. Figure 6.4 displays how: 'the key components (in the research process) are systematically related to one another in order to link evidence to theory in research' (Rose, 1982: 14).

The model in Figure 6.4 shows how your research will draw on theoretical perspectives that are outside its immediate practical context. You demonstrate your familiarity with this wider literature (A) in order to produce conceptualisations or hypotheses (B). The connection between A and B should be made clear. The research design (C) is 'the pivotal stage in the research process' (Rose, 1982: 18) and your subsequent fieldwork (D) should follow logically from it. Readers should be able to follow a clear trail of research decisions from A though to D that are convincing. Results follow (E) which should give you the outcome that you sought.

Using the feedback route from E to C, B and A enables you to legitimise your findings by referring back to the internal and external consistency of your

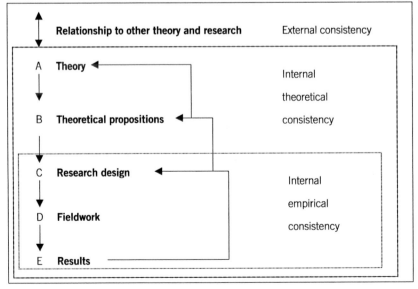

Figure 6.4 Consistency in levels of research (after Rose, 1982).

research design process. In the conclusions chapter, you can then use the coherence of your research design to justify the robustness and rigour of your research (see Chapter 8).

Readers see the full account of your research only after it has been undertaken. However, it is not unusual for modifications to be made to initial research plans. Accounting for such changes allows readers to recognise how you audited your research progress and took appropriate actions. Using or adapting the model in Figure 6.4 would have two practical benefits for you. First, it would consolidate your confidence in the rigour of your research and so add to your preparation for defending your work in the viva. Second, it signals to any reader that you have been thorough in ensuring the quality and scholarship in your research.

Research design is a strategic process. It lays out the direction and shape of your fieldwork and determines the type of data to be collected and analysed. Auditing your research design needs to move from scrutinising its internal empirical consistency before checking its external theoretical consistency. These checks should show that your research actions are both integrated and coherent and so confirm the internal consistency of your research. Only after establishing this can you then ascertain how your conclusions relate to other theory and research. Ascertaining a positive relationship between your research and external theoretical perspectives imparts strategic consistency to your research. This strengthens your later claim of making a contribution to extant knowledge.

Looking back and ahead

The research design chapter is where you justify that your research has been undertaken after careful consideration of the 'whys' and the 'hows' of that enquiry. By making these choices and decisions explicit, it demonstrates your understanding of the inherent complexity found in doctoral-level research. You are also helping readers to decipher how your research was planned and undertaken. In addition, both you and others can use the chapter as an analytic framework to assess the research itself. When you have achieved that then undertaking the research itself becomes relatively straightforward. By laying out your strategy and plan, you can then proceed to undertake your research, confident that you can justify to anyone why it was undertaken in a particular way. By doing this, already you are 'defending' your research and preparing for your doctoral viva. Thus, your doctoral research design chapter should exemplify your scholarly thinking rather than being a technical activity of simply describing the use of research methods.

Chapter 7 explains the importance of your choice and use of words to convey your ideas in your thesis.

Appendix 6.1 Explaining ethical considerations

A doctoral thesis investigated *Living through detachment: cancer patients in their final years.* The background to this research was that the candidate held a senior nursing role in a hospice and her respondents were patients with terminal cancer. These extracts are from a part of the thesis whose title was *Theoretical approach, methodology and method.*

In her research design chapter she offered her view of the research setting through these words:

My research sought to observe, and collect data, to explain how my respondents created and acted on their understandings in the highly specific context of coping with a medical condition that was terminal . . . My study was carried out with the help of interviews, observations and data from medical files in order to create a rich description of the phenomenon being focused on in this research . . . My data included demographics, age, gender, ethnicity, status, diagnosis, medical history and treatments, medication, physical therapy, blood tests, CT scans and other medical interventions . . . Altogether, it gave expression to the phenomenon's unique characteristics and events and the participants associated with them.

Due to the medical and nursing aspects of this research, an entire chapter of nine pages was devoted to the 'The code of ethics.' The chapter opened with this general observation:

Research on human beings, especially if it examines ill individuals under sensitive and difficult circumstances, necessitates regulations regarding its organisation, the selection of and relationships with patients and their families and the role of the researcher.

Next, the candidate outlined the philosophical–ethical aspects of this type of research. She identified the ethical obligations that exist reciprocally between medical staff and their patients as individuals and as groups. Then, she explained the codes of professional practice that applied to all staff employed by the hospice and set those regulations in a national and international context. Finally, she introduced the personal and individual professional ethical relationships towards patients, colleagues, employer and the profession itself. The candidate had now given a thorough description of the ethical settings in which her research was to be undertaken.

Then she provided a detained account of how she sought and gained formal approval for her research:

My request to undertake this research was submitted in accordance with national health regulations and medical experimentation on human beings . . . The committee must assure themselves that research will be conducted according to the code of ethics that are to be followed in such research . . . The regulations ensure that participants' rights, safety and well-being will be protected consistent with the Helsinki Declaration as well as to ensure that data gathering will be authentic. My submission had to contain a full list of all the research methods that I intended to use to collect data from patients. I also had to explain how these data were to be stored and for how long.

[. . .] The committee provided authorisation for my research . . . Although the opportunity existed for me to contact the committee at any time during my research it was not necessary. This provided me with (reassurance) the support of fellow professionals such as doctors specialising in geriatrics, oncology and psychiatry. It also allowed me professional independence in conducting my research without any external interference.

She explained how her sample of patients was chosen and her use of statements of informed consent with patients, their families and colleague nurses and doctors and then wrote:

Two meetings were held with staff overseeing cancer patients (doctors, nurses and social workers) before my research started. All members of these groups received an explanation of my research, research conditions, research procedures to be used, the selection of the research populations and the length and expected contribution of the research itself.

[. . .] Data gathered throughout the research was filed and kept in a manner that prevented the identification of names or any other identifying details.

Conscious to ensure that her research maintained high ethical standards, she outlined how others audited this requirement:

Due to the sensitivity of this research and concern regarding emotional reactions likely to cause damage to the participants, the attending staff in the community were requested to assess, from time to time, participants' reactions to their meetings with me. These arrangements were intended to create a situation that provided control and security for my research participants to provide trust and openness between us.

She closed this section of the chapter in this way:

Thus, my approach to conducting this study was undertaken within the approved regulatory framework. Since it was already familiar to me through my normal professional roles, the ethical guidelines did not cause me any problems in respecting the patient/respondent relationship. I followed ethical procedures as outlined in the statements of informed consent that each person associated with my research received. No complaints were made about my conduct of this research and so I am satisfied that the ethical considerations were fully respected.

Appendix 6.2   Linking the conceptual framework with research design

A doctoral thesis investigated *Patterns and perceptions of oral feedback in the EFL (English as a foreign language) classroom in three culturally different environments*. The background to this example is that the theoretical perspectives on the topic were dealt with in 47 pages of Chapters 3–6 which formed Part 2 of this thesis. The titles of the four chapters were:

- The importance of interaction;
- The concept of feedback and its role in the learning process;
- Cultural elements affecting interaction;
- Intervening variables.

Chapter 6 closed by recapping the theories that had been discussed. Certain features were identified as being significant to the classroom context:

- interactions between staff and pupils;
- two-way communication in the classroom;
- the nature of feedback between teachers and pupils;
- the significance of the out-of-school cultural backgrounds of teachers and pupils;
- the in-school cultural processes.

Then the conceptual framework for the research was introduced:

The framework that emerged from the conceptual dimensions presented in this part is that the language classroom is a complex environment consisting of a web of relationships that are both interrelated and interdependent (see Figure 6.3) *. . . The model portrays six variables that reflect their interdependency within the language classroom. While each variable contributes to the interactional web, it is only when all six variables interact that the full complexity of the learning environment can be appreciated, understood and explained.*

These words emphasised the origins of the conceptual framework, showing how the candidate had designed it specifically for that doctoral research as a unique configuration of concepts for a practical purpose. The writing of this text was intended to help readers attach importance to the variables in the conceptual framework. All the variables were so apparent in the classroom setting that their combination into the conceptual framework followed quite logically.

The next chapter was Chapter 7, whose title was: *Research design considerations*. The chapter opened with these words:

Part 2 presented a conceptual understanding of the issues relating to the topic for this thesis. The previous section drew these notions together and provided the conceptual framework on which the research has been conducted. This chapter now converts the conceptual framework into the array of issues that comprise the operational fieldwork map (Robson, 1993) . . . Evidence for the conceptual framework features drawn from the theoretical perspectives can be found in the teaching situation of classes displaying different cultural contexts. This type of data is going to be held by teachers, pupils, their interactions, relationships, schools and their principals. In order to account for the significance of culture, I have to investigate the teaching and learning processes in schools which display different cultural backgrounds. Thus, the research access has to be through data collection processes which are capable of gathering these indicators of cultural awareness.

These words provide a bridge between the conceptual framework and its purpose as setting boundaries for the fieldwork in this research.

The next chapter was entitled *Perspectives on methodology*. Here, the candidate made explicit connections between the conceptual framework, research design and the fieldwork approach though these words:

Because this study explores the complex interconnection between people's beliefs and actions and the effect of this connection on classroom dynamics, it is necessary to use a methodology that emphasises the experiences of the participants themselves – their actions, thoughts, feelings and perceptions. Qualitative analysis is concerned with how actors define situations and explain the motives which govern their actions . . . Thus, the methods which seem most appropriate for my research are those associated with ethnographic field studies. This methodology permits me, as the researcher, to meet all the basic requirements of empirical science: to confront the social context, to discover relations between categories of data, to formulate propositions about these relations and to organise these propositions into an analytical scheme that others can understand (Blumer, 1969).

Later in the same chapter, the candidate explained that the main data collection system was personal observation. Three secondary methods of data collection were used to provide supplementary data and these were documentary materials, videos and interviews. The choice of each research method was justified by showing how it accessed data that related specifically to one or more components of the conceptual framework. Thus, the function of research design was demonstrated in this thesis through detailing the origins of the conceptual framework, how it influenced the design considerations and the choice of methods as data collection techniques.

7

What's in a word?

This chapter will:

- outline responsibilities for achieving quality of your written text;
- describe how working agreements on submitting draft work can be established;
- present attitudes towards the use of words by candidates, supervisors and examiners;
- highlight styles of writing and the different meanings they convey.

Introduction

Undertaking a doctorate will involve you in two complementary processes – conducting research and writing a thesis that presents that research. Whatever the length of your doctoral thesis you are faced with a considerable amount of writing. This component of your doctoral journey demands, and deserves, as much of your attention as the research itself. There is a particular imperative behind doctoral writing: addressing the needs of your readers. This makes writing a doctoral thesis uniquely demanding due to the direct evaluative role that examiners have as your primary readers.

Academic writing is, at last, gaining its own substantial literature. This adds to contemporary knowledge about gaining a doctorate as it reminds both candidates and supervisors of this important component in a thesis. While acknowledging the help and advice that candidates can find in such texts, the technical act of writing is not the focus of this chapter. Instead, it addresses how candidates and supervisors explained their respective experiences of writing. These views are set within the observations of examiners when reporting on or commenting about the written text of theses.

Recognise responsibilities for the text

Applicants wishing to register for a doctorate will usually be required by the university to provide an outline of their research topic. Exceptions to this would be if they were applying for appointment to a team whose research focus was already established. In the former case, it is normal for applicants to expand that outline into a research proposal for consideration by an approving committee or panel. Both of these examples include applicants having to express themselves in writing about their research. The university's formal decision whether or not to accept them as a doctoral candidate will therefore have included an assessment of their ability to convey scholarly ideas succinctly.

Example 7.1 Filtering process for admission to doctoral study

Programme director   Initial enquiries vary from a few lines to pages that explain what the applicant would like to investigate. I accept them only as indications of interest. Unless it is an unsuitable topic for us to supervise or impossible to read – and they arrive sometimes – I enquire about a possible supervisory team.

Assuming that we could supervise the topic, we then ask applicants to submit a fuller proposal of four to six pages. Sometimes we also interview applicants to discuss their proposal. A committee then decides whether the research intentions and the literary ability indicate that the applicant has the potential to complete their studies successfully. We can help individuals to develop while they are with us, but only if the potential is apparent in the research proposal. Our decisions are right in the majority of cases, despite making judgements on a very small sample of their work.

The view from the director of a large well-established doctoral programme on this filtering process is shown in Example 7.1. It illustrates how from the initial stage of the doctoral process, the quality of written expression is important to those who are responsible for making decisions about academic progression. The use of the word 'potential' indicates that applicants are not, at this stage, expected to be competent and proficient writers of academic text at the doctoral level. It also implies that later, as candidates, they would be expected to develop those capabilities during their doctoral studies.

After registering for your doctorate an issue for early discussion with your supervisor(s) is to clarify mutual responsibilities for the quality of your written text. If this has not happened yet, perhaps you should instigate it. At this meeting you will arrive with certain assumptions towards assuring that high-quality text gets into your thesis. But so too will your supervisor(s).

Figure 7.1 shows the array of commonly expressed views on this matter by candidates and supervisors. For both parties, the assumptions range from pessimistic to optimistic. It is important that you discuss how your supervisor(s) prefer to receive your draft text and for you to express views on this matter, too. This will avoid any misunderstandings on either part. Once this is agreed, it will form part of the psychological contract (Schein, 1965: 43–65) of mutual expectations between you and your supervisor(s).

CANDIDATES
My text is always clearly written
I would prefer to write it in my own way
My supervisor will correct any errors and mistakes
It is my responsibility to prepare good-quality text
I will sort out the writing when the research is finished
I have to learn and apply the rules of academic writing
My supervisor will explain the ins and outs of academic writing

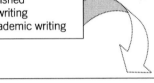

SUPERVISORS
They read other theses and learn about style
They proofread draft text before submitting it
They read books about it and attend writing groups
They replicate good style from quality books/articles
The majority work hard to acquire good writing skills
They appreciate the need to write carefully crafted text
I may have to educate my candidates in academic writing

Figure 7.1 Who holds what assumptions about academic writing and theses?

The contract between you and your supervisor may either be formally expressed and agreed or it may be informally 'taken for granted'. However the contract is expressed it will be reinforced when each party meets the expectations of the other(s). The contract will be weakened or broken if either party fails to meet those expectations. Thus, agreeing how draft text should be submitted to and returned by your supervisor(s) early in your relationship has potentially far-reaching consequences for your mutual relationship (Taylor and Beasley, 2005). Task 7.1 invites you to think about this issue.

Task 7.1 Agreements with supervisors

What type of agreements do you have with your supervisor(s) regarding the 'quality' of the text that will appear in submitted drafts?

The preferences that supervisors have on dealing with the submitted drafts text from their candidates vary, as shown in Example 7.2:

- Supervisor A was willing to accept a major and constant role in ensuring the quality of the text.
- Supervisor B offered professional advice for the first submission, but then passed the responsibility to the candidate for the quality of subsequent text.
- Supervisor C absolved herself of responsibility for matters of grammar to candidates but willingly accepted an educative role towards the academic development of her candidate.
- Supervisor D insured against a thesis being referred by examiners on the grounds of poor-quality writing through undertaking detailed checking of the text.

Example 7.2 Attitudes of supervisors towards amending submitted draft text

Supervisor A   I annotate the text when sentences have to be changed. I usually write in a few sources to be chased up as well, all via 'Track changes'. I will remind them about meanings and grammar, but they have to change it.

Supervisor B   I don't mind correcting the text for non-academic items once. After that I just put *'Please check the grammar'* or similar abbreviation near the mistake. Yes, it sometimes causes upsets. But whose job is it to write the thesis?

Supervisor C   I do not believe it is the role of supervisors to correct grammar etc. I explain that early on and then stick to it. Style? Yes. I see that as another part of the developmental process for my students and I'll advise on that every time.

Supervisor D   I agree with each candidate that they should submit their best quality text to me for comment. Most do. I always correct what I read as I go through it. It is natural for me whenever I read anything. This slows my reading but it deals with mistakes quickly. In the final drafts of chapters, I do make every correction. Once errors are submitted in a thesis, examiners will find them and it will be referred for corrections to be made. I'll have to read it all over again. So I check everything thoroughly before any of my candidates submit their thesis.

Example 7.3 shows how four candidates experienced the establishment of a working agreement on submitting written work:

- The writing capability of Candidate A determined a supervisor's willingness to supervise her doctorate.
- Candidate B's assumed expectations that the supervisor would correct the literary nature of the text were clarified very early in their relationship.
- Candidate C carried over previously agreed academic writing practices between supervisor and candidate.
- Candidate D assumed full responsibility for the literary quality of first draft text that he would send to his supervisors.

These four candidates illustrate how supervisors and candidates established mutually acceptable responsibilities and expectations (psychological contracts) towards the quality of writing that would be submitted and reviewed.

Example 7.3 Attitudes of candidates towards submitting written draft text

Candidate A   My prospective supervisor wanted to see something I had written. She received and read my master's dissertation. At our first proper meeting we discussed my work, which she liked. She told me that she had no intention to write my thesis. She would only correct first drafts. She assumed that I could deal with it then. She was blunt, but clear. I take this approach now with my candidates.

Candidate B   My supervisor explained at our second meeting that he would offer advice on technical terms and so on. That was it. He expected me to provide drafts that were fully checked for spelling and style. I felt that was reasonable even if I did not like it at first.

Candidate C   My doctoral supervisor had supervised my master's dissertation so he knew my writing style. I assumed that I would continue sending my drafts in a finished form for comment with no typos etc. That's how it's working and I'm happy with the arrangement.

Candidate D   Why should I send unchecked text to my supervisors? Isn't it my job to get it right before they see it and their job to advise me on its academic argument? What's the difficulty with that?

Examining what has been written

Mullins and Kiley (2002) and Tinkler and Jackson (2004) show that examiners invest considerable time reading and rereading theses to gain a thorough understanding of their content. Their views are confirmed by Pearce, who provides a detailed account of how examiners approach reading a thesis. After an initial reading to discover what the thesis contains, she suggests that at a second reading: 'A thesis of 100,000 words cannot be read in much less than eight hours (even without note taking)' (Pearce, 2005: 49). She lists the checkpoints that examiners may use which, in total, constitute a complete audit of how a thesis was written, plus how its ideas and scholarly arguments were advanced (Pearce, 2005: 49–64). These accounts argue that examiners explore all aspects about a thesis before arriving at a conclusion about its merit. The quality of writing is inevitably an integral consideration in that process.

Example 7.4 shows the experience of four examiners in examining the textual quality of theses:

- Examiner A offered a general assessment of writing quality in doctoral theses. He believed that in theses of lower quality it was the candidate's writing that usually detracted from the research itself. This view contradicts the received wisdom that so often focuses on methodology as *the thing to get right* and overlooks the manner in which that methodology is written up in the thesis.
- Examiner B echoed a frequently expressed view by other examiners about the pervasive nature of good-quality doctoral writing within the thesis itself.
- Examiner C's comments are unique and tell of a thesis that was excellent in every respect, but in particular it was very well-written.
- Examiner D responded to a particular style of academic writing. He believed that every word had to *work for its living and deserve its place in the thesis.* Furthermore he wanted candidates to be positive in expressing themselves in the text. Finally, he believed that doctoral candidates should *write as if they were members of the academy with the assurance of doctoral scholarship behind them.* He judged a candidate's current writing against his anticipation of their future authorship in the academy. (See also Example 11.2, Examiner C.)

These four comments are a template against which you and your supervisors could assess how these expectations of examiners compare with your own writing.

Example 7.4 Examiners' attitudes toward the textual quality of theses

Examiner A In my experience, the majority of theses are well-written. They do the job they are intended for and that is to report on research that has been undertaken. The excellent ones shine with polished text and the remainder are more frequently let down by their style of writing than their methodology.

Examiner B When you see good-quality writing on page 1, then you know the rest of the thesis will usually be the same. That is good news for any examiner!

Examiner C Very, very occasionally I have so enjoyed reading a thesis as an examiner, that I have read it again wearing my other hat as a fellow academic. Just to enjoy it once more is a bonus.

Examiner D I really do enjoy reading a thesis that is boldly written with the confidence that expert knowledge brings with it.

Example 7.5 contains observations from four examiners reflecting on their experiences.

- Examiner A used his experience to assess what the remainder of a thesis would be like from his initial visual impressions of it. He made a subjective evaluation of what he saw from this overview before reading the text in any detail. It seems that from his experience he could predict with some certainty whether the text would be good or poor.
- Examiner B also includes prediction in her recollections. In her case, she was unforgiving over poor proofreading and recognised that when it appeared it was symptomatic of a consistently poor piece of academic writing.
- Examiner C placed the responsibility for ensuring high-quality writing jointly and unreservedly with candidates and their supervisors.
- Examiner D believed that many candidates could have produced higher quality writing if they had broadened their vocabulary and then used it appropriately in their theses.

Example 7.5 Examiners reflecting on their experiences

Examiner A   A quick glance through a thesis can tell you a lot about style and presentation. The amount of thought given to headings, paragraph length and format usually, for me, shows up again in how the thesis will have been written.

Examiner B   There is no excuse for a thesis to be submitted with poor grammar, typographicals and other things like that. Once I find the fifth one I know that there will be others. And I find them! I know it should not, but sloppiness like this distracts me from following the argument and the development of ideas.

Examiner C   What really worries me is when I meet a sentence that does not make sense. I wonder what it was supposed to mean. Then I know that the thesis has not been carefully proofread. That is the responsibility of the candidate and the supervisor, not the examiners.

Examiner D   I believe that everyone registering for a doctorate should be given a massively thick thesaurus to use every time they sit down to write. It would help them and certainly make my job easier.

These four observations show that examiners place a premium on the quality of academic writing in theses. When it does not reach that level of acceptability, then, for them, the quality of the thesis itself is reduced. You will know from your discussions with other candidates, that examiners refer many theses so that minor alterations can be made to the text. A significant proportion of these minor amendments involve correcting typographical errors, grammar and the style of expressing ideas. In these cases, the thesis has not passed. The examiners have suspended their recommendation that the degree be awarded to the candidate who they had just examined. Thus, these avoidable errors have prevented those candidates from gaining their doctorate at their viva.

Conveying meaning

All of us must have smiled when we first saw these words: *I know you believe you understand what you think I said – but I'm not sure you realise that what you heard is not what I meant!* While it obviously relates to the spoken word, it applies equally to how far readers comprehend exactly what writers intended them to understand.

Now consider the different meanings in these three sentences:

A The examiners said the candidate enjoyed the viva.
B The examiners, said the candidate, enjoyed the viva.
C The examiners said, the candidate enjoyed the viva.

Punctuation alters the significance of the words and meanings in a sentence. In the first sentence (A) readers have to make up their own mind exactly what the author intended the words to convey. The use of commas in the second and third sentences (B and C) places the subject as the examiners and then the candidate, respectively. As a result, the meanings of the last two sentences are quite different, despite each sentence containing the same eight words.

When writing is unambiguous then readers recognise and appreciate that authors have endeavoured to write clearly. Visitors to the Royal Academy exhibition of Making History: Antiquities in Britain, in 2007, experienced an example of this type of writing. The items displayed in each of the galleries were introduced by an account of their context and period. These accounts were displayed prominently for visitors to read before they then moved around the exhibits in the galleries. The accounts were approximately 1,000 words in length.

Example 7.6 shows three sentences from the displayed account of the context in the first gallery. Visitors paused to read the account and many remarked on the words that it contained. It also appeared in the published catalogue for the exhibition. Comments such as *I can almost see how it must have been, What wonderful writing, So clear and informing of a visual situation* and *I wish that I could write as elegantly as that* were typical of the appreciations being expressed. Some visitors appeared to have been so impressed by the account that they even returned to this gallery and read the account again.

Example 7.6 In the mists of time

Before the seventeenth century people in Britain had limited understanding of their past and were strongly influenced by pagan or Christian beliefs and ancestral myths. . . . There was little sense of distinguishing periods in the past and little expertise in identifying its material remains. People knew nothing of the rural and urban landscape beyond their own localities; early maps did not show roads or distances, and images of places and buildings were rare. (Parry, 2007: 15)

The example had been written for a different purpose than your doctoral writing. Nevertheless, it shares a similar function of organising ideas into a particular sequence in order to be passed from the writer to the reader. Like you, Parry had to reduce complex sets of facts into succinct expressions that presented concepts for readers to consider. Take for example the eight words *early maps did not show roads or distances*. The deeper implications of those few words followed visitors around the galleries and the rest of the exhibition. In your doctoral writing, such a sentence would no doubt form a prelude to a detailed explanation of those implications. Achieving such an economical use of words produces text that readers prefer to see rather than struggling with overlong text that wanders around the subject.

Examiners hold similar views toward the text in theses that they have to read. Example 7.7 shows comments by four examiners on the writing which they read in theses. These statements all point to examiners seeing the act of writing as parallel to the act of research itself. This supports Salmon's earlier view that situated PhD work and research: 'as a process, rather than as merely a product' (Salmon, 1992: 5). She calls attention here to the way that research is a means to some other end; writing is an aid to achieving high-quality scholarly research that others recognise and accept. Thus, it requires your attention.

Example 7.7 Examiners' comments on doctoral writing

Examiner A It makes my job far more enjoyable when I do not need to read any part of the thesis twice to understand what is being meant.

Examiner B Writing is difficult. If an effort has been made to present good-quality chapters, that is sufficient for me. I do not expect prize-winning writing, just good writing that complements good research.

Examiner C Academic writing is often rather dreary and almost dead. But a thesis should give me the excitement that I always assume the candidate has for the topic. Otherwise, why take on years of study? Maybe supervisors don't mind if they read heavy-going chapters one by one. Examiners, though, have to read the whole thesis and they are often saturated by words that are used not for their meaning but to fill pages.

Examiner D Most write well, and it is reassuring to read a well-crafted piece of very extended prose. It is possible to be clear and creative without jeopardising so-called academic standards in the process.

Example 7.8 shows how three candidates experienced the task of writing. Candidates A and B encountered difficulties and addressed them in their own ways. Candidate C had served an apprenticeship in academic writing through earlier master's studies and so knew what was expected and how to produce satisfactory text. All three cases illustrate the need to consider taking advice from your supervisor(s) or academic writing groups and other sources. Exchanging draft text with colleague candidates is a helpful way to receive and give feedback that can help strengthen your scholarly writing (Caffarella and Barnett, 2000).

Example 7.8 Views of candidates on doctoral writing

Candidate A   I am not a confident writer. The idea of producing 80,000 words was worrying, though I knew it had to be done. When my first draft chapter was returned, so my wife said, it contained more red words than my black typing. It was so embarrassing. After that my drafts were read first by my son, then my wife. There were still some red words, but they were about argument and references.

Candidate B   I really thought that I could write quite well until I started my doctorate. I was devastated when my first chapter was returned with so many questions and comments. I felt deflated. I was being told to check exactly what was meant by what I had written because many sentences included far too many ideas. The large letter **M** at the end of a sentence meant that the meaning was unclear and **R** meant that it was repetition. I worked very hard on those problems.

Candidate C   I suppose I got into academic writing through my master's. It set me up for my doctorate and I've had no problems so far with my writing.

It is easy for any of us to overlook some very simple attributes of writing. Perhaps we should occasionally remind ourselves that writing is:

- a means of communicating our ideas to others;
- a form of refining ideas in order to construct new ideas;
- a way of thinking through the agency of written words;
- a means to explore ideas and so identify potentially new fields of reading;
- a way to express your views unambiguously on the page for others to read;
- an active process involving thought, reflection, revision and judgement of quality.

It is important to recognise these points as you write for your different readerships. The first readers of your draft text will be your supervisor(s). Comments on your text will be from the discipline and methodological perspectives that are relevant to your research. However, your examiners are your primary readers because they determine the outcome of your viva. Once your thesis is on the shelves of the university library, your readership widens. From then onwards, your readers include members of your discipline or profession, researchers interested in your topic or methodology and other doctoral candidates. Although you have a readership of mixed interests, it is critical that you meet and satisfy the expectations of your writing held by your primary readers. Family, friends and colleagues will be significant readers for you, personally, but they are not those for whom you are writing academically.

Creating and using titles

As you write your thesis you will constantly decide between which words to use and their order within your current sentence. This is the notion of *crafting the text*. It involves weighing the meanings of individual words and how they are used. Then you will inevitably reread the sentence and maybe alter the words – but this, too, is a writing decision and part of the crafting process.

The title of your thesis is the first piece of your writing that any reader sees. Its origin may be in your initial ideas about your topic. The words that you choose would therefore tend to describe the research as a working title that could be modified later. Alternatively, you may prefer the title to emerge and become a consolidated notion as your research progresses and your understanding of the topic matures. For these reasons, how you decide on the topic is less important than how it is expressed. Your doctoral thesis deserves a title that transmits the meaning of your research to others. The title should convey exactly what you want readers of it to understand.

Verbally adroit, enigmatic or catchy titles are not always welcome or even acceptable to your potential readers. Dunton (2004: 51) counsels caution against using overly clever titles. His reason for this is they can easily: 'fall into the trap of providing an image that is just a bit too obscure to be understood by the bulk of readers'. Since this is exactly what you should avoid, the earlier encouragement by Rudestam and Newton (1992: 127) to use those key words that: 'correctly and accurately convey the content of your study' is still very helpful and practical advice. They also suggest that the title should have no *redundant words*.

Unless there are protocols in the regulations of your university regarding the format of titles for doctoral theses, then its form of words has to be created by you and discussed with your supervisor(s). Example 7.9 shows two titles that express the work of their thesis in different ways:

> **Example 7.9** Contrasting thesis titles
>
> **Title A** Management role profiles of secondary headteachers.
>
> **Title B** Causes of failure in high technology manufacturing spin-off companies that commercialise complex military technology for export: case studies of small and large enterprises.

- Title A is short and succinct. It presents management role profiles as the conceptual focus of the research and its context is secondary headteachers. The merit of its brevity is counterbalanced by the omission of any contextual details.
- Title B is a descriptive account of the research topic. It provides considerable detail which tells readers exactly what is involved in this research. The boundaries and major variables are self-evident through groups of words – 'causes of failure,' 'high technology,' 'manufacturing spin off companies' and 'for export'. This part of the title provides readers with sufficient information to know what the research investigated. A colon before the subtext told readers that the method of presenting the data was via case studies and that they would relate to two further variables – small and large enterprises.

In their different ways, both titles have been tightly expressed with no superfluous words. Thus they reflect Rudestam and Newton's hopes for research titles to be clearly expressed.

The title of your thesis has a longer term importance than just appealing to your immediate readers. You will include it on your CV, refer to it in application forms and cite it in your postdoctoral research publications. The readers on those occasions will look at the title from quite different perspectives than your examiners. They are unlikely even to see your thesis or discover what it contains. To anticipate how those readers may view the words in your title, you should avoid it being dull, offputting or unfashionable. Looking beyond your viva, Dunleavy advises that appointment panels: 'tend to read a lot into your PhD subject, seeing it as expressive of your character and temperament. In addition, it may be hard to spin off any worthwhile publications from a completely dull PhD' (Dunleavy, 2003: 21). For these various reasons, it is important that you scrutinise the inclusion and meaning(s) of each word in the title of your doctoral thesis.

Inside your thesis similar issues of clarity, brevity and completeness apply as you provide signposts to readers as titles for parts, chapters and sections. Oliver (2004: 81–82) advises that a consistent font should be used for all titles, from the frontispiece, through parts, chapters, sections and any other subcategories plus the text itself. Point sizes and use of bold script should also be used consistently. How you use them must be guided by the protocols of your discipline and institutional conventions as you work downwards in the hierarchy of relative importance where a title is used. When this is handled correctly it enhances the words that are in those titles. When it is handled clumsily and without due care, then the confused appearance that follows detracts from the words that have been used. Thus, presentation and words have a direct affinity within the overall impression that you create in your thesis for readers.

You may decide to reflect the words in your title in critical places within your text to remind readers of your research purpose. This can be overdone though when candidates: 'keep incanting words from the title of their doctorate in their chapter titles and section headings' (Dunleavy, 2003: 87). Drawing on the title for themes to use as headings in the thesis should be used judiciously. It is nonetheless worth keeping your research in the minds of readers by recomposing the main title through alternative words and perhaps adopting them as phrases in 'lesser' titles.

Producing text

Structuring the text accompanies writing the text. It is easy sometimes to lose sight of the fact that words are the raw material from which text is created, crafted and read (Prose, 2006: 16). Each sentence will no doubt receive your full attention. The meaning of words is dependent on the context to which they refer (Tietze et al., 2003: 12) and it should influence how you choose which words to use in your writing. Your own perspective on that context then influences how you build and present arguments.

As you introduce a word into a sentence you ascribe meaning to it. No doubt you expect (hope) that your readers will gain an identical meaning to the sentence. This is where your appreciation of the lexicon will guide your use of individual words (see Task 7.2). All writers make assumptions about their readers. You have to assume that your readers will be familiar with the lexicon from which you draw your vocabulary and the way in which you use its component words. The language which you use will be expected to reflect the broader 'worldview' held by your – and their – specific academic community. When it does this then you are communicating with your readers at the correct level of shared meanings, vocabulary and format.

Task 7.2 What are the characteristics of your lexicon?

Identify 10 terms that characterise the lexicon of your discipline or field.

Putting words into the structure of a sentence for maximum impact requires thought. Cheney (2005: 101) advises writers to think of a sentence very simply as having an opening, a middle and an end. Then he suggests that writers place their important ideas and words either at the start or at the closure of sentences. This structuring presents readers with important emphases either as the sentence opens or as it closes. Less important words and ideas fill the middle ground of sentences. He argues that writers should view their paragraphs, chapters and whole work in the same way. He believes that readers should be welcomed into a substantial piece of writing with a flourish of attractive ideas. They should leave it with positive memories of those ideas. When these two features are woven into extended prose, then readers will gain value from their reading (Cheney, 2005: 107–115).

Assembling your text over the period of your doctoral programme contains at least two latent difficulties. First, as you read widely, your lexicon will expand. Then, as you progress into your research, your understanding of the topic and the associated methodology that you use will be enriched. Although your lexicon is still subject-bound, the words and vocabulary that you use will change over time. You will certainly find that some of your previous text or individual words need to be revised because you have altered your views. This exemplifies Kuhn's notion of a paradigm shift when a person's beliefs and perspectives are changed (Kuhn, 1996: 18–19, 109). Such processes of change and maturation as a writer accord with Burgess's (1973) belief that: 'It is sometimes difficult for a writer to be the same . . . over a long stretch of time.'

Using Burgess's idea Zerubavel (1999: 87) addresses the second latent difficulty with long-term writing. He identifies the need to anticipate closure of chapters and the entire work so that it does not adversely affect writing. He argues that if it does, then the result might be that: 'What may have been once a source of great pleasure and excitement can become a source of boredom and frustration.' This echoes precisely the feeling of Examiner C in Example 7.5. toward what seemed to have been rather tired writing in a thesis submitted by one candidate. Zerubavel's solution to this occurring is to reward yourself when you achieve previously agreed targets and deadlines. He suggests that: 'This could be a "treat" such as a special dinner which serves as a celebratory reward for your accomplishment.' This may not appeal to everyone, but it is a nice motivational idea all the same!

The mechanics of doctoral writing are, for Hartley (1997: 106): 'putting into practice what we already know'. As we have seen already, through the expectations of examiners and the comments by supervisors this involves candidates thinking like researchers when writing about research. This entails writing in accessible prose that introduces and accounts for the research that is in their thesis. It should not involve them in adopting the form of writing and expression that Evans and Gruba (2002: 157) call *thesisese*. This happens when candidates adopt a writing style that is overburdened with jargon, contains extra-long sentences and includes obscure words within a complicated sentence structure. Evans and Gruba remind candidates that examiners were appointed by the university 'to look for critical thinking, not obfuscation'.

Taking a professional academic rather than technical mechanistic perspective on this, Kamler and Thomson suggest that:

> Doctoral researchers need to develop resources that enable a more authoritative, impersonal stance, so that they have a choice about which way to present themselves and their work in their texts. If they are to be successful scholars in the academy, they must come to the 'just right' combination of certainty, dis/agreement, personal claim, humility and authoritative stance. The 'self' of the researcher and its representation in textual form is integral to the construction of a persuasive argument.
>
> (Kamler and Thomson, 2006: 59–80)

As you start to write, you will need to balance these expectations of readers with your own desire to express yourself in your own way.

Your supervisor(s) and certainly your examiners will look to see where you are in the text. This will show in your use of the corpus and its associated lexicon. Congruence between these respective sets of terminology and vocabulary in your writing is an indicator of you identifying with the foundations of your discipline and field. Working within your academic lexicon directly affects how you write about your topic. Examiners expect you to:

- avoid personal value judgements;
- focus on central and critical issues;
- use the accepted professional terminology and grammar;
- critically engage with the primary and secondary sources;
- cite the work of others to support and legitimise your arguments;
- present implications of research within their respective wider academic context;
- achieve appropriate balances between description, analysis and conceptualisation.

These are positive characteristics of scholarly writing and when they are evident in your text they will be recognised as such by your readers.

Then choices have to be made about how you present arguments through your writing. According to many observers of academic writing, conventions in your discipline will influence how you deal with six different modes of expression that may appear in your academic use of words (Murray, 2002; Cheney, 2005: 149–236; Murray, 2005; Kamler and Thomson, 2006: 59–80; Murray and Moore, 2006):

A **Hedging styles of writing** where the text expresses a belief and commitment about 'something'. Your words here indicate uncertainty or an opinion, but not fact. You may also wish to convey modesty in your argument or deference and respect to the ideas of others. In this form of word, you should signal their use so that intended meanings are not misunderstood. The words that may be used are: Possible . . ., Perhaps . . ., Might . . ., Believe. . . .

B **Emphatic styles of writing** are where statements may or may not be accepted by readers unless evidence supports the claims. Thus, you should only use them when their accompanying statements cannot be refuted. This style stresses your certainty and belief which you want to share with readers. The words that may be used are: Clearly . . ., In fact . . ., Definitely . . ., It is obvious that . . ., Of course. . . .

C **Attitude markers style of writing** seeks to engage with readers on a personal level. Due to this it could be interpreted as being value laden and lacking in objectivity. If your research approach were deductive, then this style of writing might not be approved of by many examiners. It often includes the use of inverted commas to give 'effect', *key words* may be italicised or exclamations marks for added effect! The words that may be used are: I agree . . ., We prefer . . ., Should . . ., Have to . . ., Must, Unfortunately . . ., Hopefully. . . .

D **Relational marker styles of writing** are close to storytelling when you wish to involve readers in actively thinking about the unfolding account. This style is more appropriate for use in social science research than in the natural sciences. It enables you to talk to your readers and so differs from the widely adopted academic tradition of writing at a distance from readers. The words that may be used here are: You can see . . ., Where does this lead?. . ., How might we understand . . ., Consider . . ., You will recall that . . ., Note that. . . .

E **Person marker style of writing** give immediate emphasis to the text as it reminds readers of the writer as a person. Used selectively, you can highlight items or issues being discussed. This style actively asserts your ownership of the text and the message being communicated. The words that may be used here are: I . . ., We . . ., Our . . ., Me . . ., Mine . . ., and also, We believe . . ., My analysis showed . . ., We can see from this . . ., It is possible that. . . .

F **The self-marker style of writing** is when you use the first-person singular in the text. This is a form of writing that divides academic opinion as to its suitability in theses. By not writing at a distance, it is perceived as making the writer – you, perhaps – more significant than the research. It is stylistically unattractive if too many sentences start with the word 'I' and it is assumed to suggest personal bias in the research. A counter view argues that it obliges the writer – you – to accept ownership of what is written. Careful and selective use of 'I' can add weight to an argument and it introduces self into the text. You have to decide between guiding your text along by selective use of the first-person singular – I decided to . . ., adopting the third person – It was decided to . . ., or resorting to the stylistically clumsy – the author/researcher/writer decided to. . .

These six approaches to the use of words in your text can be interpreted either as technical exercises in drafting written communication or emotional relationships between authors and readers. They exemplify the view that: '... all words and vocabularies are socially and politically located and value laden' (Wellington et al. 2005: 156). Thus, settling on a style of writing needs to be thought through carefully and discussed with your supervisor(s).

Once you have written some draft text then it needs to be checked. As you check and check again, you should seek to:

- delete unnecessary repetitions;
- check for misrepresentation of texts and sources;
- improve clarity of the text and quality of arguments;
- ensure that signposts are provided throughout the text;
- remove value judgements apart from those in direct quotations from others;
- proof-read thoroughly to correct typographical and grammatical errors;
- avoid obscure and vague language where meanings are hazy or blurred;
- cross-check that all sources appear in the reference list and all listed sources are included within the text.

Although automatic electronic spellchecking will identify errors, a further visual check is necessary because it usually identifies more errors and stylistic faults. Checking drafts and finished text is one of your essential tasks as a doctoral candidate. If you do it thoroughly then your thesis should not be referred for minor typographical, grammatical and presentational amendments.

Looking back and ahead

This chapter has located the act of writing and using words firmly in the context of your corpus and lexicon. This acknowledges that examiners, being conversant with both, will expect you to draw on them through the choice and use of words in your thesis. It is against this background that it becomes so important for you and your supervisor(s) to have a mutually acceptable method for exchanging views on draft and final text.

Chapter 8 explores the chapter that presents the conclusions from your research.

8

How to conclude your thesis in one chapter

This chapter will:

- outline the emphasis of chapters that appear before the conclusions;
- present the scope of the final chapter in a doctoral thesis;
- indicate the array of possible items that might appear in the chapter;
- provide a list of components for the conclusions chapter.

Introduction

For many doctoral candidates, the conclusions chapter of their thesis is possibly the most difficult one to write. The prospect of distilling all the chapters into a single highly focused chapter may seem to be quite daunting. They have to choose between so many items that could be included. Most of these were so 'critical' to their research as they wrote the earlier chapters. In retrospect, some of the previous arguments or ideas may have gained or lessened in importance since they were first introduced into the thesis. These conflicting choices have to be reconciled in order to produce a suitable text to close the thesis. This task poses a challenge for all candidates because it involves combining scholarship with textual synthesis and creative writing.

We show that the act of concluding a doctoral thesis is, of necessity, a task with multiple dimensions. When examiners read the conclusions chapter, they look for features that they consider to be essential components of a doctoral thesis. We suggest that viewing the task this way will help you to shape the structure and text of the concluding chapter of your doctoral thesis.

This chapter outlines the scope of what examiners normally expect a conclusion chapter to provide. A list of the possible components in the chapter reminds you of everything that could be included! Concluding a thesis obliges candidates to tie up the ends from where they started. We suggest ways for you to connect your opening and closing chapters to show that you achieved what you had intended. We conclude this chapter by using comments of examiners and supervisors to offer further practical pointers that can help you defend your thesis in your viva.

Before the conclusions chapter

Before you can draft conclusions from your research, a foundation has to be created in the chapters that immediately precede the chapter of conclusions. It is customary for there to be one or more chapters between the research findings and the conclusions. In this part of the thesis, examiners expect to read how you extracted meaning from the research data. These chapters that deal with this issue may have a variety of titles and this reflects the personal choice of candidates. Once you have clarified these meanings, decided on their respective titles and mapped out the likely text, then you can start to draw your conclusions.

It may seem obvious, but it is not possible to move directly from presenting descriptive facts to offering conclusions. These two elements of a thesis are linked by a deliberative process that involves meaning-making and it is found in chapters with titles such as Analysis, Interpretation, Discussion. These aspects of your research story might appear in either two or three separate chapters. The choice is yours. It is a structural aspect of the thesis on which the views of your supervisor(s) should be sought.

Alternatively, the three functions could form a single chapter. If you choose this option then the chapter could become too long, too diffuse or even too complicated to write. Either way, these chapters would represent how you have arranged your thinking 'into ascending levels of abstraction' between facts and conclusions. It is important that you guard against including conclusions anywhere in the text of these chapters. Consider these preceding chapters as taking your readers almost to the end of the academic journey. You must not expose the final part of your story – you must keep that for the conclusions chapter.

The presentation of these chapters determines how you introduce your readers to ascending levels of conceptualisation in your thesis. The first (lowest) level would present the 'actuals' as facts found by your fieldwork (Hart, 2005: 435). This information would form the chapter(s) where your research findings appear as a straightforward description of data in either textual form or text with tables histograms, piecharts and other visual forms. Hart suggests that these chapters should not combine presenting the facts with any interpretation of those facts. Thus, these chapters or single chapter would precede those chapters that introduce levels of meaning to the data.

The chapters that give meaning to your data provide the textual bridge between what you found in your fieldwork and the conclusions you then drew from that evidence. You should expect each of your readers of your thesis to look for satisfactory explanations of the process that you adopted to convert 'fact' into 'conclusions'. Examiners, in particular, want to understand the 'why' and 'how' of this process as shown in Example 8.1.

Example 8.1 Examiners' questions concerning analysis, interpretation or discussion

- We would like you to talk us through how you analysed your data.
- Can you now explain the actual mechanical processes that you used to analyse your data?
- Why did you decide to choose XYZ as the criteria against which to compare your data?
- How did you use your conceptual framework as you interpreted your findings?
- Why did you use three separate chapters to deal with analysis, interpretation and discussion? Did you consider combining them into fewer but more focused chapters?

It is worth noting that in Example 8.1, all the questions were asked in an open-ended manner. This style of questioning invites candidates to provide an explanatory response rather than a finite answer. The questions also invited elucidation on the decision making that resulted in choosing those, rather than some other, research methods. Unless candidates have adopted inappropriate forms of analysis or handled the process incorrectly, examiners will ask direct questions about the research mechanics in these chapters. Instead, their questions will be similar to those in Example 8.1 in that examiners want to:

- seek understanding if the written account of the process is unclear;
- invite explanation of the decisional process that resulted in a particular choice of analysis;
- explore the internal linkages between different components of the thesis.

Thus, examiners echo the researchers' obligation to explain how meaning is extracted from data through constant questioning that seeks categorisation, linkages and tendencies within those data (Glaser and Strauss, 1967).

Finally, a higher level of interpretation occurs when you then discuss the analysis and interpretation in order to 'explain it in terms of theoretical constructs' (Hart, 2005: 205). It is the discussion of your data at this higher level of conceptualisation when you demonstrate your scholarship by relating your interpretation of data to the theories of others. Drawing out the connections between your interpretations and relevant concepts in the literature raises the level of your thinking and argument. Once you have discussed your analysis or interpretations of data, then you have the foundation from which to draw your conclusions.

Whether your research approach is inductive or a deductive, Evans and Gruba (2002: 110–111) argue that for these chapters 'the creative part of brains are paramount to the act of writing'. Their reason for this view is that you would be drawing out implications from your evidence as a discursive prelude to the conclusions chapter. They suggest that throughout the duration of your research, you would have been thinking about the conclusions. They believe that researchers are always mentally testing ideas against findings or developing potential theories based on emerging evidence. Either way your creative brain has been quietly working and so you would have an inkling of what those conclusions might be. Drafting the chapters that appear before the conclusions expresses this creative thinking in the text.

Conclusions are just conclusions

Some of the guidance that is provided on the drafting of this chapter seems obvious. However, because it is so obvious when it is overlooked or ignored, examiners do notice. Then they ask questions that cause candidates to say 'oh dear' as they realise their oversight or mistake. The guidance on producing the conclusions chapter itself might well be called 'good practice' since that is how experienced researchers view it.

Bell has pointed out that: 'Only conclusions which can 'justifiably' be drawn from the findings should be made' (1987: 128). This simple sentence warns us all not to claim outcomes that are unsupported by our evidence. She uses the word justifiably to emphasise the need for researchers to give reasons for their conclusions. This also means that those reasons should be explicit, substantiated and defensible. Thus, you cannot offer conclusions on matters that are not part of your research.

You can avoid criticism on this point by checking that your conclusions only contain text that can be traced directly back to the chapters that presented findings/analysis/interpretations/discussion. The most obvious item that fits within Bell's rubric is for you to provide an answer to your research question(s) in this chapter.

Bell also states that: 'No new material should appear in this chapter' (1987:

128). The meaning and implication of this sentence is unambiguous. Despite this, some candidates do not heed either its guidance or warning. Something not previously featured in the text should not be included in the conclusions. Furthermore, it is inappropriate to alter the boundaries at a later stage of the research process since this has implications for the quantity and availability of data that you could collect. However, as you close your research you might decide to cite a recently published source. This does not challenge Bell's advice *if* it is relevant to your topic and illustrates that you are up to date in your reading.

A thesis is a long and word-rich document. Although the chapter of conclusions may remind readers of points that appeared earlier in the text, this is not an excuse for extensive repetition of earlier text. Isn't it odd how your mind sometimes tells you *I have read these words before. Where was it?* When that happens you often search for that earlier text. When you find it you may be pleased to have proved your memory to be working well, but possibly irritated by the texts' unnecessary double appearance. Multiple uses of the same text are unlikely to add noticeably to the quality of any argument. You can avoid this error by: 'not repeating material, which has been included in previous chapters' (Oliver, 2004: 151).

Candidates who overlook these protocols will have it pointed out during their viva. Then, after the viva, examiners will require them to amend the text of their thesis. Feedback from the examiners, at the close of the viva and in their consolidated report, would list the changes that have to be made. Example 8.2 illustrates the type of statements that have appeared in examiners' consolidated reports.

Example 8.2 Examiners' statements requiring textual alterations to the conclusions chapter

- The text must be proofread and repetitions must be removed.
- Remove material that has not been referred to in earlier chapters.
- Shorten the chapter by locating analysis into the previous chapter.
- Show more clearly how the conclusions emerge from the discussion chapter.
- Relocate any recommendations into an appendix and show how and why they might be of practical importance to certain groups of readers.

You can see that candidates who receive these types of required alteration face making textual revisions rather than undertaking severe academic changes to their thesis. Most of the actions are relatively straightforward and would be easy to make. However, behind these requirements is the fact that candidates and their supervisors too, perhaps, should have checked the textual form of the thesis far more thoroughly before it was submitted. These errors are avoidable, so perhaps the adage *You can never check your writing too many times* originated from a doctoral candidate!

Since word lengths of doctoral theses vary between universities and disciplines, it is only possible to indicate the relative comparisons between the sizes of chapters. This is a topic to discuss with your supervisor(s) so that you appreciate 'local custom and practice' and any regulatory guidelines which the university has on structuring theses in your field of research. Table 8.1 shows the proportions of pages in chapters devoted to analysis, interpretation, discussion and conclusions in a selection of thesis from nine disciplines/academic areas. The number of pages in each thesis refers only to the text and excludes preliminary pages, reference lists and appendices.

Table 8.1 shows the tendency for conclusion chapters to represent a relatively small proportion of the total words in theses. The pages that are normally devoted to analysis, interpretation, discussion and conclusions chapters amount to just over one-fifth of the length of theses. These are relatively crude evaluations of word count due to the influence of personal preferences of

Table 8.1   Proportion of pages in the closing chapters of nine doctoral theses

Discipline/academic area	A+ I	D	C	T	%C:T	%C:AID	%AIDC:T
Adolescent's development in closed communities	40		20	210	10	50	28
Nursing diagnosis of personality disorders		37	15	274	5	40	19
Patients coping with cancer	17	43	5	283	2	8	23
Curriculum development for dance and movement in kindergartens	20	27	19	295	6	40	22
Image encoding in optical stereoscopic displays		43	6	202	3	14	24
Critical biography in poetry	29	32	17	279	6	27	28
Visual literacy in developing photographers	14	46	14	255	6	23	29
Culture in family businesses	27	32	40	287	14	24	34
Oral feedback, cultural style and learning language	13	6	19	292	6	32	27
Aggregate totals	160	306	155	2684	6	33	23

(**A** = analysis; **I** = interpretations; **D** = discussion; **C** = conclusion; **T** = thesis.)

author–candidates and the way they allocated text to these structural components. Nonetheless, Table 8.1 supports Bunton's findings that concluding chapters in American doctorates averaged 3.5 pages in the natural sciences and 15 pages in the social sciences and humanities (Bunton, 1998). Received wisdom from candidates, examiners and supervisors suggests that similar totals appear in British doctoral theses. Thus, as you plan these closing chapters you need to consider the relative length and respective relationship of these final chapters to avoid an unbalanced textual emphasis between them.

Hidden scope of the conclusions chapter

Your conclusions chapter is more than simply presenting the conclusions from your research. This is clearly the primary role for it in your thesis, but the chapter serves other implicit purposes. Understanding how your readers will approach and appreciate your text provides a view of writing and presentation that is often hidden but you should take into account.

Examiners give particular attention to their reading of the conclusions chapter. There are two simple reasons for this: it is the final piece of writing produced by candidates and the final piece of examiners' own reading. They expect that the chapter will distil the entire doctoral study into a convincing case that supports your claim to have made an original contribution to knowledge. To present that case, you will need to draw on your capacity for high-level thinking and your understanding of high-level research.

Figure 8.1 shows the relationship between these two components of doctoral study. The rising diagonal progresses from the low micro-level of descriptive factual conclusion, through macro-answers to research questions to the high meta-level of thinking that characterises conceptual conclusions. To account for how you arrived at your conceptual conclusions therefore requires you to use your factual and interpretive conclusions as stepping stones to that destination.

As you provide this account, it is important that you incorporate the four complementary functions of *reminding, telling, selling* and *leaving*, implicitly, into your text. They provide a framework for you to check that this chapter does more than simply conclude your thesis.

Reminding readers

An early paragraph, often appearing immediately after the introduction of the chapter, can *remind* readers:

- why the topic was chosen;
- what the research sought to discover;

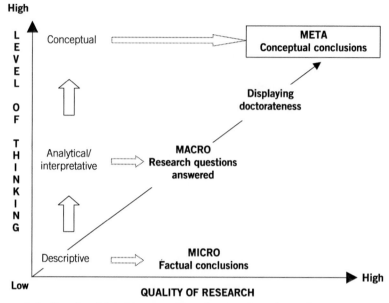

Figure 8.1   Levels of thinking, quality of research and conclusions.

- how the research was designed and undertaken;
- what boundaries were set for the research and why they were chosen;
- which research questions the research was intended to answer and so contribute to knowledge.

Including such text will ensure that readers recall the primary purposes of the research they would have met some thousands of words earlier. The text itself needs to be written in a sensitive and supporting style rather than as a verbatim repetition of previous text. If you provide this as reinforcement it will be welcomed by your readers. Omitting such gentle reminders may mean that readers have to look back to the opening text themselves. Therefore, this is a way of helping readers to recall what you had written in the opening chapters of your thesis. This simple writing technique is how you ensure that examiners should recognise the scope of your research – what it is and what it is not. If necessary, you could refer to this text in your viva to clarify the exact boundaries of your investigation.

Telling readers

Next, you ought to consider how the chapter *tells* your readers:

- what you found – as facts that answer your research question(s);
- how those facts were interpreted as concepts;

- how you have critiqued your research approach and the methodology that was adopted;
- what secondary findings emerged from your fieldwork and how they informed your conclusions;
- what items might now constitute a research agenda for you, or others, to address.

Addressing these issues will help readers to appreciate the significance of your findings and recognise your understanding how interpreting your fieldwork opened up further questions that can be answered through research.

Selling to readers

The chapter itself is a *selling* opportunity. This may be an unexpected view of the conclusions chapter in a doctoral thesis. However, as the final chapter, it has the potential to create an impression and to leave in the minds of its recipients' positive images of its value and contribution (Bernstein, 1984). As Bernstein argues, all communication is a means of conveying one's influence to others in appropriate ways. In this sense, your conclusions chapter represents a means of *selling* to your readers the impressions that you would like them to have as they finish reading your thesis.

Thus, the chapter should endeavour to *sell* to readers that your:

- research outcomes are evidence based;
- research approach(s) follow informed choices and engagement with appropriate ideas;
- argument is coherent and scholarly throughout your thesis and justify the claim of a modest contribution to knowledge;
- formulation of factual and conceptual conclusions are reasonable;
- capability to undertake doctoral research is demonstrated by the content of the thesis;
- thesis displays your potential to undertake further research independent of supervision.

These persuasive items represent aspects of writing that should be apparent from the text as they convey the merit of your doctoral research to readers.

Leaving readers with

Finally, it is important that the chapter *leaves* your readers with positive impressions. These would include having:

- ample evidence to judge the scholarly merit of the thesis;
- gained insights on your scholarship as displayed by arguments and conceptualisation;

- an appreciation of your academic resilience, through an account of how you undertook your research;
- an understanding of the contribution to knowledge that your research has made;
- a positive impression of your ability to undertake postdoctoral research independently of supervision.

When these impressions follow from reading the final chapter, they will leave readers with memories that are favourable. For examiners, such memories influence how they then compose their initial independent report on the thesis and subsequently how they approach their viva with you.

Hidden persuaders

You will have recognised that there are overlaps between some implications of the four functions above. You will influence readers differently in this chapter depending on how you deal with the significance of research questions, facts and concepts plus your own scholarship and postdoctoral capability. For instance, a candidate undertook a phenomenological enquiry in *Craftsmanship in ceramics* with a single research question: What is the nature of craftsmanship in ceramics? The central theory in this research was the notion of 'flow' (Czikszentmihalyi, 1990, 2000). Example 8.3 contains extracts from this professional practice doctoral thesis. The first is a brief explanation of 'flow'. Then, extracts from the conclusion chapter allow us to follow the reasoning that leads to his developed, and new, theory. The text gently combines the four functions to achieve writing that one examiner described as 'powerful'. It is also persuasive of the candidate's conceptual grasp in his professional context.

Example 8.3 Making the hidden visible

Flow explained in the abstract
The theory of 'flow' (Czikszentmihalyi, 1990) is a . . . means by which craftsmanship within ceramics can be understood. 'Flow' is a mental state, which can be deliberately contrived, which allows the potter to concentrate upon the work in hand without being affected by the two extremes of boredom and anxiety. It is also revealed how the contributing potters naturally strive for excellence, in the way that Dissanayake (2003) suggests is 'making special'.

Extracts from the conclusions chapter
During the research I came to consider craftsmanship in ceramics as one aspect of 'making special' which I understand as a universal

constant of behaviour. It is enormously important because it is a defining aspect of what it means to be human.

During the research I (also) uncovered the theory of 'flow.' I came to agree with potters like these in the research, who subconsciously, or consciously, work in a state of 'flow', and so avoid the extremes of anxiety and tedium, both of which can be overwhelming and destructive. They learn how to induce that state of mild euphoria, called 'flow' by Czikszentmihalyi and that feeling of well-being is so satisfying that they wish to return to the task time and time again. The additive nature of 'flow' is a powerful attractant and serves to bind the contact with pottery making.

Viewing craftsmanship from a wider perspective has validated my commitment towards work in a way that would have previously been impossible. I now know what I and other like-minded people do is part of a fundamental human need and therefore significant and life affirming . . . My contribution to knowledge has been to assimilate these points of view and synthesise them from within my own practical experience and the experience of the practitioners and so arrive at new understandings.

The new theory necessitates understanding craftsmanship in ceramics as located beyond the separate and skilled aspects of making pottery, for example slab building or throwing. This research has shown how the entire process of skilled making and judgement is *the phenomenon of craftsmanship. This process is crucial to establishing a professional practice, conceiving the things to be made, manufacture, marketing, sales, delivery and public relations. Craftsmanship therefore* is *the professional practice of potters.*

These four categories are unlikely to appear in university guidelines on structuring the doctoral thesis. However, as recurring checkpoints that examiners use, they represent valuable pointers against which you can audit your writing. They provide you with a practical template for your writing to ensure that these 'hidden persuaders' (Packard, 1957) have been included in how you draft this final chapter. Addressing these points ensures that you capitalise on the investment that you have made in your research and writing your thesis. When examiners are genuinely impressed by the argument, textual form and presentation of a thesis then they may open the viva with statements similar to those shown in Example 8.4.

Example 8.4 Examiners' opening statements

Examiner A   From the first page of your thesis, we were pulled into the story of the research by your very open and appealing style of writing. Your enthusiasm showed through also as you used your own experience of the topic to illustrate occasional points. Because of this care and attention, we felt that the thesis was a pleasure to read.

Examiner B   You have presented us with a very well-argued thesis to read. It was intriguing to see how you had woven your arguments together with your data and the literature so that this very complex topic became clear to understand.

Examiner C   We liked the way that you have presented your argument and taken us through the story of your research in a seamless way.

Examiner D   Both of us found the signposting that you had used was helpful as we read your thesis. It helped us to follow the argument so easily. We really enjoyed reading your thesis. Thank you for this.

Examiner E   We particularly appreciated how you drew the entire thesis together in the concluding chapter.

These statements do not pick out the conclusion chapter specifically for praise. Nonetheless, they reflect how examiners appreciated the thesis as a textual entity. The impression that the conclusions chapter had made on these examiners must have been supported by what they had read in other chapters. Had it been otherwise, then their judgement and comments would not have been so complimentary. Thus, the potential influence of the conclusions chapter on the academic judgement and opinion of examiners deserves special attention as you write it.

So, what should be included in the chapter?

Before you even start to outline the chapter, you will have thought about its possible components. This is yet another aspect of your doctorate where you have choices to make. Figure 8.2 contains 18 unevenly shaped items. Two of these items, the introductory paragraphs and the closing paragraphs, will remind you of the need to address your readers through elegant and convincing text. The remaining items are not in any particular order. Neither do

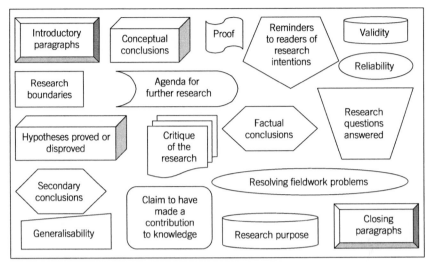

Figure 8.2 Possible (randomly organised) components of a conclusions chapter.

they touch or overlap, which might symbolise a connection between them. Instead, their randomness is intentional in order to pose, for you, some practical questions, as shown in Task 8.1.

Task 8.1 How are you going to structure your conclusions chapter?

- What are the essential components that you will have/have in the conclusions chapter of your thesis?
- What less important components will you include, how will you decide whether or not to include them and when will you make those decisions?
- What will be the order of appearance in the text for the main components?
- What is the visual structure for the chapter and what will be the headings of its sections?
- How do you intend to build a argument throughout the chapter that will convince your readers of the scholarly merit in your research?
- How many theses in your discipline/field have you looked at to learn how their authors wrote and structured their concluding chapters?
- What did you learn from that reading that will help you to structure and write your conclusions chapter?

Your conclusions chapter will be shorter in length than the previous chapters. Its role is simply to present the conclusions and not to engage in any further analysis or discussion. As a result, examiners expect the chapter to focus quite specifically on the outcomes of the research. They also expect you to acknowledge other less critical features since these, too, are outcomes. Examiners consider the following components to be essential features in a well-argued conclusions chapter.

Answers to research questions

They should provide an unambiguous answer to the question(s) that gave direction to your research. You can do this by reformulating the words of the question to provide an answer.

Examiners may not ask about the answer(s) that you have provided if it appears to be satisfactory and appropriate. However, in his viva, a candidate who had not provided an answer to his own research question was asked by an examiner: 'I understood exactly what your research questions(s) implied for this study. However, I could not see the answer anywhere in your conclusions chapter. Perhaps you could point me to it?'

Factual conclusions

State *exactly* what you can conclude from the evidence that you have collected. These are the facts from your investigation and may be expressed descriptively without analysis or interpretation.

Examiners may just want you to talk about your research outcomes and so they would ask a very open question: 'So what did you find/discover?'

Conceptual conclusions

Once you have presented your factual conclusions, then you can raise your level of thinking by providing your conceptual conclusions. You might want to devote a section to this part of the chapter in order to conceptualise your factual conclusions. This will involve you expressing the conclusions through abstract ideas and theories. You will need to align your conclusions with the components of your conceptual framework to reinforce the conceptual foundation of your research design, methodology and intellectual context. Thus, in this section of the chapter you are 'closing the conceptual circle' of your doctoral research.

Examiners often ask candidates to explain the reasoning that led them to formulate their conceptual conclusions through a straightforward request: 'Please tell us how you arrived at your conceptual conclusions and how they link your work together.'

If a candidate has not provided any conceptual conclusions, then these are the types of question that examiners might ask:

'Can you extend your factual conclusions a little bit for us? Show how they relate to the wider literature.'

'What is the link between your conclusions and your conceptual/theoretical approach?'
'How does your research relate to the literature that appeared earlier in your thesis?'
'What do your conclusions now tell you about the assumptions and theoretical perspectives that guided your research design?'

A statement of the contribution to knowledge

Use your explanation of the gap in knowledge, in a previous early chapter, to express your contribution to knowledge. It would be quite appropriate to restate the gap in knowledge and then rephrase it as a contribution to knowledge. Then, show how your evidence allows you to claim a modest contribution that is plausible and can be defended through the rigour of your research approach and methodology.

Examiners will subject your claim to scrutiny, since this is central to their scholarly role as examiners. They will explore with you the case that you have advanced. If examiners are satisfied with the quality of the argument, they might ask an apparently flippant question in order to explore this feature of the chapter: 'How big a contribution to knowledge do you believe your research has made?'

A justification for the claim of a contribution to knowledge

Your claim to have contributed to knowledge must be clear and unambiguous. The justification for it must also be unambiguous. Whether your research approach is inductive or deductive, you will have based your research design on certain conceptual assumptions. These will have been based on one or possibly two of the items shown in Chapter 2:

- application of conventional research instruments in new fields of investigation;
- combining disparate concepts in new ways to investigate a conventional issue;
- creating new understandings of existing issues;
- design and application of new field instruments in a contemporary setting;
- extending the work of others through a replication of their original methodology;
- identification of new and emerging issues worthy of investigation and explanation;
- originality in using the work of others.

It is quite proper to remind your readers of these starting points for your research. Once this text has been written, then you can show how the rigour of the research design and fieldwork allows you to draw these conclusions.

If they are convinced with the claim, they may not even ask a question on this aspect of the chapter. However, they may invite a very general response in this aspect of the research such as: 'Please tell us about the significance of your findings in (your) field of research/scholarship/profession.'

If they were unconvinced by your arguments, they would ask you to clarify and justify your claim. In these cases, they would focus their questions on aspects of the research which they considered not to be rigorous or coherently argued. The nature of the question(s) would be discipline-specific.

Examiners will want to clarify how your research has contributed to knowledge. Making such a claim in a thesis and leaving the claim there to gather dust does little to disseminate your conclusions! So if you have not already published your findings in appropriate journals or texts, expect examiners to enquire about your intentions to publish from your research. Seeking opportunities to deliver a conference paper, making a poster presentation or publishing an article are recommended ways to disseminate your work before submitting your thesis (Phillips and Pugh, 2000: 95–97, 203–204; Murray, 2002: 136–140; Dunleavy, 2003: 249–250; Neumann, 2004: 86). The public review of your work, or its publication details, can then be cited in your thesis. These items in the reference list of your thesis will show that you have already contributed to the corpus in the scholarly arena. In addition, examiners who are on editorial boards of journals often invite candidates to submit articles to their journal for publication that draw on relevant parts of their thesis.

Hypotheses and/or propositions

In the previous chapters, you would have analysed, interpreted and discussed the evidence that will test your hypotheses. In this chapter, you would then only need to show whether your hypotheses were proven – *or not*. You can deal with each hypothesis one by one and state your conclusion. Your research outcomes can be generalised and you are entitled to make this claim due to your deductive research approach and methodology. Thus, you will have shown how your research approach has tested the theories that were enshrined in your hypotheses.

However, if you adopted an inductive approach then your research would have sought to develop theory. In the previous chapters, you would have analysed, interpreted and discussed the evidence that will allow you to offer propositions. In this chapter, and usually after presenting your conceptual conclusions, you would express your contribution(s) to knowledge as single sentence statements. Each statement should deal with a separate aspect of your theoretical contribution and contain no more than two variables. In this sense, they are similar to a series of hypotheses, which you are making available for others to test in their own context. Thus, you would avoid claiming generalisability when you are actually developing theory. If others test your propositions as their hypotheses, then that investigation would be deductive and they could generalise from their conclusions.

Examiners always check that candidates provide the appropriate handling of hypotheses and propositions. It is therefore important at the close of your thesis not to stumble over the methodological differences between deductive and inductive research paradigms. Then there are those occasional candidates who are asked *What is the difference between methodology and methods?* For this question even to be asked suggests that the candidate has obviously misused these two terms in the thesis and so demonstrated a lack of understanding of these distinctively different important research terms.

Examiners want to see that your research has arrived somewhere. The consequences of testing hypotheses or advancing a set of propositions are closures to any piece of research. Unless something is 'wrong' with the methodology, examiners may not ask any questions about this part of the chapter. Occasionally an examiner may ask: 'Were you surprised by the conclusions that came from your research?'

You will recognise that this question opens up the assumptions on which you based your research. It invites you to discuss philosophical stances of epistemology and methodology rather than content features of your findings.

A critique of the research

Undertaking doctoral research is implicitly a learning experience for the candidate (Lawton, 1997: 3) Wellington et al. (2005: 41) extend this view by suggesting that 'Untangling and becoming aware of the many aspects of learning on a doctoral programme illustrates the scale and multilayered nature of the whole endeavour'. Examiners expect to see a section that provides a retrospective view on what candidates have learned from undertaking their doctorate. This can be a reflective view of how the research might have been undertaken differently. If your research were well-planned, well-executed and achieved its purposes, then examiners would expect you to defend that happy state of affairs!

Critiques are, of necessity, retrospective and use informed hindsight. Consider how your research would have been quite different had you chosen a different paradigm to describe your research topic. It would have altered your research approach, design, fieldwork, findings, conclusions and outcomes. This form of critique would show you to be 'thinking like an experienced and competent researcher' and therefore displaying the episteme appropriate to your discipline (Perkins, 2006: 42). Through this, examiners would recognise that you are demonstrating the capacity to undertake unsupervised postdoctoral research. Some candidates, though, focus their attention instead on the relatively lower level intellectual and technical issues of sample sizes, response rates and duration of the study. They are not exhibiting the episteme appropriate to their discipline and examiners would recognise this.

Vivas could close with examiners asking either this question or posing this statement: 'How would you critique your research?' Alternatively, 'We would like you now to critique your research for us.'

An appropriate handling of generalisability

If you adopted a deductive approach to your research then you would have collected data in order to test theory. Your conclusions would therefore be high in reliability. As a consequence, it would then be possible for you to generalise from your conclusions. Alternatively, if your research approach were inductive, then you would have sought to develop theory. As a result, your conclusions would be high in validity but low in reliability. Your conclusions would, therefore, not be generalisable. However, you could capture the essential elements of your conclusions and express them as propositions. Examiners become quite unhappy if they see claims for generalisability emerging from essentially inductive research!

When both deductive and inductive approaches are adopted in staged research, then the chapter will account for combinations of methodological outcomes and focus on the final methodological approach regarding generalisability. It is essential that you respect the methodological differences between inductive and deductive approaches to research as you write about these last methodological stages in your thesis.

One examiner was obviously enjoying a viva where the candidate had already been told that he would be awarded his doctorate. She obviously had decided to move the general discussion onto an even higher methodological level when she asked: 'I note that your research was entirely based in a quantitative approach. How generalisable would you consider your conclusions to be?'

You might speculate on how the ensuing discussion between the candidate and the two examiners proceeded!

An agenda for further research

In the process of completing your research, you may have recognised the need for further research. Time constraints, funding or opportunity may have prevented you from including these topics within your doctoral research. Many candidates include a section that explains the nature of further research that has emerged from their investigation. Others, who have investigated a self-contained topic through action research for instance, may be unable to include such a section. Thus, the nature of the topic and methodology determine the inclusion or omission of agendas for further research. Examiners would recognise this.

In his concluding chapter, one candidate restated his three research questions as goals. Then one short paragraph linked his answers to those questions in this section that dealt with a research agenda:

> During the development and conduct of this research, each of these three goals were achieved, though, as outlined in the following section, further work is desirable for this research area to progress to fruition.

This extract was the candidate's introduction to then outlining the main components of that agenda. This candidate had therefore helped his readers to recognise that he had achieved what he had intended to do. He saw that further postdoctoral research was yet to be done. In his viva, the examiners commended him on the explicit way that he had made these links between his intentions and possible further research.

Overview of the conclusions chapter

As you introduce the chapter, it is essential that you re-establish the context of the research which you have undertaken. First, you should use the chapter's introductory section to remind examiners of the purpose and origins for your investigation. In your opening chapters, these purposes would have been explained. It would be quite acceptable for you to repeat the same words to introduce the conclusions chapter so long as you make that clear to readers. If you prefer not to duplicate the text, then an alternative approach would be to rephrase those earlier words. Either way, it is important that you frame the arguments in your conclusions within these initial research parameters.

The introductory section is also an appropriate place to restate the boundaries that delimited your research. This is another reminder to readers that your conclusions relate to what is within those boundaries; after all, they are the chosen context for your research. You could even see this text as an attempt to insure against questions about matters that lie outside that boundary.

At the other end of the chapter, you have to decide how to close your thesis. Some candidates use a headed small section to summarise the whole chapter. Others do not have such a formal method of ending their thesis. For them, the chapter itself serves as the closure of the thesis and so a section dealing with future work, for them, could be the final piece of text.

Even carefully planned research can discover something that was not expected. This would not necessarily be a primary finding, but could justify being mentioned as a secondary finding. Secondary findings could be the trigger for further research and be explained in that context. You could introduce the sentence that leads into the secondary findings by using this type of comment: 'As a by-product of my research, my secondary findings unveiled . . .'

This chapter is the right place, finally, to disclose how you problematised the research that you have now completed. Wisker (2005: 178–179) reminds us that: 'Learners who contextualise their learning relate it to themselves and their own world. They become reflexive, self-aware and more flexible.' Similarly, doctoral candidates who recognise the intricacies of the research act, the pluralist nature of the research process and the potential problems in undertaking research will be able to disclose their views.

This could be provided in an explanation of, maybe, a couple of pages that summarised how you had learned both about research and yourself while undertaking your doctoral research. It would involve you reflecting on having to handle diverse theories and large quantities of data as a learning process rather than purely as a logistical exercise. Doing this you might distinguish between superficial and deep levels of learning. Perhaps you would also acknowledge the associated consequences of only just being able to cope and fully grasping the intricacies and implication of those concepts and data (Wisker et al., 2003a, 2003b).

Looking back and ahead

In this chapter, we have illustrated how examiners view the concluding chapters of doctoral theses. Your style of writing will inevitably reflect how you intend your readers to appreciate your doctoral research and its scholarship. However, to achieve that we have presented the obvious components that have to be included and the underlying features that you need to consider. The concluding chapter really only tells readers about the destination and outcomes of the research that was outlined in the opening chapters of your thesis. Thus, it deserves careful thought and planning as you decide how to shape and then write it. Please remember that it is the last chapter that examiners will read before they start to assess your entire thesis.

Chapter 9 deals with just one page of your thesis – the abstract.

9

The abstract

This chapter will:

- explain the purposes of the abstract in doctoral theses;
- outline the expectations that readers have of abstracts;
- provide a template for drafting an abstract.

Introduction

Doctoral candidates in all British universities are required to include an abstract in their theses. However the format of the abstract is prescribed by all universities and of the many components in your thesis, the technical specifications for your abstract are non-negotiable! Although abstracts are of just one page in length, they serve many purposes and so deserve equal attention as the rest of your thesis.

This chapter explains the functions of the abstract and we suggest ways that you can assemble the text for, and draft, your abstract.

Significance of abstracts

Your abstract will serve a number of purposes. First, it will summarise your thesis and convey the essence of the research on a single page of text. Second, it will provide examiners with initial insights on your research and writing style. Third, it will convey specific essential information that you have selected about your doctoral research. Finally, it will act as a filter for potential readers who may wish to access your thesis but who need to know more about it before doing so.

Because your abstract has these purposes, the task of drafting it deserves equal seriousness to that which you devoted to the rest of your thesis. Therefore, you should avoid Dunleavy's criticism of doctoral abstracts as often being *very badly written*, because their authors: 'normally only write them in a hectic rush to get finished'. He suggests that they are frequently seen as: 'another piece of boring university bureaucracy' (Dunleavy, 2003: 203–204). The regulations of your university will indeed prescribe a standardised format for layout and structure of abstracts. The reason for this extends beyond the confines of your university. Other scholars may be interested in your doctoral topic through their electronic or hard-copy searches of library stockholdings.

Abstracts should be 'self-explanatory' (Herbert, 1990: 97) and 'complete in [their] own right' (White, 2000: 137). In these words, Herbert and White both imply that abstracts should provide a complete overview of a thesis. Their views accord with those of Punch who concludes that abstracts: 'are a brief summary, whether of a proposal or a finished study. It is not the introduction ... but rather a summary of it ... (it provides) a brief overview of all the essential elements' (Punch, 2000: 68). Thus, while Murray (2002) observes that: 'The logical structure underpinning the abstract may seem obvious in such a short text' Oliver (2004: 94) argues that abstracts fulfil the role of being: 'a synopsis of the entire thesis, including the analysis of results and conclusion'.

Recognising these complementary factors emphasises the potential for abstracts to influence the opinions of readers before they encounter the text of your thesis. In this context, Dunleavy (2003: 203) confirms that other researchers: 'rely heavily on the abstract' in determining whether or not to request a complete thesis from another library. It is these wider roles of the abstract that the necessity for it to convey 'what your thesis is all about' becomes an absolute imperative for you.

It is against this background that university regulations will state exactly where the abstract must be located within the Preliminary pages of your thesis. It will normally be either the first or the last item of these pages. In either case, the abstract is the first piece of continuous prose that readers will encounter in a thesis. Oliver (2004: 94) states very clearly that the abstract is: 'an essential part of the thesis and will probably be the first part which will be read by examiners'.

In their assessment role, examiners are required to check that you have complied with the regulations that apply to the presentation of theses. They can withhold their recommendation of the award until any such omission has been corrected. Some universities specifically ask examiners to confirm that *the abstract is satisfactory*. This places particular importance on the abstract 'being correct' when a thesis is submitted. After their first reading of your abstract, examiners: 'will read it again to get an overall flavour of the research, and once in detail while writing [their independent] report' (Bergquist, 2004: 210).

Thus, you should not underrate the significance of your abstract as a component in your doctoral experience.

Visualising the abstract

The primary readers of your abstract will be your examiners. At a secondary level of importance are those other researchers who may interrogate the abstract as a prelude to, perhaps, requesting sight of your thesis. Then there are your family and friends who may wish to know what you have been writing about and the abstract could just tempt them to start reading!

University regulations usually limit the length of the abstract to a single A4 page and protocols will prescribe the type and content of headings that appear above the text. It is customary for these headings to include:

- the name of the awarding university;
- the faculty/department in which your doctorate was registered;
- the name of the degree;
- your full name;
- the title of your thesis;
- the month and year when the thesis was submitted for assessment.

You should also note any line/paragraph spacing, plus font and point specifications, that apply to the abstract. The text of your abstract should not include references or quotations.

The text of the abstract addresses the questions that prospective readers would like to ask about your thesis. Only four succinct paragraphs are necessary to provide a perfectly adequate answer since:

- Paragraph 1 answers the question: **What was the purpose of your research?** Readers expect to discover the rationale for the study. By stating why a gap in knowledge existed and the specific gap towards which your research was directed you can then present the research question(s) as the imperative for your study. By outlining the rationale, context and boundaries readers can then appreciate the delimitations of your research.
- Paragraph 2 answers the question: **How was your research designed?** Readers expect to discover which research approaches you adopted for your study and why. An outline of the paradigm/conceptual framework(s) and associated assumptions will provide the strategy for your research approach. Then, explaining how your study was undertaken requires a simple description of the research methods and a brief account of the fieldwork.
- Paragraph 3 answers the question: **What were your findings?**

Readers expect to discover the nature of your aggregate findings. You should also present general details of your significant factual conclusions.

- Paragraph 4 answers the question: **What were your conclusions?**
  Readers expect to discover what your research discovered. The significance of your (main) conceptual conclusions can show how you have added to or developed theory. The results of testing hypotheses *or* the type of general propositions being proposed would support this position. This paragraph should close with a sentence that emphasises your contribution to knowledge.

By answering these four questions, your abstract will be succinct, focused and sharply argued. As a result, it should provide any reader with a clear overview of your doctoral research. However, as Parahoo wisely reminds us: 'Readers should not ask too much from an abstract as details are provided in the rest of the [thesis]' (Parahoo, 2006: 403).

Drafting the abstract

As Dunleavy pointed out, the abstract is possibly the last piece of text that most candidates write for their thesis. You could, of course, draft the first paragraph after writing your introductory chapters, followed by the other paragraphs when their respective components of your thesis are written. This approach has the potential to result in a piecemeal piece of writing that may need revising – usually when the next paragraph appears.

However, reserving that writing task until you have completed the first draft of your thesis has four advantages since you gain:

- the benefit of a retrospective overview on the thesis when you know the outcome of your research and have determined its conclusions;
- a consolidated and complete text that is unlikely to undergo any major alterations to methodology, arguments or conclusions;
- a detailed knowledge of the literature appropriate to your field of investigation that have informed the conceptualisation in the thesis;
- an up-to-date knowledge of developments in your field against which you can confidently align your conclusions and so justify your claim to making a contribution to knowledge.

Thus, we suggest that although you can make notes in a file called 'abstract' at any time, do not draft it until you have a complete first draft of your thesis.

These four questions provide a practical framework from which you can draft your abstract. However, your university will stipulate the length of doctoral abstracts, which will vary between 250 and 400 words. This means that you have less than 100 words in which to answer each of the above questions.

As you write your thesis, you could anticipate how certain words or phrases capture exactly what you would like the abstract to convey. You could place these words or phrases into a category (file) which will become a 'bank of text' that might be useful as you draft your abstract. This bank of text could be easily classified to provide the four answers required for the abstract. With this text already placed into surrogate paragraphs producing the first draft of the abstract should be relatively straightforward.

A retrospective approach that you might adopt is to revisit the architecture for your thesis (see Chapter 4). The introductions for the parts and chapters represent potential sources of text for your abstract. The summaries for certain chapters can also be trawled for what Finn (2005: 126) refers to as 'the main message' in their arguments. These various paragraphs will include succinct arguments and crafted phrases that can be lifted, reworked and categorised under one of the four paragraphs of the abstract. So considering *What have I already written that can be used?* may be a time-saving way to assemble your abstract.

Table 9.1 indicates the possible locations in your thesis of text that could, perhaps, be included in each of the four paragraphs of the abstract.

Table 9.1 Locations for text in your abstract

Component of abstracts	Possible sources of text
Para 1 What was the purpose of your research?	Statements of aim, context, boundaries to the investigation, gaps in knowledge, context, boundaries to the investigation, research questions.
Para 2 How was your research designed?	Research design and methodology chapters, paradigms, explanation of the conceptual framework, assumptions and philosophical stances on the issue, methods chapter.
Para 3 What were your findings?	Chapters dealing with fieldwork, analysis or discussion.
Para 4 What were your conclusions?	Chapter of conclusions and those sections that deal with the contribution to knowledge and generalisability.

Given that you will not be writing many words on any of the paragraphs, this places your abstract in the category of 'tiny texts' (Kamler and Thomson, 2006: 85–86). This type of writing: 'compresses the rhetorical act of arguing into a small textual space using a small number of words'. But, as Kamler and Thomson argue, an abstract: 'is "large" in the pedagogical work [it] can accomplish'.

If you have produced a well-argued focused thesis, then preparing the first draft of your abstract should be straightforward. You may need to spend time polishing the text, so that it reads to your satisfaction and your supervisor is happy with it, too. Some candidates, however, are unable to prepare a synopsis of their thesis on one page. For them, as Wellington et al. point out: 'It is often a warning of a larger difficulty about the thesis itself – the argument is indistinct, the focus is unclear or the significance is not articulated' (Wellington et al., 2005: 174). In those cases, such candidates should revisit their thesis to locate, review and, possibly, rewrite some text before drafting their abstract. Their inability to produce a first draft of their abstract also suggests that they might not be able to defend their thesis successfully at their viva. Thus, it implies a connection between a well-written, carefully argued thesis and a candidate's ability to draft their single-page abstract with relative ease.

At this point in your reading, you are invited to take a break and tackle Task 9.1.

Task 9.1   A very provisional draft abstract

Take some time out from your research or your writing just for while. Using the four paragraphs as a template, prepare an intermediate draft of what you would put into your abstract now. Discuss your draft with your supervisor(s) to see how far they concur with your current thoughts. Keep the draft to revise – and learn from – when you are ready to produce your substantial abstract.

Why not market your thesis?

Writing your abstract is an opportunity to sell the scholarly quality of your thesis to prospective readers. The abstract is more than just an administrative requirement for inclusion in theses; it presents the merits of your thesis to your readers. It also shows how your contribution to knowledge met the specified gap in knowledge that was your original reason for undertaking the research. Therefore, view your abstract as a device to convey your confidence in the quality, scholarship and doctorateness of your thesis. Use it to influence how your readers will approach the substantial text of your thesis through already possessing positive views of *what your thesis is all about*. Thus, why not use the abstract in a positive way to market what your thesis contains? You can achieve this through ensuring that the text is:

- factual, but not descriptively detailed;
- free of references;
- jargon free and clearly written;
- informative, but not argumentative in writing style;

- written in an appealing style that engages with your various potential audiences.

These protocols all contribute to presenting a positive image of your work. They are recognisable indicators to others of your scholarship. Thus, use the regulations of your university to ensure that the layout of your abstract fully meets the expectation of your examiners and other readers, too.

Higher education institutions in the UK provide the British Library with a copy of each candidate's thesis and abstract, following the approval of a research degree award. This is an ever-increasing archive of successfully completed research. It is also an accessible reservoir of theses for investigation by scholars – including yourself, of course. Thus, your abstract affords insights on your research to scholars around the world as a form of free advertising!

Two examples of abstracts are provided as appendices to this chapter. Appendix 9.1 shows an example of the early draft for an abstract. Detailed comments that were made by the supervisor are shown in the text. The supervisor's alterations and suggestions indicate what the candidate has to do in order that the text would meet the requirements of a doctoral abstract. This abstract neither complied with the university regulations nor provided a coherent picture of the research and thesis. Appendix 9.2 is an example of a good abstract that addressed the four questions through text that was simple, clear and direct. Read the appendices and then tackle Task 9.2.

Task 9.2 Comparing a poor with a good abstract

How do the two abstracts that are shown in Example 9.1 and Example 9.2 differ in terms of their content and structure?

Looking back and ahead

In this chapter, we have shown how the abstract provides a synopsis of the critical features in your thesis. The abstract is more than simply a succinct summary of your thesis; it is a (revolving) door through which some people are drawn into the thesis, but it keeps other people out, too. Thus, it deserves your serious attention as it is compiled, drafted and included in a prescribed place within your thesis.

Chapter 10 shows how, by closing the research circle, candidates confirm their understanding of doctoral research thereby elevating their appreciation of interconnectedness within research processes.

Example 9.1 An amended poor abstract

UNIVERSITY OF RUTH

Faculty of Education

ABSTRACT

Doctor of Philosophy

Developing and using evaluation for quality assurance in colleges

By Charlie Watch See regulations. No qualification letters, please. Thanks.

This research was undertaken into the evaluation systems for the management of further education colleges. Why? Use your reasons for undertaking the research; show the gap in knowledge that existed. It aimed to Be bold. What were the research questions? explain how senior staff used existing methods to assure themselves of the quality standards that were. The words – in place – are meaningless. Omit. It examined how the regulations which the government agencies had introduced operated in practice and how managers used them in their job (DfEE, 2001) See regulations. No references please. It looked at Meaning? the curriculum as well as resource planning and the management of premises. The research was undertaken over a three year period in selected colleges located in the East of England.

The ten lines, below, should be compressed into a more focussed paragraph that answers the question: How did you design and undertake your research? The research describes how colleges approached the task of establishing internal guidelines for Heads of Department and section leaders and then how these policies were implemented through the year. Data included minutes from meetings of Senior Management Teams (SMTs) and Governors, Government policies, interviews with eight Principals, twenty seven members of SMTs, heads of Departments in each college, and their quality assurance staff. These meetings were all conducted in the colleges with their full approval and following formal ethical clearance. This paragraph is far too detailed. State your research approach, explain that it was a multiple-method investigation, indicate the sequence of stages, mention that you triangulated your data and omit the final sentence.
The data that were collected was very detailed. Over sixty hours of taped evidence was collected and transcribed, read and analysed. Fifteen files of policy statements, minutes and college reports were used to support the interviews. Omit this paragraph. It describes rather than conceptualises your research.

All of this was collated and categorised before being analysed and interpreted using the NUDIST package. You need to explain your findings in one paragraph. State quite directly what you discovered. Make sure that it then leads into the final paragraph.
It was apparent that most of the colleges were adopting government policies quite well. These two words are vague language. What do they mean, Charlie? They found the guidelines helpful Value judgement. Avoid such phrases. and Heads of Department, in particular, were most appreciative Value judgement of the assistance that these documents provided in managing their Departments. Senior management teams were less impressed since they wanted more rather than less autonomy in how strategies for their colleges were designed and implemented. Your thesis contains conceptual conclusions that were evidence-based. Use them here to show how you have theorised your findings The three hypotheses were proved. Omit this sentence, it is just detail and does not add to understanding what you discovered.

You are well inside the word limit. So, structure your Abstract to show, in paragraph 1 Why you chose to investigate quality assurance initiatives by senior managers in colleges and how the adoption of Government guidelines on evaluation influenced that process. Then, state that no published work existed on this topic in UK.
Para 2 should explain that your research approach was deductive, sequentially staged, used multiple methods and extended over four years. Your hypotheses were drawn from gaps in knowledge about national practice in these areas and tested within a representative sample of XYZ-sized colleges in England.
Para 3 can be descriptive. Briefly, mention NUDIST to illustrate how your analysis was undertaken. Also, don't forget to state that you triangulated the data. Then present your main factual findings.
Para 4 must contain your conceptual conclusions – briefly. State also how these are generalisable since you had adopted a deductive approach.

Deleted: I

Deleted: ate
Formatted: Font color: Black
Deleted: a system of
Deleted: , BA (Hons) L'pool, M.A.

Deleted: in place
Deleted: It
Deleted:).
Formatted: Underline

Deleted: SMT minutes, governor's minutes,
Deleted: 8
Deleted: enior
Deleted: anagement
Deleted: eams
Deleted: all the
Deleted: s
Deleted: ¶
Deleted: as

Formatted: Underline
Formatted: No underline
Deleted:
Formatted: Underline
Formatted: Underline

Formatted: Underline
Deleted: n
Formatted: Underline
Deleted: 288 words
Formatted: Font color: Blue

Example 9.2 A 'good' abstract

University of Ruth
Faculty of Management

ABSTRACT

Doctorate of Philosophy

Mentoring by founders of family-owned businesses in the entertainments industry

By Julian Warboys

The majority of businesses in the United Kingdom employ less than 100 full-time staff. Family-owned businesses represent both a majority of these firms and particularly in the entertainments industry. Despite their increasing contribution to the gross national product, research into how experience is shared, or passed on, by founder members is non-existent. The national press and trade journals provide descriptive accounts of how the firms operate but without either a national perspective or any cumulative insights. This research answers the question how do founder members employ mentoring techniques to develop other members of family-run entertainments' firms.

The research approach was ethnographic. The research strategy addressed how founder members recognised the need for professional development of their family members and acted on that finding. A professional association was used to identify national, regional and locally-based firms who's trading exceeded 25 years and operated in a direct competitive environment. A representative sample of 35 firms provided in-house meetings for repeat interviewing with founders, mentees and selective 'other staff'. All were family members. Data were used to create case studies, cameos and vignettes of professional practices. The 87 respondents included 36 female founders or family members.

Older founders gave more attention to developing staff as a positive investment in the future of their firms then younger founders. Formal qualifications were not normal preparations for a career in the entertainments business. There were no detectable gender differences in attitudes towards mentoring. Views of how the family influenced managerial roles and behaviour were mixed across the age ranges and entertainment specialisms of the respondents.

Levels of perceived collective confidence in family cohesion were significant determinants of managerial behaviour, and were critical features in establishing successful family businesses. No firms employed personnel specialists, yet all engaged in staff development in order to remain competitive. Personal enthusiasm of founder members, emphasised through acceptable operating cultures, represented the rationale that justified mentoring in all fields of operations. Family members wished to learn from successful 'product champions' where mentoring was an inter-generational responsibility. Propositions were derived from the conclusions.

10

The magic circle: putting it all together

This chapter will:

- explain the significance of the informal impressions that examiners have of the thesis from their initial reading of it;
- outline the importance for research to be coherent and integrated;
- identify how you can audit your research and thesis to ensure that it demonstrates methodological rigour and scholarship;
- present a cyclical and interactive model of the research process rather than one that is linear or static.

Introduction

Some candidates see writing a thesis as a task that stretches away into the future. At the end of that process they foresee a viva that is attended by examiners who ask questions about their thesis. Such a view portrays the entire process as linear, with one 'bit' of it following immediately after another 'bit'. But research is not always like that. Instead, doctoral research can be viewed as a holistic process of many interrelated components which is not necessarily linear. Understanding that perspective will enable you to exploit the inherent relationships that are found within doing doctoral research and writing your thesis.

All research displays a sequence of activities and processes that together make up the overall activity. This is inevitable. However, within these processes, there is another innate feature that deserves recognition – the interconnectivity of parts. When we think about any research activity, it is easy to see that it comprises numerous 'bits' that display varying levels of interdependency.

Further thought enables us to identify that this dependency contains differing semblances of order (Mulgan, 1997: 11). The explanatory value of this view is that it emphasises the effects research activities have on one another.

We have seen, in Chapter 8, how you can influence the impressions that examiners have of your work. These tactics will only be successful, though, if your research is itself of high quality and coherent. But to achieve these features, you will have to demonstrate certain levels of argument, scholarship and technical capability in research. This chapter presents ways to emphasise the interdependency of those components in your research and so present a clearly coherent piece of doctoral research.

Impressions count

Examiners' initial reading of your thesis will provide them with 'a general overview of the thesis first' (Pearce, 2005: 50). However, until your examiners meet at the viva, they may not have seen each other's independent report(s) although local practices may permit this to happen. On this point, Pearce (2005: 66) observes that: 'It is by no means standard practice for examiners to exchange their pre-viva reports verbatim, but many do as the quickest way of establishing if there are areas of common agreement and consent – or not.' The exchange of their initial views, either before meeting at the university for the viva or informally over a cup of tea or coffee, reveals examiners' impressions of the candidate's work. These exchanges are a prelude to their more serious discussion of merit, scholarship and quality in the thesis.

This lead-up to disclosures of stance or position reveal the underlying impressions that examiners hold towards the thesis. The following examples of these conversations illustrate how relatively neutral items open the exchange before one examiner (E1 or E2) moves attention to more important matters. However, even the less scholarly items convey impressions that examiners will take into the viva itself. Example 10.1 traces the opening words between two examiners before they discussed their respective initial independent reports.

In this short conversation, note how E1 conveys appreciation of how the thesis was presented by associating 'good' presentation with academic quality. E2 agrees. It illustrates how background matters provided a common view of shared impressions between the examiners that would have then influenced how they discussed their independent reports before the viva itself.

Example 10.2 is part of a discussion between examiners who were mystified over the submission of an unsatisfactory thesis. It shows how one examiner (E1) tried to discover something that explains the submission of a poor-quality thesis. E2 accepted this information and both examiners seemed to conclude that the candidate had chosen to submit early without his supervisor's advice or support. They would have asked the candidate about this issue in the viva.

Example 10.1 Examiners' first exchange of views: presentation and quality

Examiner 1 *Can I mention the thesis? For once, I came across no typos or things like that, even in the reference list. What a change. What a delight!*

Examiner 2 I agree. It is a shame when attention has not been given to how a good piece of work is presented. I remember telling someone that her thesis would have deserved a clear pass but for poor spelling, grammar, pagination – the whole lot. You name it and she had it.

E 1 *So what happened?*

E 2 We referred it for a major grammatical overhaul. Of course, when it was resubmitted both of us had to read through it again.

E 1 *But this time we have been in luck.*

E 2 We have and the thesis is very good too, isn't it?

E 1 *It is excellent. Maybe the two go together. Shall we talk about our reports?*

E2 Good point. Yes, let's start on the rest of it.

Example 10.2 Examiners' first exchange of views: why did things go wrong?

Examiner 1 *I joined the institution just this term and found that the dean had nominated me as the internal examiner for this piece of work. It is not a very good example for me to start with is it?*

Examiner 2 No, it isn't. Do you know the supervisor?

E 1 *No, I don't know him personally. I asked the dean about him and it seems that he provides a reasonable service. This means that he holds regular tutorials, he has a few completions and he published two papers in this area last year. He should be OK.*

E 2 Why was the thesis submitted in such a dire state then? It is almost as if the candidate knows nothing about research, the topic or academic writing. It is a complete mess.

> **E 1**   *I did find out something that may explain it. His bursary ends in 3 months' time and he has a job to go to. It is a good job, too. They want him to start as soon as possible. Maybe he exercised his right to submit, put it all together and submitted. I got a feeling in the office that they were surprised that he had submitted very suddenly and when his supervisor was unavailable too.*
>
> **E 2**   OK. That helps. It may also tell us why the thesis is in such an unfinished state.
>
> **E 1**   *Be that as it may, it cannot excuse the state of his thesis. Where do we start on a piece of work like this?*
>
> **E 2**   I agree entirely. How about we look at his first chapter?

These two examples illustrate the contrasting views of how a doctoral journey might finish. In Example 10.1, the examiners recognised consistency throughout the thesis in presentation and research quality. Incidentally, the outcome of the viva was that the candidate gained her doctorate with no amendments. In Example 10.2, the examiners concluded that the candidate's haste to submit had overlooked attention to research quality and to presentation. The examiners referred the thesis for major alterations and the candidate gained his doctorate following a second viva.

Both examples represent different types of investment by candidates in their doctorate – care and haste. They share the common feature of closing the journey that each candidate had embarked on some years earlier. External examiners, in particular, are usually unaware of a candidate's personal history or academic circumstances when they read the thesis and prepare their independent report. Although such information will not influence their academic decisions, it may help examiners to appreciate the candidate's circumstances.

Earlier research in Australia by Mullins and Kiley (2002) showed that experienced examiners normally expect that when a thesis is submitted to be examined it will 'deserve' to pass. Their evidence for this was that examiners recognise the: 'three or fours years of effort by a talented student and that its production has been an expensive process in terms of resources and other people's time'. Their findings also showed that 'first impressions count'. However, although they are not irreversible: 'They did influence the examiner's frame of mind for the rest of the thesis. Experienced examiners decide very early on in the process whether assessment of a particular thesis is going to be hard work or an enjoyable read.'

These views emphasise the importance of examiners' first impressions.

Perhaps the idea of impressions being important in the doctoral process is not one that receives serious attention. But it only means that examiners are acting like other human beings who often make what Gladwell (2005: 16) calls: 'instantaneous impressions and conclusions . . . whenever we confront a complex situation'. Impressions may be ephemeral. However, they are important if examiners place such views alongside the harder indicators of scholarship in your thesis. But it is only during reading the thesis and meeting these harder indicators that examiners' impressions are formed. Thus, you should ensure that your examiners receive favourable impressions as they read your thesis for the first time.

Integration and cohesion

Examiners arrive at impressions about a thesis before they then devote time to detailed reading and annotating items on its pages. Their initial reading has guided them to a conclusion. It may be based on just encountering the presence of doctoral features that examiners hope to see. During this canter through the text, examiners may not delve deeply into the finer points of scholarly argument or sophisticated numeric work. They attend to this in later readings of the thesis.

Winter et al. (2000) presented a comprehensive list of views that examiners held towards 'the satisfactoriness or otherwise of doctoral work'. The clusters of positive and negative features appear in full in Appendix 10.1. The components of each feature are unsurprising, comprehensive and relatively straightforward. They are merely research indicators that show linkage between concept and fact. For instance, consider the concept of presentation in the positive features list of Appendix 10.2. The indicators of positive presentation are shown thus:

- The thesis is clear, easy to read and presented in an appropriate style.
- It contains few errors of expression.
- The thesis also displays flawless literacy.

Thus, collectively the features and their respective indicators form a template of good, or bad, practice for candidates.

Based on the questions that examiners ask, the evidence presented by Winter et al. shows that candidates should incorporate the positive features in their thesis. They saw these features as 'the fundamental criteria for a PhD' that formed the basis for 'originality and publishability'. Similarly, candidates 'should avoid' the negative features appearing in their text. Winter et al. suggested that: 'The features indicate that what examiners seem to be looking for is a form of intellectual rigour (throughout the doctoral thesis).'

However, as we have seen some theses still exhibit many of the negative features. Sadly, for their respective authors, these are the ones that examiners refer or fail.

Throughout the paper by Winter et al. (2000) is the view that rigorous research is what examiners hope to find in a thesis. They propose two indicators of rigorous research – integration and cohesion. If these are present, then the thesis will display the other positive features of intellectual grasp, engagement with the literature, grasp of methodology and presentation. The consequence of these desirable features is that the thesis is likely to have made an original contribution to knowledge or understanding of the subject in topic area, in method, in experimental design, in theoretical synthesis or engagement with conceptual issues. If these features are evident, then parts of the thesis will also demonstrate publishability or the potential for publication. Conversely, research that is not rigorous will display most or even all of the negative features.

In the same article, Winter et al. draw on their experience as action researchers. They say: 'At the heart of all good action research lies the search for better questions and, once found, these form part of the outcome of the research rather then its starting point' (Winter et al. 2000). He illustrates this through the words of Gaardner (1997: 31) 'An answer is always the stretch of road behind you. Only a question can point the way forward.' Here we see a connection between starting, arriving and restarting as a circle in the research process. In recognising this interconnectedness, you can show, in just a sentence or two, your wider vision of research.

Most examiners are quite happy to acknowledge excellence in theses that they read. Since they are assessing theses against essentially generic criteria this explains why the sentiments which they then use are often alike. Their individuality, though, comes through in the depth to which they express their satisfaction with the thesis which they have read. When examiners are satisfied with the qualities of a thesis then their initial report will normally contain between 150 and 400 words. As a result, their comments are succinct and they highlight those features that they consider to be of merit. Example 10.3 shows the approach that two examiners took to drafting their initial report.

It follows from these views that examiners identify the salient features of a thesis to include in their initial reports. To do that, they will mention those features that left a positive impression. Thus, the initial reports provide insights on the components of doctoral research that examiners extract from reading the thesis.

Example 10.4 shows four extracts from the initial reports of examiners. In each case, the reports were of less than one page in length and focused on the positive aspects of the respective theses that were to be examined. The four examiners emphasised aspects of the respective theses that collectively accord with the positive features in the typology of Winter et al. (2000). This suggests that despite coming from different scholarly traditions, disciplines

---

Example 10.3 Examiners' view of the independent report

Examiner 1 I want my colleague examiner to see instantly what my impressions and conclusions are about the thesis. This can be done in about half a page. Issues of detail can be raised later in our discussion and during the viva itself. So I always try to highlight the strengths that make it worthy of my recommendation for a doctorate. Why write more?

Examiner 2 I try to write more or less what I would say if the other examiner asked me 'What did you think of the thesis?' If it is generally OK then I suppose I would write a couple of hundred words. Occasionally I might give some reasons for my views, but it is not needed at this stage. Conclusions are what I would want to hear if I asked the question!

---

and institutional settings, examiners exhibit generic approaches to assessing the merit of doctoral theses. The importance of this for you is that it provides another set of criteria against which to compare your own research and thesis.

Example 10.4 Extracts from examiners' reports that were favourable

Examiner 1 The thesis is confidently presented and the case for the research is clearly argued. The layout of the thesis is helpful, with the central research questions defined early in the text and appropriate contextual information is provided. Everything fits together as it should do. This allows the reader to follow the development of the research and understand the significance of the findings. An understanding of the extant knowledge in the topic's area is demonstrated and a gap in the knowledge is carefully defined. The conceptual framework is defined and justifies the limited range of research methodology and methods. The conclusions clearly arise from the data. She explicitly avoids any claim to generalisability and the contribution to knowledge is carefully made. Overall, in my opinion the thesis meets the criteria for the award of a PhD.

Examiner 2   I found this a good thesis. There is a clear statement of purpose, it is well-structured and well-argued. There is an effective critical review of the literature. The rationale for choosing the research methodology is clear and explained. The candidate demonstrates an effective understanding of the criteria and standards that research needs to be tested against and these criteria are thoroughly explored. The thesis is well-written and presented. I knew where the research was going all the time and therefore I recognised exactly how the conclusions were produced. It makes a very welcome contribution to understanding how workloads are a vehicle for continuing professional practice.

Examiner 3   This is an exceptionally well-written, constructed and presented thesis. A succinct account is provided of problems and issues that are relevant to managers in further education colleges. She has written with a great deal of intelligence, sensitivity and reflexivity in relation to her own experience as a researcher and professional educator. By making use of a wide range of relevant literature she has been able to link successfully many practical issues to theoretical ones . . . The strength of the thesis centres around her ability to not just report research findings but to try to develop theoretical models and typologies. These are easily understood and accessible not only to professionals in FE but also to outsiders . . . The thesis hangs together as a whole. Perhaps not surprisingly, her research findings offer few surprises, except that these paint an increasingly complex picture of the many issues to be faced by those working in further education today.

Examiner 4   This is an impressive thesis and I am struck by the originality of much of the work. The candidate has demonstrated, with a high degree of rigour, a knowledge and understanding of both the issues she has sought to investigate and of the methodological complexities inherent in undertaking this work. The seriousness and conscientiousness with which she has approached her research is to be commended. She tackles methodological issues in a totally informed manner. She is also to be commended for her application of constructivism and how she addressed the shortcomings of reflection as a central factor in improving professional practice. The conclusions are significant and the recommendations are appropriate and cogently argued. The major strength of the thesis is in the research process and the communication of that process to its readers.

If examiners' initial reports are very long it usually signals difficulties and problems with a thesis. The extracts in Example 10.5 are all from one examiner's report. Although the examiner believed that the thesis showed originality and the discovery of new facts, he was not satisfied with many other aspects of the thesis. Throughout his initial report, he acknowledged the merit and strengths of the thesis. However, he was critical of how the candidate had written, argued and presented the thesis. He also identified precisely the shortcomings that were in the text and the arguments which, in his opinion, required attention. There was evidence that the examiner was thorough in his reading when he identified an item requiring further explanation, which had appeared six times over 94 pages. Finally, see how this examiner, despite his severe criticism of the thesis, explained protocols and provided the candidate with encouragement in his last comment.

Example 10.5 Extracts from an examiner's unfavourable report

[The report contained nine pages.]

In pursuing his topic, the student has uncovered and explored some fascinating material that has the potential to make an important contribution to the field. With this in mind, I wish my comments to be as instructive and constructive as possible to allow the student to successfully complete the degree . . . There are serious problems with the referencing. The student has failed to use the standard terminology and archival citations that are usual for scholarship in this field . . . Throughout the text author's names are misspelled. This is inexcusable . . . The congress was held in 1898. The language is German. There is no evidence that the student speaks or reads German. Why cite this item? The information is incomplete. Why is this listed as an 'archival source' when it was published and openly available to everyone? . . . Why use a 1928 translation of the central character's works, when there are far better and more complete translations easily available from the last decades? Related to this: the student does not seem to be familiar with historiography – a problem that I will refer to later . . . He does not seem to understand that a 'literature review' in itself does not suffice. The relevant scholarship has to be engaged throughout the text, otherwise it does not fulfil one of the basics requirements of the PhD . . . Appendix 1 must be integrated into the text or left out completely. It does not advance the thesis in its current form . . . I strongly suggest that the entire scheme of the thesis be reconfigured. A great deal of the first section, up to page 75, can be cut out . . . The literature review needs to be totally rewritten since it does not engage with the most relevant literature on this topic.

[Then specific comments were made about details on named pages.]

p 51: returns to nationalism. Why? A number of questionable assertions follow

p 71ff: crucial points raised here. They should appear much earlier in the text

p 88: fascinating

p 92: jumping around to different time periods – the point is to explain change over time, or use similar experiences in order to make a specific case

p 96ff: 'Limiting the land purchase' – best section by far

p 136: citations needed

SEE 144, 183, 197, 214, 223, 238 note and explain the importance of criminalisation in context

p 198: repetitive and unclear text

pp 267ff: The 'List of personalities, terms, and names, newspapers and magazines.' This is filled with errors. It is better to have a short and accurate description as the name appears in the text. This is a PhD, which means that it will likely be used by scholars and researchers seeking in-depth information and analysis. Should it be published in a more popular form, then this type of appendix might be useful.

Example 10.6 shows how two examiners handled the weaknesses of the thesis quite obliquely. Nonetheless, the examiners identified items for serious discussion in the viva. Their concerns are located in the technicalities of their respective disciplines. Although both examiners were satisfied that the thesis had academic merit, they were not totally convinced by the quality of the argument throughout the text. The candidate had to explain and defend these positions in the viva.

Example 10.6 Extracts from two examiners' mildly critical reports

[The report contained 490 words, plus a page of typographical errors.]

Examiner 1   My first concern about this thesis is that it far exceeded the maximum word limit ... It is possible that the work can be defended on the grounds that it is the only comprehensive analysis of this musician's work as a whole. But, it is weakened by the quantity of work which has been done on this topic in relation to individual texts ... The thesis might be viewed as an extended statement of the obvious. Looking for music in this musician's work is rather like looking for gold in Fort Knox ... There are some logical problems in the argument that I think can be addressed in the viva ... There is a tendency towards tautology and totalisation. The key critical concept of *'signifying(g) on'* is so all encompassing that it loses purchase, especially because the thesis deploys it in 'microcosmic' and 'macrocosmic' ways.' It becomes as a kind of refrain beneath which a range of vague logical relations are concealed ... While the argument aims to demonstrate particularity, it regularly fails to do so ... I would like to ask the candidate for an account of revision, intertextuality, musical structure, narrative circularity and other theses as they appear in the 20th-century novel more generally ... The thesis is rather circular in conceptual and argumentative terms.

[The report contained 310 words.]

Examiner 2   While the thesis is well-written it often relies on secondary sources at the beginning which are interrogated, leaving the second half as a rather tautological response to the assertions of the first. Furthermore, the very meaning of an authentic mixed culture identity is never really put to the test, allowing answers too easily to escape probing ... There are a number of areas that do need further discussion. These centre on the concepts of authenticity and the problems of the relationship of politics to artistic production and especially revolutionary consciousness. On the literary/music side, some time might be spent considering the structural equivalence of the two practices which are not quite answered in the text.

The rolling audit

All of us accept the need to check the quality of our research and writing. But how thoroughly do we tackle that task? How often do we check the same piece of research? The adoption of QAA guidelines has enabled higher education institutions to introduce procedures that emphasise good practice in quality assurance. Each institution will have refined the guidelines to reflect their own perspective on the doctoral process and doctoral supervision. Copies of these guidelines will be available for you to access in the graduate school, or equivalent, of your university.

Within the rhetoric of regulations and procedures, the words 'audit' and 'monitor' mean 'check'. Checking your research and the thesis should be a regular part of your doctoral journey. As Oliver (2004: 165) reminds us: 'The main purpose of this (checking for coherence and internal consistency) is to try to ensure that elements in one part of the thesis are consistent with the relevant elements in other parts.' The significance of Oliver's view is that it accords exactly with the features of a thesis that examiners expect to find.

Let us consider the practical actions that you can take to check your doctoral research:

- Make checking an integral part of your approach to undertaking your research.
- Allow time for checking your text as you plan, draft or revisit a chapter.
- Check to confirm that what you have done, are doing or will do is what you had intended.
- Use your checking to recognise deviations from your plan and then decide if they are to be accepted or corrected in line with your plan.
- Avoid leaving your checking until it is too late to alter what you have done.
- Be consistent in how you check your work so that you can recognise whether or not you are making progress with your research and writing.
- Discuss your findings with your supervisor(s) or your trusted critical friend(s) to receive opinions from others on what your checks show.

These seven checkpoints are simple for you to use and practical in their consequence. They do not take up much time. Collectively, they can help you to avoid those unnecessary mistakes that sometimes occur – even in doctoral theses. Checking will provide you with self-generated evidence about the quality of your research and thesis. However, it is essential that as you self-evaluate your own work you are prepared to recognise its weaknesses as well as its strengths.

Spending time on this activity will pay dividends for you, because:

- it provides a diagnosis of the doctoral status of your research and thesis;

- it represents an agenda of items to discuss with your supervisor(s) from which you can then take corrective action;
- it will build your self-confidence in recognising the quality of your work;
- it will deepen your understanding of research as a process and this will prepare you to defend your work in you viva;
- it presents you with evidence to use in accounting to the university for your academic progress.

Thus, checking your work has valuable outcomes and practical benefits that will help you to achieve your doctorate.

A checking system of doctoral work should ideally reflect similar characteristics to those that examiners use as they evaluate theses. This was the assumption behind the design of the audit instrument that appears as Appendix 10.2. The document represents a self-audit of doctorateness, which you can discuss with your supervisor(s) once your work is underway. It is likely to be of most value when you are about half-way through your doctoral journey. At that time, you may be able to complete up to question 12 or 13. If you complete it again after 6 or 9 months, then you should be able to answer the remaining questions. You may also, possibly, wish to revise your earlier answers as you would then be more advanced in your research and so have a deeper appreciation of it.

In these different ways, the instrument allows your understanding of doctoral level research and doctorateness to become apparent. Obliging you to think about these features helps you to identify how and where your thesis could be strengthened. Thus, by completing it you will gain evidence that shows your progress towards the required scholarly characteristics of all doctoral theses.

By comparing your responses to the instrument at different times you should be able to recognise how your thinking has changed. The second completion of the instrument will allow you to reflect on your development as a researcher. You could then account for this in a Personal Postscript or Reflections on my Intellectual Journey. This two- or three-page item could be included in your thesis after the conclusions chapter. Most examiners are genuinely interested to hear about the candidate's personal journey and development and they appreciate such a closure to a doctoral thesis. Others (a few) consider this sort of text to be an unnecessary distraction that has no place in a doctoral thesis. Take advice from your supervisor(s) on this point once your examiners have been agreed.

Completing the audit instrument

The audit instrument was originally developed in electronic form to accommodate various lengths of response from those who completed it. You might find it useful to transfer the instrument into an electronic format for your own use. Once you have done this, it will be available for you to complete maybe twice before using it as a final check on the coherence and quality of your doctoral work.

Read the entire document to appreciate how the issue of doctorateness is explored from different perspectives. You will note that questions seek closed/open-ended responses, multiple-choice answers or discussion. Responding to those questions will provide evidence on your research progress to date, your current research activity and the plans that you have for the remainder of your doctoral study. The entries that you make should be succinct and to the point. Do not provide long descriptive responses that display neither the conceptualisation of issues nor the level of thinking expected of doctoral studies.

The questions, collectively, address the notions of doctorateness that were introduced in Chapter 3, research design in Chapter 5 and conclusions in Chapter 8. These questions seek explanations and reasoned justifications rather than just factual responses. In drafting responses to the questions, your thinking will follow similar lines to those that examiners will expect of you in the viva. When you have completed the instrument, you will have checked the research that has been completed. This picture will help you to see what has yet to be done. Your responses will consolidate your theoretical perspectives and approaches. These are personal to you, your research and your thesis. Thus, when you have completed the audit instrument you will have an individualised account of your doctoral work. But isn't this exactly what a thesis contains?

There are other practical uses for the audit instrument. Keep copies of it on your writing desk as a point of reference. Refer to it often as you plan and write chapters. Check that you have given appropriate emphasis to critical factors. Use it to remind yourself what your entire research is all about. Allow it to trigger ideas that you can think about. If possible, hang it on a door where you live, so that you see it regularly and so reinforce your doctoral quest. See it as your own personal reference book for your doctoral thesis. Use it as a rolling check on your research.

Strategic overview

Having a strategic overview of your entire research process is important. Not only does this help you in planning the research, but it provides you with a framework against which to assess progress. It also has a personal benefit for you; it provides a means for you to visualise how your research fits together. Finally, it explains the cohesion in your research that can be defended in your viva. Being able to refer examiners to the page and figure where you present the overview of your research is to be forearmed – just in case. But being able to do that signals to examiners that you really do understand the cohesion that is in your thesis.

Bouma (1993: 7–8) holds a similar view: 'To do research involves a process or series of linked activities moving from beginning to end. Each researcher will be able to describe a pattern, a reasonably regular way in which they go about "doing research".' If you have made the practical links between the various stages and components of your research explicit, then they can be described as Bouma implies. But, delving deeper, you can trace their conceptual interconnectedness. Taking this further, Koch (2004) advocates using: 'an audit trail as a creative way to shape the text. If signposts are offered along the way, readers can decide whether a piece of work is credible or not.' These explicit links allow you, as Parahoo suggests, to: 'give details and rationale for the key decisions (that you have) taken' (2006: 411).

Together, these views advocate having an explicit framework for your research that combine methodological and relational factors. If you were asked in your viva *Why did you undertake your fieldwork in that way?*, then the examiners want to hear you explain the decisions that determined how your fieldwork was conducted. You should have no difficulty answering this question if you have a mental picture of your research and a figure of it in your thesis that can be referred to. Moreover, it would present the evidence that examiners use to judge if candidates really do understand the intricacies of doctoral research.

When research is viewed as a system of interconnected parts, then it can be portrayed as shown in Figure 10.1. The model shows the normal sequences

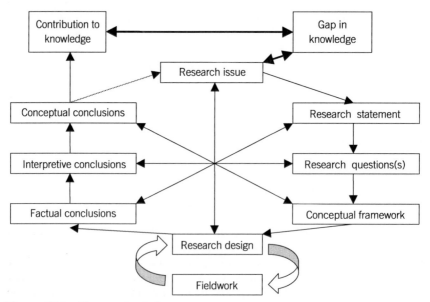

Figure 10.1   The magic circle.

of research actions around the outside circle of boxes. There are two possible starting points for the sequence. You may have an idea about a possible research topic. Thinking more about it and reading opens up the topic and you appreciate that it represents a gap in knowledge. Alternatively, you may suspect, know about or even stumble on a lacunæ in your area of interest. As a gap in knowledge you could then refine that into a specific research issue to be investigated. Either way, you will journey between these two factors as you establish boundaries for the topic of your research.

Moving clockwise around the model shows that your research statement is derived from the research issue. This statement is normally expressed as a single sentence encapsulating answers to the Kipling questions regarding your research topic (Kane, 1985: 15). It may be a challenge to capture all your research intentions in one sentence. But she argues that if it takes more than one sentence then you may have a multiphase piece of research that is somewhat more extensive than you had intended. Alternatively, she suggests that you have not have thought the issue through clearly enough and should do so in order to produce a satisfactory and workable research statement (Kane, 1985: 20).

Producing research questions that are clear and capable of being answered leads you into the theoretical perspectives you have gleaned from the literature. In turn, this enables you to devise your conceptual framework which is central to how your research is designed. The iterative relationship between fieldwork and research design acknowledges how these features influence each other throughout the duration of your research.

The data that are collected then enable you to generate factual, interpretive and conceptual conclusions. These conclusions should allow you to make a modest, reasonable and defensible claim for a contribution to knowledge that closes the gap in knowledge. Your contribution to knowledge should also relate specifically to the originating research issue and its boundaries. This closes the circle of your research.

While the circle of factors offers a neat picture of the research, there is another far more important level of meaning latent inside the circle. The four diagonal double arrow-headed lines connect pairs of factors that are influential on one another. These are:

- **Research issue – research design**: You should be able to show how the boundaries and focus of the issue are apparent in how the research was designed. The result of this is that the fieldwork should be seen to investigate and gather data on that issue and not some other issue. This represents a check on the internal empirical consistency of your research (Rose, 1982: 32) (see also Chapter 5).
- **Research statement – factual conclusions**: You should be able to show how the research statement relates directly to the factual conclusions that are drawn from your evidence. Both are concerned with fact – what is to be investigated and the facts that were found that related to that statement.

The direct relationship between these two research components demonstrates that your research possesses internal empirical consistency (Rose, 1982: 32) (see also Chapter 5).

- **Research questions – interpretive conclusions**: Answers to your research questions should emerge as you interpret, analyse and discuss your evidence. This relationship represents a higher level of thinking than the descriptive text that is associated with the previous pair of factors. It demonstrates the internal theoretical consistency of your research (Rose, 1982: 32) (see also Chapter 5).
- **Conceptual framework – conceptual conclusions**: This relationship determines the scholarly and theoretical level of your research. Among the set of conclusions it is the most critical, since it demonstrates the relationship and relevance of your research to other, external, research and extant theories (Rose, 1982: 32) (see also Chapter 5).

The model enables you to plan both an integrated and coherent piece of research. It also enables you to check the consistency of how that plan was carried out. Then, you can use it to audit the accounts in your thesis of these essential scholarly research features. Undertaking these checks and activities should give you confidence that your research is methodologically rigorous. This closes the circle of research as a process. It also provides you with a simple model to use and brings you to the point where you can tackle Task 10.1.

Task 10.1   Applying the magic circle to your thesis

Using the magic circle, can you identify where the links between the components of your research are explained in your thesis?

Looking back and ahead

This chapter has outlined a view of research that emphasises the interconnectedness of the primary research stages. It shows that if you explain these connections in your thesis they enable you to demonstrate cohesion in how you conducted and then presented your research. Examples have been provided to show how you can audit your work as a prelude to defending your thesis in your viva. Thus, the magic circle gives you another way to achieve your doctorate through checking, auditing and ensuring scholarship in your thesis.

Chapter 11 uses these ideas to illustrate how you can prepare for your doctoral viva.

Appendix 10.1 Positive and negative features of theses

Positive features

Intellectual grasp

- Grasps the scope and possibilities of the topic.
- Shows diligence and rigour in procedures – catholic and multifactoral approaches to problems.
- Shows readiness to examine apparently tangential areas for possible relevance.
- Grasps the wider significance of the topic – how the analysis is related to its methodological and epistemological context.
- Shows iterative development allowing exploration and rejections of alternatives.
- Possesses an internal dialogue – plurality of approach/method, to validate the one chosen.
- A broad theoretical base is treated critically.
- Demonstrates a coherent and explicit theoretical approach fully thought through and critically applied, i.e. noting its limitations.
- Gives a systematic account of the topic, including a review of all plausible possible interpretations.
- Demonstrates full mastery of the topic, i.e. that the candidate is now an expert in the field.
- Indicates the future development of the work.
- Maintains clear and continuous links between theory, method and interpretations.
- Presents a reflexive, self-critical account of relationships involved in the inquiry and of the methodology.
- Connects theory and practice.
- Displays rigour.

Coherence

- Displays coherence of structure (e.g. the conclusions follow clearly from the data).
- Skilfully organises a number of different angles (required by the extended length of the work).
- Is cogently organised and expressed.
- Possesses a definite agenda and an explicit structure.
- Presents a sense of the researcher's learning as a journey, as a structured, incremental progress through a process of both argument and discovery.

Engagement with literature

- Displays comprehensive coverage of the field/secure command of the literature in the field.
- Shows breadth of contextual knowledge in the discipline.
- Successfully critiques established positions.
- Engages critically with other significant work in the field.
- Draws on literature with a focus different from the viewpoint pursued in the thesis.
- Maintains a balance between delineating and area of debate and advocating a particular approach.
- Includes scholarly notes, a comprehensive bibliography and accurately uses academic conventions in citations.

Grasp of methodology

- The methodology is clearly established and applied.
- The methodological analysis indicates the advantages and disadvantages of the approach adopted.
- Uses several methodologies for triangulation.

Presentation

- The thesis is clear, easy to read and is presented in an appropriate style.
- Contains few errors of expression.
- Displays flawless literacy.

Negative features

Lack of intellectual grasp

- Lack of a clear distinction between objective and subjective material.
- Lack of clear idea of 'data'.
- Conclusions stated too early and not brought together.
- Dogmatic presupposition of issues.
- Failure to follow up and evaluate alternative lines of argument.
- Failure to defend properly the validity and generalisability of innovative research methods.
- Apparent unawareness of the limitations of the work undertaken.
- Description rather than theoretical analysis.
- Lack of background knowledge (the candidate should demonstrate a knowledge of the subject that is broader than the actual topic area).

Lack of coherence

- Lack of focus, stated aim, 'tightly managed' structure or coherent argument.
- Lack of integrity in research design.

- Lack of clearly formulated conclusions.
- Ill justified changes of direction.
- Lack of initial focus/conviction.
- Pursuit of 'originality' at the expense of control over the material.

Poor engagement with the literature

- Uncritical use of references.
- Misrepresentation of texts.
- Lack of rigour in referencing and bibliography.
- Lack of up-to-date knowledge of other research in the field.

Lack of originality

- No original contribution to knowledge.
- No theoretical contribution.
- Encyclopaedic knowledge but no personal spark.

Lack of generalisability

- No discussion of how findings are applicable to other situations.
- Does not move beyond questions and findings to making suggestions.

Methodological weakness

- Inappropriate statistical analyses.
- 'Prejudice' (e.g. gender class, racial, regional), i.e. unexamined social stereotyping.
- Lack of a 'robust' methodology.

Poor presentation

- Disjoined, unstructured writing.
- Badly written, 'with no concern for the reader'.
- Style too discursive, prolix, obscure or too anecdotal.

Originality and publishability

Originality

- Pushes the topic into new areas beyond its obvious focus.
- Makes an original contribution to knowledge or understanding of the subject, in topic area, in method, in experimental design, in theoretical synthesis or engagement with conceptual issues.
- Solves some significant problem or gathers original data.

- Reframes issues.
- Is imaginative in its approach to problems.
- Is creative yet rigorous.
- Goes beyond its sources to create a new position which critiques existing theoretical positions.
- Uses the empirical study to enlarge the theoretical understanding of the subject.
- Contains innovations, speculation, imaginative reconstruction, cognitive excitement: 'The author has clearly wrestled with the method, trying to shape it to gain new insight.'
- Is comprehensive in its theoretical linkages or makes novel connections between areas of knowledge.
- Opens up neglected areas or takes a new viewpoint on an old problem.
- Something new must have been learned and demonstrated, such that the reader is made to rethink a stance or opinion.
- Shows 'a spark of inspiration as well as perspiration'.
- Shows development towards independent research and innovation.
- Is innovative in content and adventurous in method, obviously at the leading edge in its particular field, with potential for yielding new knowledge.
- Makes a personal synthesis of an interpretative framework.
- Shows depth and breadth of scholarship – synthesising previous work and adding original insights/models/concepts.
- Argues against conventional views, presents new frameworks for interpreting the world.
- Applies established techniques to novel patterns or devises new techniques, which allow new questions to be addressed.

Publishability

- Demonstrates publishable quality or potential for publication.
- Publishable in a refereed journal with a good scholarly reputation.
- Written with an awareness of the audience for the work.
- Stylishly and economically written.

Source: Winter et al., 2000

Appendix 10.2 Audit instrument

DETAILS

Name	Start date: (d/m/y)

First supervisor Second supervisor	Other(s)

1   **TITLE**   What is the provisional working title of your thesis?

2   **RESEARCH QUEST**   What is your principal research question, and any
        associated subsidiary research questions?

3   **ORIGIN OF THE RESEARCH QUESTION(S)**   How does your primary research
        question derive from and link to your theoretical perspectives and indicate
        any appropriate single seminal paper or framework that you will cite?

4   **SPECIFIC RESEARCH QUESTION(S)**   How do your research questions
        derive from the issues that you are investigating and so determine the
        boundaries for your research?

5   **STRUCTURE**   What were your considerations in selecting the structure of
        parts and/or chapters for your thesis? Please name the parts that you have
        in your thesis and indicate which chapters have been written.

6   **ASSUMPTIONS**   What are the main research assumptions that you have
        generated, or may yet generate, from items 2, 3 and 4 above which will
        inform your research design?

7	**RESEARCH DESIGN** Are you therefore:

7a	*mainly* testing or developing theory?
7b	following a conventional or innovative methodological approach (compared to the way this type of research question might normally be investigated)?
7c	using a context that is familiar or unfamiliar with the norms for the subject domain?
7d	following mainly an inductive, deductive or mixed approach to your research?
7e	intending to extend, challenge or refute existing knowledge/practice?
7f	focusing more on reliability than validity?
7g	adopting more of a quantitative or a qualitative approach?

8	**EVIDENCE** What is the nature of your research evidence?

8a	What primary evidence will you seek to collect?
8b	How will you use/evaluate this evidence?
8c	What difficulties might you encounter in your data collection process and how will you avoid/resolve those difficulties?
8d	How will you use the secondary evidence that emerges during your investigations?

9   **METHODOLOGICAL APPROACH**   How will your choice of research methods and tools and techniques give added value to your research (e.g. textual analysis, data mining of questionnaire data, conjoint analysis, etc.)?

10   **METHODOLOGICAL CRITIQUE**   How will you demonstrate, justify and critically support your methodological stance?

11   **GAP IN KNOWLEDGE**   What is the gap in knowledge that you are seeking to fill and why does that gap exist?

12   **CONCEPTUAL FRAMEWORK**   Summarise and explain how theoretical perspectives helped you develop the conceptual framework(s) on which your research is based.

13   **OUTCOMES**   What are the likely/possible outcomes, or what might be the nature of such outcomes from your research?

13a	as factual conclusions?
13b	as conceptual conclusions?
13c	as conclusions that might inform or enhance professional practice?

14   **CONTRIBUTION TO KNOWLEDGE**   At this intermediate stage of your research how has your perception of the likely contribution(s) to knowledge been influenced by your early research activity and how has it changed?

15   **GENERALISABILITY**   What is the likely generalisability of your research findings?

16   **PROBLEMISATION**   In what ways have you acknowledged the potential or actual problems that are inherent in the research process and then explained how they have been tackled, within the draft text of your thesis?

17   **PERSONAL DEVELOPMENT**   How will you report and critique your personal journey during this doctoral research and your own personal development?

18   **COMPLETION OF YOUR THESIS**   What are the main issues that you need to address and resolve before completing the first draft of your thesis?

19   **ACTION PLAN**   Please provide a detailed indicative plan that shows the actions which you propose to take, with their respective provisional dates, in order to complete the first draft of your thesis.

20   **SUBMISSION**   When do you expect to submit your thesis for examination?

[Appendix 10.2 © Trafford and Woolliams, 2001.]

11

Preparing for the viva

This chapter will:

- indicate some of the administrative procedures that can assist you throughout your doctoral studies;
- propose that scholarly preparation for your viva should extend over the entire duration of your doctoral studies;
- illustrate how examiners conceptualise the process of examining;
- introduce some technical strategies that you can use to prepare for your viva.

Introduction

This chapter explores how you might prepare for your doctoral viva. It proposes that preparation should actually start when you register for your doctorate. Within this longer term 'preparation', there are two distinct and complementary aspects of preparing. First, you have to appreciate the administrative framework that your university has created for postgraduate studies in general and doctoral degrees in particular. Second, your scholarly investment in becoming a doctoral researcher is a cumulative preparation for its defence. Both require your attention, since each affects the other and both are of equal importance.

The viva occurs at the end of your doctoral journey. It is a rite of passage. We argue that this provides a wider view from which to understand the entire doctoral process. The chapter shows how the administrative procedures associated with doctoral study can be used to your advantage. Then, it draws on arguments from earlier chapters to reinforce your understanding of the research process as a doctoral researcher. Together, these two approaches will help you to prepare to defend your work confidently in the viva.

Understanding the administrative arrangements

It is important that you familiarise yourself thoroughly with the regulations of your university as soon as you register for your doctoral studies. Keep a copy of the university's research student's handbook, or its equivalent, in a safe place for easy access and reference. Check the website that holds information from your graduate school and central administrative services, or their equivalent, on a regular basis. These two simple actions will keep you up to date with the administrative arrangements that apply to your doctoral studies.

You should use the prevailing administrative procedures for doctoral studies as a guiding framework throughout your doctoral registration. These matters are not central to determining the scholarly outcome of your viva. However, if you ignore them they may hold up your progress and cause you sleepless nights. Thus, they are important to know about, act on and respect!

Soon after you have registered for your doctorate, do find a moment to discuss the administrative set-up for doctoral studies with your supervisor(s). These things should have been included during an induction event for new candidates that no doubt you attended. But it is always useful talking about these practicalities in a face-to-face meeting to clarify anything that you missed or are unclear about.

For instance, make sure that you understand the procedures that will affect you most directly, such as:

- how to handle your annual re-registration;
- financial arrangements that apply at each stage of your studies;
- arrangements for and timing of the annual monitoring of your progress;
- normal registration periods for doctoral studies and the procedures for extension – just in case you need to use this facility;
- arrangements for supervision – though these will be agreed by discussion with your supervisor(s);
- records that you are expected to maintain as evidence of your studies and progression – research diaries, log records of meetings with supervisors, laboratory records, equipment usage and breakages, fieldwork visits, etc.;
- intermediate stages for mid-point progression or confirmation of candidature;
- recommended maximum word count for your thesis;
- schedules for the appointment of examiners and arrangements for fixing the date of vivas;
- the procedures for submitting your thesis, the protocols that have to be respected and the timescales that apply.

The received wisdom of other doctoral candidates gives a picture of how these things work. However, do check with your supervisor(s) that these views are accurate and reliable. Please do not overlook the responsibility and role of your supervisor(s) at this time. They are your point of contact into how your university's administrative framework actually operates. Their advice should be worth seeking and receiving.

It is important that you appreciate the regulations that will apply to your type of research degree registration, such as:

- MPhil progression to PhD;
- MRes progression opportunities;
- specific arrangements that apply to professional doctorate degrees;
- specific arrangements for part-time and full-time doctoral candidature;
- specific arrangements for doctorates by published works.

You should expect to be advised of changes to these regulations by members of the doctoral programme teams or by your supervisor(s). But do check regularly that you know about any changes to your particular doctoral programme – just in case.

Being familiar with these sets of regulations should provide you with knowledge of the administrative context for your doctoral studies. Think of them as the vehicle in which you will travel along the route to achieving your doctorate. You should note the critical dates of this journey in your diary. For instance, there are certain dates that will definitely apply to you:

- completing the annual monitoring report/return;
- submission of required materials for the mid-point progression or confirmation of candidature processes;
- submission periods in which to submit your thesis;
- lead times between the submission of your thesis and the likely date for the viva.

You could even include advance reminders to yourself in the diary as a safeguard against missing any of these checkpoints. Bentley observes on this role for candidates quite explicitly: 'It is normally considered your responsibility to make sure that everything that needs to be done, gets done' (Bentley, 2006: 118). This is very sound advice.

Within the regulations, you will also find the administrative arrangements for appointing examiners. In most universities, it is customary for supervisors to discuss the choice of suitable examiners with their candidate. This is not usually part of a formal consultative process, but a respectful act of courtesy. It checks that, in principle, the proposed examiners are generally acceptable to you. Assuming that you are acquainted with the individuals through their work or personally, this should be a formality. Very occasionally, candidates do have serious reservations over the proposed examiners due, for instance, to diametrically opposed intellectual approaches to research in their area, or deep-rooted differences in personal values and beliefs. If you found yourself in this position, then your reasons must be discussed with your supervisor(s). Those reasons can then usually be included in the formal deliberative process of considering and deciding on the names of your examiners.

In an ideal world, an examining panel would contain expertise in your topic area and the methodological approach of the research. In the real world, demarcation between these specialisms is usually rather blurred. In approving your team of examiners, the university will take into account:

- the individual and collective examining experience of the proposed team;
- the individual and collective supervisory experience of the proposed team;
- the joint topic/discipline expertise in the team;
- the relevance and level of the proposed team's publications and research to your research area;
- their scholarly and personal independence from you, your research and, possibly, your department or faculty.

Universities have to balance different levels of examining experience so that, in total, the team as a whole possess a certain number of doctoral examinations. This would balance the experienced examiner with the novice examiner in order to arrive at an acceptable membership. These criteria are safeguards that protect the integrity of the examination process and the international standing of your degree.

Your supervisor(s) will draw on two other factors from their own experience:

- the proposed examiners' awareness of the intellectual frontiers in your subject and their ability to judge whether your thesis makes a contribution to knowledge and scholarship sufficient to justify the award of a doctoral degree;
- the proposed examiners' professional maturity, wisdom and humanity so that they are able to make the examination process a worthwhile and developmental experience for you, irrespective of the outcome (Joyner, 2003).

However, when choices have to be made among potential examiners, then: 'Experience of successful supervision is a better qualification than having examined research degrees' (Joyner, 2003). Your supervisor(s) will use these criteria as the names of examiners are proposed and discussed with you.

The decision to approve the recommendation of your examiners is a formal act in the university. The details of these practices vary considerably because they are university-specific. This decision may be made either by the Chair of the research degrees committee, a panel that selects from a shortlist of suitably qualified persons or deans of faculties. Thus, discover the extent to which you and your supervisor(s) are entitled to influence any stage of this administrative and academic process. Then, you need to discuss how and when you would have the opportunity to become involved – whatever that means in the context of your university's prevailing administrative practices.

If you are a staff member in the university where your doctorate will be examined, then certain additional regulations will usually apply. In your case, the examination panel will normally contain either two external examiners or three examiners with one being an internal examiner from the staff of your university.

The views of candidates on how their viva panels were composed reflect the ways in which local customs and practices determine the appointment of examiners. Example 11.1 illustrates the extremes of administrative procedures that resulted in these comments.

Example 11.1 Candidates' involvement in the appointment of their examiners

Candidate 1 My supervisor told me that we had to decide who my examiners would be. He already had one of his colleagues in mind from the faculty. He was totally unfamiliar with my field of research or any of the writers in it. I proposed someone whose work I knew and who had published extensively in my field. That was it and my nominee was approved as my external examiner.

Candidate 2 We talked about possible examiners, but my supervisors had more knowledge of who was suitable than me. I accepted the reasons for their nominations. A committee considers all nominations and my supervisor had to justify the names that were proposed. Approval is really just a formal confirmation of the recommended names made by supervisors who are experts in the discipline.

Candidate 3 My research field is relatively new and still quite small. We all know the professors and readers, we all attend similar conferences and some of us present jointly with our supervisors. We all know everyone's publications. Selecting examiners from such a small group could be incestuous, but occasionally a thesis fails. This suggests that examiners do maintain academic standards, doesn't it? Nominations cannot be declined due to the small pool from which to choose.

Candidate 4 As a committed Marxist my research approach was, I suppose, quite predictable. I had no part in suggesting names for my examiners, this was done by a school committee. My supervisor missed that meeting due to illness and so he took no part in the decision making. The external was someone whose Leninist views had been carefully demolished in my thesis and who throughout the viva took affront at my justification of what I had written. I still feel that my referral can be traced back to that committee and the absence of my supervisor when the decision was taken.

Candidate 5 My supervisors and I agreed on internal and external examiners who were both experienced and had published in my area. Their names were proposed to RDC for approval. Later, one of my supervisors told me that the dean had added a third examiner who only asked three questions in my viva. Two were so unbelievably simple that I wondered if they had deeper meanings. Since I could not find one I gave a simple answer that seemed OK. The third question was way outside my research and I declined to answer it. Then the examiner insisted that I did and so I explained that it related to something that I had not investigated. The other external examiner agreed with me. After that, the third examiner took no further part in my viva.

Candidate 6 The university requires a faculty committee to receive a minimum of three nominations for each external examiner appointment. Full CVs have to be provided with an accompanying half-page statement. The supervisor does not attend this committee. I helped to identify two of the nominees and my supervisors found the other one. All three were rejected and we started again. It is very much a lottery.

These accounts show processes in which candidates and supervisors have quite different levels of involvement and responsibility:

- Candidate 1 was recognised by the supervisor as being the expert in the field. Their jointly proposed name of a preferred examiner was forwarded by the supervisor to a higher level for ratification.
- Candidate 2 represents a democratic allocation of responsibilities between the supervisor consulting the candidate and then the committee accepting expert advice from the supervisor.
- Candidate 3 describes situations common to any newly emerging discipline where the choice of suitably qualified examiners is limited, initial selection is handled democratically and so approval is inevitably automatic.
- Candidate 4 appears to have suffered from the supervisor not being present at the decision-making committee, which then possibly chose to appoint an external examiner on the basis of political considerations.
- Candidate 5 was involved by the supervisor in identifying possible external examiners. The intervention of the dean to introduce a third (inappropriate?) examiner without informing the supervisor represents an unhelpful and non-collegial act.
- Candidate 6 was involved by the supervisor in the initial listing of possible

examiners, but the power of the approving committee to overturn all the nominees rejected the informed expertise of the supervisor.

Although in some universities candidates are not consulted on this matter, informal discussions between supervisor and candidate are usually seen as being helpful. Thus, this administrative process is one in which you may be able to make a useful contribution.

Your supervisor will be informed when the examiner appointments are confirmed within the university system. This usually happens before you have submitted your thesis. You need then to check the submission arrangements, which will include:

- scheduling the viva after a minimum number of weeks following your submission to allow for examiners' reading time of your thesis;
- arranging the date of the viva by coordinating the availability of the examiners, yourself and the Chair, if your university has such a role in vivas.

The room that is allocated for your viva and the time of day when it will be held may not be announced until a couple of weeks before the viva. The administrative task of finding a suitable date for your viva often takes some time. You would, of course, be consulted over your availability to attend that event on the proposed dates!

In many universities, candidates may request to make a short visual presentation at the start of their viva. There are reasons for and against using this facility at the opening of a doctoral viva. Our advice is that you and your supervisor(s) should discuss exactly how such a presentation could add value to your viva. A useful place to start would be to ask the question *What will it contribute to the examiner's understanding of my thesis?* Your answer must recognise the position of your examiners; they will have read your thesis, written their independent report and agreed their agenda of questions to raise with you. Thus, you need to be sure that making a visual presentation to them will positively influence their opinions in your favour.

Where examiners have judged a visual presentation to have been successful, it:

- lasted no more than 5 minutes;
- contained six visual screens or fewer;
- opened with brief details about the candidate – qualifications, current position, research contracts, publications/conference presentations based on the thesis;
- expanded the four paragraph themes in the abstract to show: what was investigated and the research question(s); how the research was undertaken and the research approach; what was discovered and its significance in the discipline; what factual and conceptual conclusions were drawn from the evidence;

- closed with a brief statement the showed the gap in knowledge and the contribution to knowledge that the research had explored.

Those few examiners who had witnessed good opening visual presentations at doctoral vivas frequently mentioned these six points.

In contrast, more examiners had witnessed, or heard about, opening presentations that added nothing to, or, indeed, actually detracted from, the merit of the candidate's submitted research. The reasons for these views are not surprising. Examiners do not appreciate long or poorly delivered presentations that repeat what is written in the thesis. They consider this as an intrusion onto the purpose of the viva and on their own time too. Their resulting impressions of the candidate are unfavourable. Some examiners admitted that this may then have influenced what transpired in the viva itself. In these circumstances, the candidates had made a bad start to their viva.

On balance, you should only make a visual presentation at your viva if you are competent in using the technology, clear in why it is to be used and succinct in your delivery. Most examiners do not expect you to make a presentation and so it may be worth not challenging this widely held examiner convention.

However, if you do intend to make a presentation then there are some precautionary things that you should do. Once the room for your viva has been announced, check that it has the appropriate visual aid technology to meet your technical and presentational needs. In particular, ensure that there is compatibility between the university's projector systems and your own technical systems. Simple questions about the availability of a projector for you on the day, plug compatibility, length of leads or access to extension leads plus how the system works, are easy to check and resolve in advance. But any one of these issues could also create a potential disaster for you at the very start of your doctoral viva. You must have satisfactory answers to all these technical questions before you can assume that your presentation will happen as you would want it to. And then, you have to deliver your presentation faultlessly.

Visualising the viva strategically

Before you become embroiled in the stories and mystique of the doctoral viva, stand back and ponder just for a moment on what it really represents. Instead of thinking about matters of location or duration, focus instead on how examiners conceptualise the process of examining. Asking examiners how they connect their independent report with their questions in the viva shows that the former clearly influences the latter as the comments in Example 11.2 indicate.

Example 11.2 Examiners preparing for the viva

Examiner A Reading the thesis again in preparation for the viva usually triggers additional questions in my mind. These tend to be more of a philosophical sort that require answers of a deeper level than I had suggested in my first report. But they would be put into the pot with the other examiners' questions as we form an agenda of points to raise in the viva itself.

Examiner B I am always looking for aspects in the thesis that show merit or weakness. Merit is easier to recognise because it is what scholarship is all about. As a journal editor, very similar checks are applied as I read a submitted article or a thesis. If the good points are plentiful in the thesis then my questions in the viva are really just confirming that the candidate can justify and explain their research. Weak theses always take more of my time. I want to understand why it is weak and why things have been overlooked or omitted! My tentative agenda for the viva is always based on my initial report.

Examiner C When I first read a thesis, the impressions that I get certainly influence how I proceed through to the final chapter and into the accompanying details. Really poorly expressed argument or major blunders of methodology are rare in my experience. They stand out when they do happen. My attention will be on trying to detect exactly how the candidate has tackled their research. If I can get behind the words and identify with their thinking, that usually tells me more than what is written on the page. In the viva, I will follow up these impressions to fill in my picture of the candidate as a potential postdoctoral researcher. That is what we are really attempting to assess, isn't it?

Examiner D My first reports are always short. They give salient points of strength or weakness in the thesis. Doing that tells me all that I really need to know. It is similar to a credit and loss account. In the viva, I then probe to gain a better view of how they did their research. I want them to speak to me as someone with years of experience from doing their research. Their own. Good students do that. Weak or poor ones cannot. The balance is confirmed in the viva. It always shows there.

These four individuals had each examined more than 10 doctoral theses in a variety of universities and they were from different disciplines. Their respective approaches to connecting their initial reports with their investigatory approach in the viva showed that:

- Examiner A emphasised philosophical underpinnings;
- Examiner B sought evidence of scholarship;
- Examiner C projected postdoctoral capabilities as an independent researcher;
- Examiner D looked for maturity in research understanding by candidates.

These features embody thinking about the examination process at a sophisticated level. None of the examiners dwelt on issues of method or even methodology – unless, by implication, it had resulted in a weak or poor thesis. Their attention was drawn towards factors that were the consequence of high-level good research practice.

Consider how these factors are critical to your success in achieving your doctorate. Focus on the evaluative criteria that would be in the examiners' mind as they read your thesis and prepared themselves for your viva. Once you have done that then you should consider three questions that all examiners would recognise.

What distinguishes a doctoral thesis that passes from one that does not?

We have shown already, in Figure 2.1, how examiners' questions emphasise four overlapping features in a doctoral thesis. We termed Quadrant D 'demonstrating doctorateness' since it represents higher level thinking. It portrays ways in which conceptualisation has been used in the thesis. The evidence that examiners use to check if these features are present was shown in Figure 3.2, where 12 components form a template of characteristics that, if present, demonstrate doctorateness. As a result, if these various features are present then a thesis would be judged as scholarly. A thesis that lacked one or more of these features would not be judged as scholarly. Thus, positive evidence of doctorateness separates pass and fail categories in a thesis.

What connection is there between a candidate's understanding of the research process and the nature of doctorateness?

This question is at the centre of what makes doctoral research different from other research. It differentiates between understanding as a cognitive process and the technical actions that are associated with fact finding. When examiners read your thesis they should recognise that all these features of doctorateness are apparent. This tells them that you have understood how complex research processes are comprised of interdependent parts. It also allows them to see how you have integrated arguments and concepts throughout the text in a coherent manner. Your examiners will then know that you understand, as a researcher, why you had designed and undertaken the research in the ways that you explained in your thesis.

Examiners expect that in your thesis and, during your viva, you will 'make your thinking visible' (Perkins, 2003). In doing so, you will inevitably explain your use of conceptual connections as you expose your cognitive processes to scrutiny by others (Vygotsky, 1978). This, in turn, shows how your level of understanding enabled you to think like a doctoral researcher. The evidence for this would be that you understood the philosophical principles that are central to your discipline. If you were able to do this then you would justify your deliberations within the accepted ways of knowing typified within that discipline. Thus, you will have signalled your capability to undertake postdoctoral research that is independent of further direct supervision.

Examiners will seek a satisfactory account of how your research was designed, planned and undertaken, as the foundation for doctorateness. This task involves examiners seeking evidence which: 'establishes that by your thesis work and your performance in the viva you have demonstrated that you are a fully professional researcher who should be listened to because you can make a sensible contribution to the development of your field' (Phillips and Pugh, 2000: 152). When this happens it: 'allows a mature and detailed academic discussion between examiners and the candidate. Such discussion signals the candidate's entry to a community of scholarship, and it also provides useful feedback that may help improve subsequent publication of the research' (Finn, 2005: 168).

Thus, the examiners will have recognised your maturity and confidence in the episteme of the discipline – the system of ideas and ways of understanding that others in that discipline also use (Perkins, 2006: 42–43). This is why experts in your topic or methodology are appointed as your examiners. Their expertise provides them with the insights and experience to recognise scholarly ability or to identify any shortcomings in the thesis.

How does a candidate's ability to use the lexicon of research, appropriate to their discipline and field of research, influence how they are able to defend their thesis in their viva?

As your ability to think like a researcher develops, your understanding of the essential principles and philosophies of your discipline will deepen. This will give you the confidence to handle them as scholarly tools of your trade. With that confidence, you will have internalised the language that is specific to your discipline, too. Subsequently, the style of your writing will reflect the lexicon of the discipline and the research process itself. You will be able to 'talk the language' of research (Perkins, 2006).

Your viva is when you have to combine your thinking, understanding, lexicon and confidence into defending your research. Examiners will expect you to know what you are talking about, including its meanings, nuances and the underlying philosophies. They will also anticipate you being able and willing to engage with them in an informed and scholarly manner. Your ability to engage confidently in a scholarly dialogue of questions and responses will convince them of your doctoral capabilities.

This would manifest itself particularly as you develop responses from description into 'conceptually coherent accounts of the theories being used'

(Murphy and Medin, 1999: 427). Professional maturation processes are typified by candidates who think like serious researchers and, as a result, 'come to terms with their (conceptual) experience' (Cohen et al., 2000: 13). Thus, the cognitive aspect of questions and answers is what really typifies scholarly dynamics in a doctoral viva.

These three questions go to the heart of the viva's function. Answers to them have to explain the nature of high-quality research, then, what it means to act like a researcher and, in particular, to recognise the significance of doctoral research as an integrated process, have to be teased out. Finally, distinctions have to be made between the textual account of research, belief in its merit and ways in which it can be defended.

Thinking about these questions should have taken you on an intellectual journey that raised your thinking to a strategic level. Using such a framework to visualise your viva brings you close to the way in which examiners themselves view the viva. Thus, you can concentrate on preparing for your viva at the strategic level of thinking that seems to typify how examiners approach the viva.

Preparing for your viva

Now that you have finished your thesis you should prepare for your viva. We believe that this frequently heard exhortation is misplaced. Our book has argued that you should view your entire doctoral experience as preparing for your viva. Using questions and approaches that examiners apply in their evaluative role can guide you along the preparatory journey to your viva. Taking this longer view accepts a very hard fact: once your thesis has been submitted for examination, it is then too late for you to make any further alterations to its content. Thus, any preparations can only be of a supportive, technical or emotional form. Table 11.1 illustrates the case for this longer view.

Perhaps the long view was best expressed by a doctoral candidate who said:

> When I first thought about doing a doctorate, I bought a small pocket-sized notebook and a stubby pen. Anytime I had an idea, or browsed bookshops and read something interesting, I made a note of it. Occasionally, I would have a really good question that I could not answer. They went into it too. What a boon my little book was when I finally started my doctorate and during it as well. I still have a little book in my pocket and make notes in it, it has become a habit now, I suppose.

Most experienced supervisors adopt this view towards preparing their candidates for the doctoral viva. Lawton's view of a PhD being 'a worthwhile learning experience' (Lawton, 1997: 3) captures their use of preparation as a constant learning and developmental experience. For them and their candidates, the

Table 11.1 Our long view of constantly preparing for your viva

If the scholarly merit of the thesis determines the outcome of the viva – then producing a thesis that is based on explicit scholarship *is* your preparation for the viva.
If your supervisor(s) constantly ask the Kipling questions to challenge you and foster your intellectual development – then answering questions, defending points of view and engaging with scholastic ideas and their applications *is* your preparation for the viva.
If undertaking constructive reviews of the thesis can reinforce understanding of its cohesiveness and synergy – then achieving deep understanding of research as an integrated process *is* your preparation for the viva.
If critical rereading of the text of thesis strengthens its arguments and improves its presentation – then auditing the thesis for meaning, clarity and presentation *is* your preparation for the viva.

activities that need attention between submission and viva are essentially administrative and supportive, rather than being preparatory in any academic sense.

Once you have drafted your thesis and then submitted it for examination, you may experience a moment or two of mixed emotion. The relief of knowing that you have written many thousands of words, undertaken research on a new field of knowledge and found 'something' will be exhilarating. For a while, you will be rightly delighted and proud of your achievement. Then, perhaps, your feelings will be tempered by the knowledge that your examiners will shortly receive your thesis and start to assess its scholarly merit.

The quality of your preparation for the viva should be evident to your examiners through their reading of your thesis. While they do that, you have other tasks to deal with. These activities will support and facilitate your defence of your thesis in the viva. They can be divided into two complementary sets of actions.

First, there are actions that can sharpen the defence of what you have already written. In Chapter 10, the audit instrument was shown as a device for you to monitor progress during your doctoral study. Why not use it again as a self-help audit of your submitted work? (See Appendix 10.1.) Completing it without referring to your thesis would be a practical memory prompt as you produce a final profile of your doctoral research. This time, though, the completed document will provide you with a concise aide mémoire – just in case you need to remind yourself what your research was really all about! It would also be a working document to discuss with your supervisor(s) during the time before your viva.

Most candidates produce a summary of their thesis before their viva. This can take many forms:

- **A condensed summary** – an A4 page containing the critical items that they intend to use as a checklist to ensure that they have dealt with those points which they want examiners to receive.
- **A broad summary** – an A5 double-page with carefully placed listings of the

key points in chapters that provides a complete picture of their thesis in one broad glance.

- **A mind map** (Buzan, 2005) – providing on one or more pages overviews of the thesis or significant parts of it by projecting identified associations of sub-features from a central feature that portray the relationships in an easy-to-see-and-understand manner.
- **Chapter summaries** – noting their respective content and collectively representing an extended synopsis of the thesis.
- **A minimalist overview** – using 3×5 flash cards for rotation as visual memory prompts to identify selective primary names and dates that you might mention, a conceptual model or two, some quotable quotations and abbreviated hypotheses or propositions.

In these systems, you could identify specific pages, figures, tables or chapters by different colours for ease of reference when you needed to access one. Each method has either advantages of brevity and ease of access or practical limitations due to size and access. Which of these you use is obviously a matter of personal choice.

The task of reducing your entire thesis into a few words, models or notes will certainly reinforce your knowledge about your work. This is an excellent reason for devoting time to any of these methods that summarise your thesis. Many candidates also want the emotional reassurance that they have something they can use as a prompt to their memory if necessary. Being smaller than the thesis, manageable and easily accessible, each of these methods serves that aim very well. Scheduling this task as a form of revision in the time between submitting your thesis and the viva is a valuable exercise in itself.

Second, there is the well-tried and trusted method of tagging pages in the thesis. This very simple task involves sticking relatively small coloured papers onto specific pages that you might want to refer to in your viva. You could also select the first page of each chapter to help you find discrete blocks of text. Alternatively, if turning immediately to a figure, model or table would be important for you in the viva, then you would tag those specific pages instead – or as well. Writing on each tag what it gives you access to then allows you to select the page(s) that you want to look at.

Two very practical considerations now arise. Do make sure that the stickiness of your tagging paper is fresh, has not dried out or become no longer sticky! Tags can fall off their pages if they do not adhere as intended. Also, when you have tagged your thesis treat it carefully so that the tags are not rubbed off their page. This last point applies particularly as you pack and unpack your thesis on the day of your viva.

The disadvantages of these various systems occur when candidates reach a saturation point in their textual retrieval systems. Combinations of these choices often result in overloading the thesis with access points into the text. It is self-defeating if candidates are unable to find what they seek in their own thesis during their viva due to the complexity of their own 'information system'. When such episodes occur, and they do, they are also embarrassing for everyone in the viva room – examiners, candidate, supervisor(s) and Chair. Furthermore, examiners would have gained an impression of these candidate's heavy reliance on mechanical props rather than deep understanding of arguments in their thesis. Thus, while these systems are helpful, you should use them with caution. If you decide to use any of them make your system as simple as possible and try it out long before the day of your viva to see that it works for you.

The investment of time in producing any of these prompts is well spent because they help you to restudy your thesis. They will remind you of connections and arguments that took time to produce and were intellectually satisfying once they were produced. However, most candidates do not even open their thesis during their viva. Furthermore, they seldom refer to their notes that usually are lying beside the thesis. The reason for this is due to them giving full attention to the examiners, the questions that are being asked and how their responses are received. Thus, these summary prompts serve more as an investment in unravelling the thesis than as a source of directly helpful material that is used in the viva.

The previous preparatory tasks were textual but the next preparatory task is oral. Without referring to your thesis, you could talk through your responses to the 12 critical questions that we presented in Chapter 2, as follows:

- Why did you choose this topic for your doctorate?
- How did you arrive at your conceptual framework?
- How did you design your research?
- How would you justify your choice of methodology?
- Why did you decide to use XYZ instrument(s)?
- How did you select your respondents as your main/materials/area?
- How did you arrive at your conceptual conclusions?
- How generalisable are your findings and why?
- What is your contribution to knowledge?
- We would like you to critique your thesis for us.
- What are you going to do after you gain your doctorate?
- Is there anything else that you could tell us about your thesis that you have not had the opportunity to tell us during the viva?

You could invite someone who was willing to spend an hour or so with you asking these questions. Encourage them to ask follow-up questions and so create some spontaneity for your responses. To gain more benefit from this task, you could record the session and play it back. This would allow you to assess how you had handled the questions. You could also judge the clarity and duration of your replies plus the extent of the lexicon that you had used.

Your examiners may pose these questions differently than they appear in this list and they will certainly ask additional questions, too. But by answering these questions you will be preparing yourself to cope with generic aspects of research in your thesis. Recalling your responses will help you to anticipate answers to related questions as illustrated now by one candidate.

Example 11.3 demonstrates how a candidate exploited one question to provide information that he really wanted the examiners to know about at the outset of his viva. He had prepared for this type of linguistic tactic before his viva. He had decided that he wanted the examiners to hear the reasons he believed were crucial to his decision to undertake doctoral research. He was fortunate in seeing an opportunity to introduce those views alongside his answer to a related question. Planning of this type is useful, but don't be too disappointed if the appropriate occasion to slip your ideas into another answer does not arise.

Example 11.3 Answering two questions with one response

Examiner   We would like you to start by telling us something about yourself. [This was the opening question at a PhD viva concerned with trialling a medical drug.]

Candidate   Well, I went to university as did all my friends. I read medicine because I had always wanted to be a doctor. It was hard work and at times I really wondered why I had chosen such a long and exacting 5 years of study, with even more ahead of me . . . After my houseman years I gained my fellowship in my early 30s . . . being of a mathematical bent I have always been interested in what really large samples of medical data contain and can tell us. When the opportunity came for me to be part of a 6-year cardiac outcomes trial that was testing a control drug for hypertension with some thousands of patients, I jumped at it.

Many things fascinated me about this project: it would have an enormous database, it was testing hypotheses related to how patients responded to specific drugs, the introduction of placebos provided control group comparisons and every patient was selected against absolute criteria of medical suitability. The most exciting (can I use that word here?) part, though, was that a hypertension drug had not been previously trialled longitudinally for 6 years with GP-recommended patients whose diagnosis was so specific and exactly controlled. It was a perfect laboratory for clinicians and for statisticians. Recognising this, I chose the relationship between the GP, their patients and national clinical trials as my doctoral research topic. It was under-researched, important to our professions and is still lacking in adequate rigorous explanation.

In this example, the candidate initially directed his response to the question. Then, he expanded on his career choices and divulged his interest in statistics. This gave him an entrée into explaining the attractiveness of a project that contained a potential gap in medical knowledge. In turn, this allowed him to finish by justifying his choice of a doctoral research topic. No doubt, the examiner would then have had to rethink what the next question could be since this candidate had provided answers to numerous other possible questions. Many examiners prefer you not to be as expansive as this candidate had been, but rather to answer only the question(s) that had been asked by one or other of them. Thus, you should attempt to judge how acceptable such a mode of answering would be to your examiners. Caution and risk are opposite ways of responding to questions in this situation. You ought to avoid jeopardising your position by deliberately imposing yourself too early or too strongly onto your examiner's intentions for the way that your viva might precede.

There is one final action to take before your viva. Ask your supervisor to show you the room in which you will have your viva. If you have reservations about its suitability then you should explain this at the time. You will, of course, have to justify any reservations to your supervisor(s) who should then be able to take appropriate action on your behalf. It is unlikely that you will be unhappy with the room that has been allocated for your viva, but it does sometimes happen.

Example 11.4 Don't look out of the window

The supervisor always took his candidates to see the room where their viva would be held so that when they entered it again the setting was familiar. One of his candidates was a photographer who saw that a window filled one side of the room. Beyond the window was a public path, willow trees and a meandering river. The sunshine produced constantly moving shadows. The candidate looked at this scene and immediately said: *'Tomorrow, may I sit with my back to the window?'* He explained that the patterns of sunlight, pedestrians on the path and the moving willow branches would be professionally fascinating but academically distracting. His supervisor passed his request to the Chair and examiners who accepted it without question. On the following day the candidate entered the room, walked around the table and sat with his back to the window. He then thanked the Chair and the two examiners for accepting his request. He said afterwards that this episode *'showed sympathy for me. It also established another side to my professionalism in another setting. This certainly did me no harm at all in their eyes. I am so glad that we visited the room yesterday.'*

Example 11.4 shows how, when a candidate saw his room on the day before his viva, his very simple and timely request saved a possible difficulty for everyone on the viva day itself.

Using 'mock' vivas

Then there are 'mock' vivas as a way to prepare your oral abilities. If you are invited to have one, it is essential that the purpose of this exercise is clear and acceptable to you. Murray offers just such a justification: 'The advantage of the mock viva is that it helps you adjust to the more formal verbal style of the oral examination. It helps you develop your skills for more extended focussed discussion' (Murray, 2002: 263). She points out that the experience itself of answering formal questions in a formal setting can provide 'insights into what your viva will really be like on the day'. She balances this by pointing out that there is no: 'guarantee that your examiners will run things in the same way or respond to you in the same way'.

Mock vivas offer different benefits if they are held:

- during doctoral studies in workshops or seminars where your presentational abilities to advance and defend ideas would be developed;
- as a component of the transfer process from MPhil to PhD or mid-point progression/confirmation of candidature within doctoral programmes where a formal atmosphere introduces a more scholarly dynamic to the discussion;
- after the first draft of your thesis has been produced where its purpose is to explore the cohesion of the thesis and your ability to explain scholarly content and arguments. This use of the mock viva can identify areas of the thesis that require further attention before it is ready to be submitted – but only after you and your supervisor have discussed whether these are acceptable changes to the text. You would certainly get value from defending your entire thesis in this way as it confirms your conceptual grasp or indicates the need to improve your discursive abilities;
- after your thesis has been submitted where its purpose is to sharpen your response to questions, engage scholastically with others and cope with a prolonged period of answering questions. Due to the timing of this mock viva, you cannot alter the text of your submitted thesis if an accepted outcome is that something 'needs to be strengthened'. However, if this was an outcome, at least you can decide how to handle this point if the examiners ask about it in the viva itself – so the mock viva would be a forewarning thereby giving you the opportunity to get your defence in first!

Sometimes mock vivas have a parallel purpose – developing the examiner capabilities of prospective internal examiners in your university. It may also involve supervisors as surrogate examiners, so that they can experience the other side of supervising. These are both commendable corporate purposes for holding mock vivas. You need perhaps to be wary of such developmental events where you are not at the absolute centre of its purpose and outcome. Thus, your thesis and your forthcoming viva should be the prime reason for holding a mock viva in which you are the candidate.

As Tinkler and Jackson remind us, you might be the candidate in a mock viva, an observer of someone else's mock viva, an examiner in a mock viva, a non-participant observer of mock vivas for other candidates or a viewer of video recording of mock vivas of yourself or other candidates (Tinkler and Jackson, 2004: 129). These variations in form and function offer you and your supervisor a choice of how you might experience a mock viva in preparation for the real thing.

However, as Wisker explains, holding a mock viva places obligations on the organisers and those who participate to make it into an academically relevant exercise. She describes systems where doctoral candidates observe the mock vivas of other candidates. Here, the outcomes are collectively analysed to show how a candidate coped with questions, used scholarly language and defended the ideas in their thesis (Wisker, 2005: 329). This level of mutual openness to engage in sharing views on 'academic performance', while commendable, would require you to be a member of an established doctoral community of practice for it to work well (Wenger, 1998; Leshem, 2007).

Mock vivas can only seek to replicate the real thing; they cannot guarantee similarity with different examiners holding different academic agendas, on a different day and particularly when you would have a different emotional outlook towards the event. These counterbalancing positions may be reduced somewhat, though it would require serious commitment to the developmental advantages of the mock viva. With your supervisor(s) it might be possible to arrange a mock viva that:

- occurs after the thesis is drafted but before it is submitted, so that any proposed changes to your text can be discussed with your supervisor(s) and, possibly, incorporated into the thesis;
- involves two experienced examiners who are willing to read your entire thesis;
- receives an independent report from each examiner before the viva;
- is held in the room or one identical to the room in which your actual viva will be held;
- is Chaired/conducted in a similar manner to the actual viva and follows identical procedures and practices that normally occur in vivas at your university;
- can continue until the examiners are satisfied that their obligations to examine the thesis and explore it with you have been met;
- closes in the usual way, with you withdrawing from the room and the

examiners agreeing on their judgement and the contents of a report which they would convey to you on your return to the room.

Mock vivas that achieve this degree of effort will consume many hours of staff resources and require considerable goodwill from all the participants. Some institutions believe that if a mock viva is to serve a genuinely developmental and scholarly purpose, then these are the conditions under which they should be held. Unpublished evidence from one of those institutions suggests that these aims can be met (Wilmoth, 2006).

You might feel that you want to have the experience of *being formally examined on your thesis*. This should then be the explicit reason for setting up an exercise that will provide you with such an experience. Both Murray (2003: 90) and Wellington et al. (2005: 190) argue that at their viva, candidates are expected to speak the language of their discipline fluently and with confidence, knowledge and conviction. The collectivist atmosphere of workshops is unlikely to be able to provide you with the formality of this process while a properly organised mock viva could. Thus, the use of mock vivas can range from Mickey Mouse affairs through to carefully conducted near-mirror events of a doctoral viva. Their use for you is something to discuss with your supervisor(s).

Task 11.1 will help you to prepare for your viva.

Task 11.1   How will you prepare for your viva?

How you are going to prepare yourself for the viva? What technical, academic and social strategies are you going to adopt?

Looking back and ahead

This chapter has presented the idea that understanding the administrative arrangements relating to your doctoral studies cannot be overemphasised. They are means to an end and you should use them in that way. Our respective supervisors exemplified the idea that we had prepared for our viva throughout the duration of our doctoral studies. When we had completed writing our theses we each asked our supervisor: *How can I now prepare for my viva?* We each received almost similar answers: *There is nothing that the examiners can ask you that I have not asked you at least twice and you have answered to my satisfaction at least twice. There is nothing more for you to do now.* This reply echoes exactly the long view of preparing for your doctoral viva that this chapter has proposed.

Chapter 12 is devoted to the dynamics of the doctoral viva and your role in that event.

12

Dynamics of the doctoral viva

This chapter will:

- consolidate the arguments and theories in the previous chapters to create a framework for defending your thesis;
- unravel the 'mystery' of the viva by suggesting why the viva is under-researched;
- outline how to cope with the potential difficulties on your viva day;
- provide you with strategies that help you to cope with the dynamics of the viva day.

Introduction

The doctoral viva serves many purposes. It is little wonder that some candidates are confused over how it operates. Knowledge about what occurs in the viva room is akin to views about the confessional: everyone believes that they know what happens. In reality, their knowledge tends to be based on second-hand accounts from those who have not entered a confessional themselves. It is worth reminding ourselves, again, that Burnham observed so aptly: 'The viva is one of the best kept secrets in British higher education' (Burnham, 1994). This may be because, as Baldacchino suggests: 'Writings about the viva encounter have been conspicuous by their absence' (Baldacchino, 1995).

This chapter untangles the layers of influence that meld the dynamics of your doctoral viva. It demystifies the process by identifying discrete stages that you can influence as you prepare for and take part in your viva. Seen this way, preparing for your viva is a positive approach to achieving your doctorate. This will help you avoid the uncertainty in this candidate's comment: 'My biggest fear about the viva is not really knowing what to expect' (Tinkler and Jackson, 2004: 12).

The previous chapters have illustrated how you can produce a thesis that reflects doctorateness. This consolidating chapter draws together the main ideas and approaches that have appeared earlier. It uses them to remind you to anticipate, influence and control the dynamics of your viva day. It isolates significant critical factors that determine these dynamics. Examples show how candidates, supervisors and examiners handle these factors.

The under-researched doctoral viva

As researchers, we all know that the doctoral viva is an under-researched phenomenon. There are reasons for this: few people have the opportunity to undertake real-time research into its procedures and dynamics; universities are understandably reluctant to allow researchers access to such sensitive occasions whose primary purpose is the formal examination of a doctoral thesis by invited specialists (Park, 2003). Thus, first-hand accounts of vivas are limited to those who attend – candidates, examiners, supervisors and, in certain universities, Chairs of doctoral vivas.

After the viva, candidates want to get on with their career and life. Their interest in writing about their viva experience, consequently, has low priority. Examiners are experienced academics or practitioners with a commitment to their primary occupation. Their interest in the viva stems from professional concerns, as they often say, 'to act as a monitor of scholarly standards and ratify possible advancements in my field'. This view typifies an examiner's twin concerns about assessing doctoral quality and developments in their discipline. Writing about such short professional encounters is unlikely to rank high in any examiner's priorities.

Supervisors are usually academics whose main interests lie in their disciplines and rather than 'an examination process of which I am not a part', as one examiner explained. Chairs host events in which they, too, have no central academic role. Their interest in the viva qua viva was expressed by one Chair as: 'Just my small contribution to the running of the university.'

Traditionally, stories of the occasional unpleasant viva pass around more rapidly than accounts of the majority of vivas that are successful and harmonious (Major, 1994: 8). As a result, many candidates acquire knowledge about what occurs in doctoral vivas from individualised and often sensationalised second-hand accounts. Overhearing these accounts, your research antennae should alert you to use your research skills in exploring the stories' authenticity. When you do that, you will conclude that these stories are potentially unreliable and certainly non-generalisable! You will also have gained first-hand evidence that informed views on what transpires in doctoral vivas are relatively scarce.

Research-based evidence about vivas

However, there are some accounts of how vivas operate. Hartley and Jory's (2000) research showed that over one-third of psychology candidates had negative experiences. Revisiting the same respondents, Hartley and Fox (2002) concluded that even when the examiners were *fair* and *even-handed*, some candidates still felt that their viva was not a positive experience.

Models that do explain the doctoral viva have highlighted the contrasting styles and motives that examiners bring to the occasion. Jackson and Tinkler (2000) proposed a professional model that exhibited 'competence, judgement and honour' and a process model that emphasised compliance with explicit institutional polices and procedures. They also concluded that examiners may not always follow such policies, even where they do exist (Tinkler and Jackson, 2000).

An alternative view by Wallace and Marsh (2001) distinguished between those vivas in which examiners are chummy towards their candidates and others in which examiners operated a trial-by-ordeal approach to candidates in vivas. Despite examples of variable practice, it is worth remembering that: 'The majority of examiners are pleasant and fair in PhD. vivas even if they are often rigorous and challenging in their questioning' (Tinkler and Jackson, 2004: 128). Their finding accords with the general opinion of experienced supervisors, too, when they recall how examiners conducted their candidates' vivas.

This array of contradictory evidence nonetheless provides you with some knowledge about the operations of the viva. It points to one fact around which the conduct of the viva revolves – the attitude of the examiners and their likely behaviour towards you as the candidate. It is against this background that myth and mystery about the viva thrives.

In your viva, examiners will challenge you on different parts of your work. This introduces a dynamic view of the viva since: 'The process will be rather like a negotiation. Your examiners will complain that they don't like something that you have written and you will need to defend your work – negotiating a corrected version (of the thesis) that everyone agrees with' (Bentley, 2006: 98). Taking this perspective, the viva is when and where your grasp of the entire doctoral research process, as argued in this book, must sustain and justify your defence.

However, do not overlook the traditional primary purpose of the doctoral viva. Underlying all the regulations and procedural statements in a university, the viva still exists 'to test your understanding and the general adequacy of the material contained in (your) thesis' (Burnham, 1997: 198). It is in this context that candidates attend their viva to defend their research in their thesis. This is a reminder to hold on to the notion of ownership for the doctorate in the scholarly and physical form of your thesis.

Inevitably, the outcome from each viva has a direct personal and professional significance for every doctoral candidate. These outcomes are also of great interest to their supervisors and their university, plus, of course, their families. For these reasons 'the stakes are high, particularly for the (candidate)' (Park, 2003). Thus, this chapter places the candidate – you – at the centre of the viva process and in possession of some influence over how the viva can operate in your case.

On the day

The dynamics of your viva results from three influences: your cumulative scholarly development throughout your studies, your handling of the day itself and the attitudes of examiners towards your thesis. How you cope with the day takes shape from when you get up in the morning. Everything that happens to you after that will influence your feelings, your arrival at the viva, your assessment of the room and your handling of the viva itself. The role of the examiners cannot be ignored, but don't underplay the critical influence that *you* have on the day. Figure 12.1. portrays the cumulative nature in these six determinants of dynamics in your doctoral viva.

So don't be tripped up on this important day by the simplest of oversights.

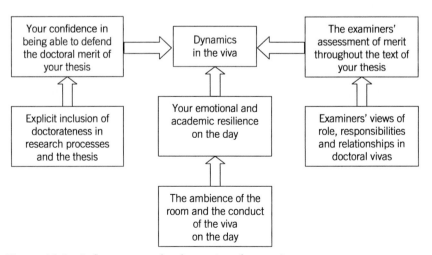

Figure 12.1   Influences on the dynamics of your viva.

As you leave where you live, check everything you need – thesis, notes, pens, etc. Then make sure that they are *all with you* as you depart for the university. These items are the technical tools for your defence. They must be with you in your viva and not left at home.

Similarly, remind yourself of the viva's date, time and location. You may also have to meet a university administrator or the Chair prior to the viva. If you have not already visited or seen the room, check with your supervisor(s) where it is and how to reach it from a point in the university that you know. This is particularly important if you study either part-time or at a distance and are unfamiliar with the university campus.

Example 12.1 shows how two candidates arrived at their viva room with difficulties that were of their own making.

Example 12.1 Avoidable problems on the day

Cameo A I arrived in the morning at the university for my 2 o'clock viva before realising that my thesis was 40 miles away at home. I then drove home and back, instead of relaxing on my favourite seat, in the sun, by the lake and the ducks, on the campus. What really irritated me was that everything was on my table ready for me to pick it up before I left. I was so annoyed.

Cameo B I spent over an hour with my colleague examiner and the supervisor, searching the building for our candidate who had not arrived at the room. The supervisor had seen him earlier in the morning so he was obviously around somewhere. The supervisor finally discovered him sitting in the adjacent room, but out of sight from the door's glass window, waiting, as he thought, 'to be called in for my viva'. The viva was a mutually frosty affair.

Cameo A This candidate had anticipated what to take to her viva but had then not checked it was with her as she departed for the university.

Cameo B This candidate had not taken due notice of the instructions about room location and timing that he had received from the university. Then he chose not to wait outside the room, but instead sat where he could not be seen unless someone entered that room. The examiners were unimpressed by his respect for the occasion. His embarrassment at what had happened accompanied him into his viva.

These candidates could have avoided the potential adverse effect from their bad starts to the day by more careful personal planning and checking of simple but important arrangements for the viva day.

Your supervisor(s) may suggest meeting to discuss any last issues before the viva. This is a useful opportunity to do that and to be in familiar company as well. It has the additional advantage of you knowing where you are, how long you have before your viva plus the assurance of reaching the viva room on time. Most candidates spend time this way in preference to being with friends/acquaintances. You have to judge how to spend any free time before your viva. You may have to be insistent to deter well-wishers from interrupting your thoughts and final personal preparations. Explaining what you want to do 'right now' and that you will meet them later ought to persuade most friends to respect your wishes.

In contrast with these cases, Example 12.2 shows how two other candidates ensured that they were at their viva at the right time.

Example 12.2 Planning to arrive on time

Cameo C   A part-time candidate was so looking forward to his viva that he woke well before his alarm rang. He decided to get up and later left for the 4-hour drive to the university, diverting from the motorway to see a historic town that had always interested him. After a leisurely mid-morning break that included walking around an archaeological site, he arrived at the university. This is how he remembered that journey: *'It was such an unhurried drive, and the site visit took my mind completely away from the afternoon's meeting. It was just what I needed because I arrived refreshed and happy with myself.'* He reached his supervisor's room slightly ahead of the agreed time for a brief chat before accompanying his supervisor to his viva.

Cameo D   One candidate told his supervisor that he would be outside his viva room 30 minutes before it was due to start. The supervisor arrived to find him sitting in a nearby armchair, with a coffee, reading a novel. After exchanging some pleasantries, the candidate said *'So you'll be back in about 20 minutes for my viva?'* before reopening the novel at his reading page. The supervisor left.

These cameos show how other candidates plan and arrive for their vivas in ways most acceptable to themselves:

Cameo C illustrates how doing something enjoyable and relaxing was ideally suited to the needs of this candidate and prepared him emotionally for his viva.

Cameo D provides a picture of a totally relaxed candidate for whom the prospect of of having a viva offered no worries.

These cameos portray how four candidates handled arriving at their viva. In each case, they appear to have known how to reach the viva room, but in Cameos A and B, quite avoidable personal mistakes upset their plans. Cameos C and D show different personal approaches to reaching the viva room on time. You will recognise how personal control of these situations resulted in their calm and confident emotional state of mind.

Considerable circumstantial evidence suggests that the final few hours before the viva are important to candidates. These hours are when candidates remind themselves of the critical features in their thesis. The notes that you have made to sit alongside your thesis during the viva (see Chapter 11) should be used for this last-minute revision. They will also remind you of important ideas that you want to use as reminders to use, perhaps, during the viva.

A general view by supervisors is that time spent, yet again, rereading the thesis in detail is potentially unhelpful. It will not extend a candidate's knowledge about the thesis; neither will it strengthen their understanding if they do not already have such knowledge or understanding. Some weaker candidates have admitted that revision of this sort produced mental saturation and propelled them into their viva in a state of confusion. Occasionally, this final intense concentration even triggered sudden overwhelming worries about 'not knowing' and this was emotionally distressing. Others, though, regularly use this revision method to good effect as they prepare for important academic occasions.

The value of last-minute revision is therefore very individual. It may be a comfort for those who gain reassurance through immersion in the familiarity of their thesis. As many candidates have explained: *It is good to know that I am in control of the information in my thesis.* For others, it is potentially unhelpful. You have to decide how you want to spend those hours before your viva and then control how you use it, as shown in Example 12.3.

Example 12.3 The hours before the viva

Cameo E My family accompanied me to the university to wish me well and to see where I had studied. They met my supervisors and some of my friends in the cafeteria. It was a nice comforting time for me and I went into my viva with *'Good luck,'* and *'I love you'* ringing in my ears.

Cameo F So many people were in the open area where my supervisor and I were talking. Some wanted to check that I was OK, others wished me well and a few made small talk. This was not what I needed at all. Before I became irritated with my friends, and maybe my supervisor too, I asked if we could go somewhere more private to continue our conversation. He agreed and we moved to a nearby tutorial room and closed the door.

Cameo G   I arrived at the university much earlier than the appointed time for the viva. The vivas of two other colleagues I knew were scheduled to be held before mine. Their family and friends were waiting outside the rooms anxious for the candidates to come out. The crowd, the voices and the stressful ambience did not really suit my state of mind at that time. My supervisor suggested that we leave the place and just go out somewhere to have lunch. We found a close-by pub and sat chatting about all sorts of things, enjoying a light relaxed lunch, not even mentioning the viva! When we came back I was much more at ease and ready to go in and discuss my thesis.

Example 12.3 provides cameo recollections by three candidates of how they spent the final hours before their viva. Each candidate quite consciously influenced how those hours were to be used and in whose company they would be at that time. They deliberately controlled that experience in their own interests. Depending on where you have reached in your doctoral journey, use Task 12.1 to determine how you propose to spend those hours before your viva. The examples highlight the importance to you of being aware of and sensitive towards location, personal orientation, social groups and preferred activity on the day. Your choices will directly influence the day's dynamic.

Task 12.1   The morning before your viva

Assume that your viva is due to be held in the afternoon. What would you expect to do that morning so that you arrived at the viva relaxed, unhurried and ready to defend your thesis?

Understanding the roles of those attending your viva

Local regulations prescribe who can attend your viva and their respective roles. Each of these people have prescribed responsibilities in the examination process and you ought to appreciate how they relate to you as the candidate (Grabbe, 2003).

Traditionally, most universities appoint one internal and one external examiner for doctoral vivas. However, for staff member candidates, an additional external examiner would be appointed. Remind yourself how these roles and responsibilities are described in the regulations. Examiners fulfil a constitutional role when, under the university's formal charter, they recommend the award of a doctoral degree that also changes the public title that you then legally possess and can use. Their contractual responsibility places legal obligations on them through undertaking specified examining duties. Their scholarly roles are to ascertain the worthiness of submitted theses in making an independent and original contribution to knowledge while also protecting the academic standards of the university.

Additionally, they have a technical role of ensuring that theses accord with the protocols of presentation for doctoral degrees. These roles are discharged through their reports and asking questions of candidates in vivas. Thus, as Baldacchino observed: 'The (doctoral) examiners are essentially gatekeepers to the profession' (Baldacchino, 1995). They discharge these roles in the viva. Figure 12.2 shows how your thesis and the viva are interconnected through these roles being discharged by your examiners.

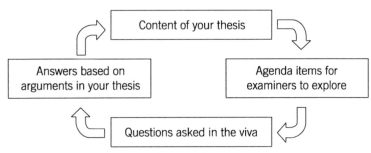

Figure 12.2 Iteration between thesis and viva.

Since the thesis is the focus of the examination process, it is also often the cause of problems in the viva as shown in Example 12.4. The unprofessional situations that are described raise serious questions about how those examiners interpreted their roles and responsibilities. They also should alert you to the (slim) possibility that your examiners might act unprofessionally. If, sadly, this does happen then your diplomatic and negotiation skills need to be exercised to rectify the situation. At the extreme, you could signal your concerns non-verbally to the Chair – if there is one – and to your supervisor(s) in the expectation that they would intervene.

Example 12.4 An experienced examiner's observations on other examiners

I have seen some emotional outbursts during vivas, but more frequently the opposite – anger and frustration. On many occasions, the

> anger on the candidates' part was justified; one examiner clearly hadn't read the thesis, another was very ethnocentric and wanted to know why the candidate hadn't cited her work! Then there was an examiner who was unwilling to accept any answer that the candidate provided. It was very difficult and embarrassing. But, most of the examiners I have worked with have been open-minded, and genuinely respected the work that candidates have produced. In spite of various generic models of vivas and typical questions to anticipate, every viva seems to be a one-off. This is why being an examiner is so interesting!

The presence of Chairs and supervisors should be institutional safeguards against such situations. Some situations arise, however, that a Chair may be quite unaware of and are typified by issues and worries that are taken into the viva room by candidates. As one candidate observed rather pointedly about her forthcoming viva:

> Right from when I registered for my doctorate, I spent my time becoming a better scholar, and so I have no intention of becoming a doctoral victim in my viva. The viva is just another event in my life and for the university too. Examiners have responsibilities to the university, but I have rights. The viva is simply an intellectual encounter between me and my examiners.

Candidates possessing a positive mindset regarding the viva experience, nurtured throughout their studies, should avoid victim attitudes towards the viva event.

This view reflects an inner-directed confidence by the candidate in the quality of the thesis that is not academic arrogance but possession of an internal locus of control (Rotter, 1966). In contrast, candidates with an external locus of control experience a day organised by others and a viva almost completely shaped by their examiners. As outer-controlled persons, these candidates tend not to accept what happens: 'bewail their "bad luck" and (even) cry foul' (Trompenaars and Hampden-Turner, 1997: 232).

The appointment of independent Chairs introduces a welcome demarcation between the functions of examining and numerous other activities that ensure a smoothly conducted viva. Their presence is to facilitate your viva and they have no personal or professional examining function in that process. They perform a range of supportive tasks, which can include:

- ensuring the room layout is acceptable to the examiners and candidate;
- ensuring privacy for the duration of the meeting;
- distributing the independent reports to examiners and to the supervisor(s) when they enter with their candidate;

- meeting and greeting examiners, the candidate and supervisor(s);
- dealing with any refreshments that are provided before, during and following the viva;
- welcoming the candidate to the university, the room and then introducing the participants to one another;
- providing advice on the interpretation of regulations, as appropriate;
- ensuring consistency in proceedings and equity for examiners and candidate alike within the rubric of their university's regulations;
- overseeing the closure of the viva and, often, announcing the examiners' recommendations to the candidate;
- ensuring that the examiners' decision is conveyed to, and understood by, the candidate – unless university regulations provide procedures for this to happen at some other time;
- dealing with the administrative aftermath of the viva.

The twin roles for Chairs are therefore hosting the viva event on behalf of the university and ensuring a satisfactory occasion for all participants. Chairs observe the proceedings to ensure that examiners do not place candidates under undue or discourteous pressure. Thus, Chairs remove non-academic tasks from examiners who can then concentrate on their primary role of examining.

Permitting supervisors to attend vivas is an acknowledgement by universities of the developmental value that such observation offers. After the viva ends, the candidate and supervisor(s) are usually invited to leave the room while the examiners decide on their recommendation. Then the candidate and their supervisor(s) are invited back to hear the outcome of the viva. The presence of supervisors becomes important if examiners require candidates to make alterations to their thesis.

Supervisors will listen as these details are outlined and so they can clarify with the examiners if anything is unclear. Very occasionally, a supervisor may question a recommendation that examiners offer if it does not accord with what transpired during the viva. Their intervention at that time can avoid subsequent misunderstandings of what a candidate is required to alter in the thesis. They may also influence the wording of the examiners' consolidated report and this would determine exactly what subsequent amendments have to be made to a thesis.

During the viva itself, supervisors may only speak if invited to do so by the Chair or an examiner. This is rare. When it occurs, the issue normally concerns the availability of technical equipment, access to specific resources in partner institutions or institutional budgetary matters. In these cases, the original question would not be directly related to the candidate's thesis. Thus, it would be quite legitimate for you to pass such a question via the Chair to your supervisor(s). Their responses would normally be factual and brief and should resolve the matter.

Being present at their candidate's viva enables novice supervisors, as one observed, 'to experience the scholarly debate as an onlooker and recognise now what happened in my own viva'. This extends their appreciation of how theses are examined and contributes to their development as supervisors.

Then there is you – the candidate. Your roles in the viva need to meet three sets of expectations:

- your examiners who hope to engage with you as you successfully defend the scholarship in your thesis;
- your own capability to respond appropriately to every question that examiners put to you.

Your long view preparation for your viva should prepare you to meet your first two role expectations in a mutually satisfactory way (Schein, 1965). If you meet these, then you will also have met the third one, too – your own expectations of successfully defending your thesis.

Getting into the viva room

Rooms used for vivas come in all shapes and sizes from grand board rooms, via someone's office, to 'whatever is available'. Example 11.4, in the previous chapter, shows the advantage of visiting the room before entering it for the first time at your viva.

Example 12.5 Coffee and questions in a viva

I had not seen the dean's room before being ushered into it by his secretary. It was quite large with a small desk, bookshelves along one wall and Venetian blinds on the windows. At the end of the room was a coffee table with cups, jugs and a plate of biscuits. Around it were five people and one empty chair. My supervisor stood and introduced me to the dean, the internal and external examiners and a 'representative from the university who was there to observe the proceedings'. He indicated that the empty chair was mine. The dean asked if I would prefer tea or coffee and then served me, before offering me the plate of biscuits. Throughout my viva, the courtesies of being entertained were respected and at one moment pouring tea took precedence over one of the examiner's questions. Despite the unexpected civility of the occasion, my viva was conducted in a very business-like and academic manner. It was all rather nice.

Example 12.5 shows how a candidate was hosted in a dean's office where his doctoral viva also took place. The faculty's arrangements for this viva seemed to privilege the occasion by creating an informal relaxed ambience without overlooking the academic purpose of the viva. The candidate appeared to have responded favourably to this situation.

Example 12.6 shows how entering their viva rooms may not have been quite what candidates had anticipated.

Example 12.6 On entering the room

Candidate A The room that I entered was narrow, rectangular and long. It contained a polished oak table the length of the room leaving little space around it. One examiner sat at each end of the table with the Chair in the middle facing the door. Two chairs were jammed against the table opposite the Chair. I sat down glancing at my supervisor in mounting dismay, thinking '*How can I possibly relate to people when I can't see both of them at the same time? This is quite wrong.*' My supervisor's face conveyed a feeling similar to my own. Then, the Chair welcomed me, introduced the examiners and announced that I would be recommended for my doctorate at the end of the viva. Suddenly, the room became more acceptable. Afterwards, I complained bitterly to the Chair that an inappropriate room had been allocated for such an important event. I do not know what happened to my complaint.

Candidate B My supervisor was ill and unable to attend my viva. Regrettably, I did not know the inside of the building where my viva would be held and so I walked a long roundabout way to the building. I climbed the stairs to the second floor which made me out of breath. When I reached the corridor, the internal examiner, who I recognised, saw me and said '*Come right in, we have been expecting you.*' Being 15 minutes early might have been a good sign but I was out of breath, needed the toilet and was not ready to answer questions. When I sat down, I was perspiring and uncomfortable. At least the examiners gave me time to relax and put out my notes before the viva started. I was quite tense and not as composed as I had planned to be. After 10 minutes, and sensing that the viva was going well, I mentioned to the external my hasty arrival and how unprepared I had been at the start of the viva. Both examiners instantly apologised and enquired if I needed anything. I asked if they had any objection to me going to the toilet. Returning to the room, I found that someone had refilled my glass of water. We resumed the viva with smiles and a relaxed atmosphere. I was OK then.

Reasonableness suggests that Candidate A was entitled to object to such an unsuitable environment for her viva. Her supervisor shared that view and might have intervened on her behalf but for the Chair's announcement. Perhaps it was arriving 'in a state' that caused Candidate B to overlook the normal common courtesies to which she was entitled. Later, she chose an appropriate moment to intervene and during her absence an examiner had acted courteously. These actions rectified an unfortunate situation. Had her supervisor been able to attend then Candidate B should not have had this experience. These cases support the value of your supervisor(s) attending your viva. If you are asked if they may attend, say Yes.

Example 12.7 provides two contrasting entrances to the viva room – one by a candidate, the other by a supervisor.

Example 12.7 In the first minutes of a viva

Viva 1   The candidate had been an officer in the armed forces. Entering the room, he turned to the examiners and said: *'Gentlemen, once I was the defending officer in a courts martial of someone who was obviously guilty. I was less scared then than I am now.'* The examiners reassured him that he need not be worried since his thesis was good. At that, he pulled a book from his briefcase and placed it in front of the examiners, saying: *'This was published last week right on my topic. But I can tell you that it is not as good as my thesis.'* The examiners laughed as they told him that they too had read the book and arrived at the same conclusion. With some relief, the candidate joined in the laughter.

Viva 2   The supervisor received copies of both examiners' initial reports as he entered the room with his candidate. He had previously arranged to smile warmly at his candidate if both reports were favourable; no smile would indicate a less welcome outcome. Both reports recommended a pass. Overjoyed, he attempted to smile at his candidate who was looking at him expecting to see good news on his face. Instead, she saw (or thought she saw) a grimace that become more severe as he fought to control it and convert it into a smile. His candidate recognised the signal and concluded that the examiners did not like her work. This galvanised her into a series of brilliant answers that prompted one examiner to announce: *'You are going to get your doctorate. We liked your work, so why don't you relax and just enjoy the occasion?'* Only then was the supervisor able to provide his warm smile signal of success.

The unexpected always poses a challenge. The candidate in Viva 1 was perhaps fortunate to have seen the book, but his handling of the news allowed him to show how up to date he was with his literature. He was also fortunate in that it prompted a welcome response from his examiners. The supervisor, in Viva 2, intended to convey restricted information to his candidate but the plan backfired on both of them. Viva 2 warns against introducing potentially dangerous tricks into an arena where tricks have no place. These examples should encourage you, first, to keep up to date with your literature and, second, not to rely on tricks but the inherent merit of your scholarship.

Your examiners will have titles. These may be academic, religious, military or of another form. Custom suggests that when you initially meet them, their formal title should be used. This recognises their formal status and it signifies respect. Many examiners respond by inviting candidates to refer to them by their preferred forename. Until this offer is made by the examiner(s) to you, continue to use their formal titles as a safe option. Honouring this convention avoids you upsetting examiners who may prefer the use of their formal title. They might see a doctoral viva as being precisely when titles should be used. Thus, whatever your personal preferences are on this issue, do not upset an examiner's perceptions of self-status as you shake hands on entering your viva room.

Looking at the examiners

Each of us relates to other people in our own way. We chose intuitively which approach to use. This is automatic once we have seen the context, the people and assessed the situation. It is especially significant if someone is relatively near to us in a room. So let's think about the viva room that will contain two or three examiners, maybe an independent Chair and your supervisor(s).

Before your viva, you should know whether an examiner's expertise is the area of your research or the methodology of your thesis. Your supervisor(s) should be able to advise you how the examiners may relate to each other in the viva. This could revolve around such factors as presumed seniority, professional or personal friendship, examining experience and (assumed) approach to examining. Checking the web may provide additional information to create a profile image of the examiners before you meet them.

When you are shown into the room, keep your right hand free to shake hands with the examiners. This will avoid pausing as you meet them to put down a briefcase or your thesis and any accompanying notes. Getting flustered when you first meet your examiners is good neither for you nor for them.

Then you have to think about your place at the table. Take your time to sit down, making sure that you are comfortable. If the chair is uncomfortable, then change it if necessary. Remove notes, notepad, pens/pencils and the thesis from your briefcase/bag arranging them for easy access. This process may seem to take a long time, but it is usually less than a minute! Why not look up as you are attending to these things and acknowledge the examiners with *Almost finished* or a suitable smile? Finally, check that you have a glass of water nearby. If water is not available for you, then it is reasonable for you to ask for a bottle or a jug. The Chair or supervisor(s) could collect this, with a glass, too, of course.

You may feel inwardly nervous and anxious. Most candidates experience some nervousness. Examiners expect this. Some make no comment about it. Those who are interpersonally sensitive would ask how you feel or suggest that you relax. Some even share an experience from their own viva, explaining how they felt in your position, as a form of reassurance.

Only you can decide when you are ready to start. It is unwise to allow yourself to be pushed into starting your defence before you are fully ready. Remember that it is your opportunity to defend your work and others are present to enable that to happen. They are not there to threaten your intellectual equilibrium in the opening seconds by posing sudden questions. If this happens, then finish what you are doing, and once again, you could use another smile or simply say: *I am ready now. Sorry if I kept you waiting.* The power of a sincere smile works wonders on these occasions.

At this moment, look pleasantly at each examiner inviting an opening question. This should signal your confidence in your work and that you are looking forward to engaging with them in discussing your work. Be positive. The image you are conveying now is of the doctoral candidate about to defend their doctorate.

However, the opening question might be asked too early for you. Without rebuffing the examiner, glance up, saying: *I am almost ready. Do you mind if I just have another moment to arrange my papers/open my thesis/take a sip of water/ remove my spectacles?* You really do need to be mentally and technically prepared to deal with the first question in your doctoral viva. Thus, do not be bounced into a hasty response to your opening question. It is your viva and you must not lose control of it before it has even commenced!

Questions in the viva

Before your first question, one examiner usually makes an opening statement thanking you for submitting your thesis for them to examine. A feature or two will be mentioned as having interested them and then the first question will be put. Over 80% of opening questions take the general form of: *We would like you to explain why you chose this topic for your research topic.*

Examiners differ in how they ask this question, but whatever words they use the question serves two purposes. First, it breaks the ice allowing you to choose what to say and it allows you to set the context for your research. Second, it gets you talking by providing a low-risk issue to open the viva. Examiners will then explore aspects of your answer by asking follow-up questions. Since you will have dealt with this issue thoroughly in the opening chapters of your thesis, you can give an informed and confident reply to this first question. Your viva is now underway.

Your complete attention on the examiner's questions inevitably restricts how you follow the questioning process itself. During her viva, one candidate had not noticed an imposing picture on the wall immediately facing her and between the heads of her examiners. Years later she said: 'I have retained a clear image of both examiner's faces and their eyes. I did not notice the picture until after the viva ended when we returned to the room.' She had focused her complete attention on her examiners for the 1 hour of her viva. You are likely to have a similar experience.

Within the questioning process, there are four distinct phases in doctoral vivas, as shown in Figure 12.3. Questions in each phase of the viva serve

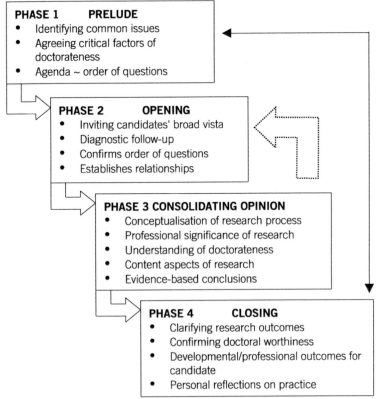

Figure 12.3 Sequential phases of questions in doctoral vivas.

Source: Trafford, 2003a

different discursive and communicative purposes and allow for feedback. Phase 1 is when examiners decide on an outline agenda for their questions before the candidate enters the room. Phase 2 is when examiners and candidates seek to get to know each other through how initial questions are presented and answered, plus associated body language. Phase 3 represents the substantial part of the viva during which engagement and interchange of academic opinions occur. Phase 4 is when examiners and the candidate summarise or reemphasise their central issues to each other, before the viva closes. Relating back to earlier phases enables examiners to introduce different angles on the issue being discussed.

This model explains the differences between vivas in the natural sciences and the social sciences and humanities, as shown in Figure 12.4. This illustrates how the sequencing of questions in natural science vivas customarily follow a linear route through the thesis. Examiners raise their respective questions from their agenda in sequential page order, often starting on page 1. An examiner's explanation for this approach was: 'It has a logic since I would expect the thesis to build its research case in a linear manner and so asking questions that trace that linearity can follow the author's reasoning that should have been put into the writing.'

In the social sciences, the sequencing of questions is iterative between the phases. Examiners often take issues from one phase as the lead into a question from a different phase. An examiner explained the rationale for this style of questioning as: 'Research is so often iterative itself and when it is written up this shows. In any viva, ideas are touched on and sometimes left on the table to be raised later. This exemplifies the process of examining, and answering too, as being a discussion about ideas and their use.' If you have the opportunity, use these models to anticipate how the questioning process is moving in your viva. It may help you to detect the direction of further questions that examiners might ask.

You could perhaps recognise how the four quadrants (see Chapter 2) explained the questions that examiners are asking. Expect to have some questions in Quadrant B, Theoretical Perspectives, and C, Practice of Research. These quadrants represent your research process in action. When examiners ask questions in Quadrant D, Doctorateness, it indicates that they are engaging with you at a conceptual and scholarly level. Continued questioning in Quadrant D normally acknowledges their acceptance of your conceptual grasp and the scholarly merit of your thesis.

Less experienced examiners have a different emphasis in questioning than more experienced examiners. This is illustrated in Table 12.1. In this viva, twice as many of the experienced examiner's questions focused on doctorateness (Quadrant D) than on other aspects of the thesis. The less experienced examiner, in contrast, asked fewer than 10% of the questions in Quadrant D. Extrapolating, crudely, from this evidence, suggests that less experienced examiners will ask you to defend questions from their own safe areas of research expertise – Quadrants A, B and C. These questions address relatively

Natural sciences ~ deliberative linear progression between phases

Social sciences ~ deliberative iteration between phases

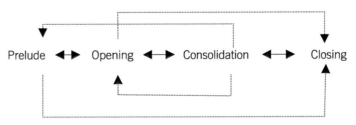

Figure 12.4 Two approaches to sequencing questions in doctoral vivas.

Source: Trafford, 2003a.

low-risk aspects of your research and are therefore more direct for you to defend. Experienced examiners tend generally to ask conceptually probing questions. Thus, expect the conceptual nature of questions that you are asked to be determined by the respective experience of your examiners.

Some vivas are memorable for non-academic reasons, as shown in Example 12.8. These two vivas illustrate the warm-hearted nature of vivas. Examiners enjoy the moment just like anybody else. They also make mistakes as does everyone. The viva is no different, so don't expect it necessarily to be too grand an event.

Table 12.1 Distribution of questions per examiner and per quadrant

Examiners / Quadrants	A	B	C	D	% questions
Less experienced	3	4	4	5	34
More experienced	1	4	6	20	66
Total questions	**4**	**8**	**10**	**25**	**47**
% questions	9	17	21	53	100

Source: Trafford and Leshem, 2002a

Example 12.8 Laughing at vivas

Viva 1   The viva was 10 minutes old when Professor Green said to the candidate: *'I now want to ask you my key question.'* The candidate became even more alert as he listened carefully to the question – and also to Professor Brown's immediate answer to the question. After a moment's silence, both examiners laughed. The candidate joined in quietly and then said: *'Professor Green, I could have answered your question but it would not have been as eloquent as Professor Brown's.'* The examiners applauded this response, everyone smiled at what had happened and the candidate relaxed ready for the remainder of his viva.

Viva 2   The candidate sneezed and apologised in a husky voice for her cold. As she answered each question, her voice became weaker and quieter. In sympathy, the examiners lowered their voices and after 15 minutes the viva was being conducted in whispers. Then one examiner whispered *'Can you speak up, I could not hear what you said.'* The other examiner clapped his hands and said: *'Maybe all of us should raise our voices just a little so that we can hear what each other is saying?'* The candidate smiled, both examiners laughed and the candidate joined in. The viva resumed, with everyone speaking at a slightly higher pitch.

You have some advantages over your examiners in your viva. This is due to your intimate knowledge of your work and thesis. You should be completely conversant with the nuances of your arguments, their implication and relevance to your conclusions. You should also be able, quickly and easily, to locate the section or page(s) to which their questions and your responses refer. This strengthens your ability to defend your work confidently by:

- protecting the intentions and boundaries of your research;
- reflecting questions back that are unrelated to your research;
- seeking clarification if the meaning of questions are unclear;
- giving direct answers to direct questions;
- explaining your answer to ensure understanding of technical details;
- expanding an answer to consolidate your response in its research context;
- developing your response to embrace related concepts that strengthen the reply;
- using the words 'my evidence shows that' to confirm your findings and avoid opinions;
- sharing your research experience with examiners by referring to their own work;

- being open-minded to ideas that propose different perspectives on your work;
- engaging with the collegiality of examiners and their research experience;
- answering questions that relate to your work and avoiding those that do not;
- coping with challenging questions through careful reasoning and explicit analysis.

You have to judge whether your responses are directed back to the person who asked it or to both examiners. Use your knowledge of the examiners and your short experience of seeing them in action to classify questions. Ask yourself if your answer will be more significant to both or just one examiner. If it would be significant to both, then use your eye contact and other forms of non-verbal communication, such as hand or body movements, to involve both examiners in your responses.

If the question is specific to one examiner's expertise, then direct your response initially to that person. Examiners wish to confirm whether your understanding and conceptual grasp of doctoral level research topic is substantial and genuine. You have to convince both examiners of that scholarly capability. Thus, it is imperative that both/all examiners are included in your responses since they will jointly be involved in deciding the recommendation for your award at the end of the viva.

As Murray points out: 'Perhaps what is being tested in a viva is the students' ability to reorientate themselves to this new (for them) communication event' (Murray, 2003: 145). She argues that vivas are a different form of presentation event from that which candidates would normally encounter. To prepare for this she advocates that candidates *repeat practice* in presenting their knowledge to others (Murray, 2003: 144). Preparation like this is important to help you become familiar with predictable categories of questions (Trafford and Leshem, 2002b) (see Chapter 3). Then you can answer those questions that invite you to extend ideas, models and conceptualisations in the text itself and so build on the merits of your work. In your viva, this is direct engagement by examiners with you in genuine scholarly discussion. Questions have moved beyond examiners discovering if you understand the research process. They have decided that you do. You have, therefore, defended your academic position.

When you provide satisfactory responses to the predictable questions that examiners ask, you are confirming their opinion of scholarly merit in your thesis. However, candidates who do not provide satisfactory answers to these questions will not impress their examiners. For these candidates, their examiners will be unconvinced of their conceptual grasp and the scholarly merit of their thesis (Trafford and Leshem, 2002b). Successful defence of your thesis therefore involves you anticipating examiners' questions and providing answers that confirm your thorough understanding of doctoral-level research processes.

Dynamics in the viva

Some people describe the doctoral viva as a confrontational event. This implies that there will be winners and losers. The same people assume that examiners will dominate the discussion and candidates would be compliant in this process. Both views are unfounded as typifying the majority of vivas. There is no doubt that some examiners are aggressive in manner and mode of questioning. However, some candidates have reserved personalities, being neither effusive nor challenging of opposite opinions. If these personality types meet in a viva then its dynamics may, just may, fit into a confrontational format.

Received wisdom suggests that examiner–candidate relationships are, in the overwhelming majority of vivas, harmonious, display mutual respect and participants are satisfied with the outcomes. It acknowledges that disagreements arise over interpretations and use of ideas in the research or thesis. The challenging and defending of academic positions, by examiners and candidates alike, justify vivas occupying their unique place in the universal academic tradition of scholarship. But you should have been engaging in this form of intellectual and scholarly discussion throughout your doctoral journey. Thus, encountering it in your viva should pose nothing unusual for you. Think of it as a continuation of your previous discussions, but with other academics.

Examiners expect candidates to 'defend their work'. Their questions may seek clarification of fact from your research, to which you would provide a factual response. That is easy. The majority of their questions, though, are of a higher order of thinking. They require you to interpret what you found and to conceptualise the significance of those facts. At this altitude of thinking, your defence moves beyond explaining to justifying your position through relating your work to that of others. Using the referent of peer-reviewed publications from the corpus, reputable publishers' books and international journal articles, which, of course, you have cited and can confidently introduce into your answers, justifies your response by scholarly association. This is a powerful way for you to defend your scholarship. Examiners recognise it, too.

Your viva is a scholarly event. Examiners will be disappointed if you do not display scholarship in defending your work. This is the foundation of successfully engaging in defending from a scholarly position of recognised authority (Richardson et al., 1990). Taking the long view of preparing for the viva will ensure that your thesis displays the characteristics of doctorateness. This will be found in your research competence, conceptual grasp and self-efficacy which produces scholarly and individual academic strength 'in knowing and understanding' (Higgins, 1994: 2). These features will be evident in your thesis. Thus, the long view will have developed your academic resilience through workshops, presentations and academic exchange.

It is the features of resilience and conceptual grasp that are so necessary to sustain you through your viva. Each supports the other. You will recognise this as you handle examiners' questions and then realise, as many candidates have recalled, that: 'It is not so bad after all. I can answer the questions.' When this happens then you have located your responses within higher levels of thinking than purely descriptive accounts of research. From the perspective of examiners you will therefore have: 'progressed from description to conceptualisation and similarly from micro-levels to meta-levels of thinking. The outcome from these shifts in candidates' thinking would be conceptual understanding' (Trafford, 2008: 285). Demonstrating these features shows 'scholarly self-confidence' and 'a deeper understanding of themselves, and others, as researchers' (Sillitoe and Webb, 2007).

Murray (2003: 89) supports this position when she points out that: 'The written thesis should act as the foundation and source of oral answers in the viva.' She then reminds us – you – that: 'The thesis is the record of your work done. In a sense, all the answers must be there. Certainly the starting point to all answers lies there.' Her comments confirm that there are boundaries to what examiners can reasonably expect you to discuss. You will have stated your research boundaries unambiguously in your thesis and now you can use them in your viva to protect the cohesion and scope of your research.

If you choose to answer a question that is outside those boundaries then it can place you in a potentially dangerous position. First, your response cannot draw on evidence that you have produced through your research or written about in your thesis. This exposes you to talking without evidence-based arguments that are grounded in your doctoral research. Second, in order to respond you will have to answer from your own opinion or other information that you may posses. This could be peripheral to, or even distant from, your doctoral investigation and so you are departing from your knowledge base that should be at the centre of the viva discussion. Third, by answering the first question, you are tacitly indicating a willingness to answer other questions on the topic – which, of course, are also likely to be outside your research boundary. One question can then lead to another one on the same area. Finally, your response to an initial inappropriate question may influence how an examiner then views your knowledge in that area. Thus, you have not advanced your cause by answering that question and may even have damaged your position in the eyes of the examiner who asked it.

You should be on safe ground as you respond to questions that relate to what you have written about in your thesis. This is the primary purpose of you and your examiners being together in the same viva room. If either you or they depart from that specific area for discussion it may not be of mutual benefit. You may, though, chose to answer such a question because it enables you to touch lightly on the topic before then adroitly sliding your response back into your own research area.

However, if it is obvious that the examiners have moved into a discursive mode with you, then they may be inviting you to open up the discussion away from your topic. This occurs when they are satisfied that you deserve to pass. In these situations, the examiners wish to move their relationship with you away from examiner–candidate to one of professional collegiality. Here, they have acknowledged your recognised expert knowledge. If this happens in your viva, you will recognise it by the obvious change in formality, a more relaxed body language of the examiners and their less formal mode of questioning. Some examiners would not adopt this relationship because they prefer to remain in a rather formal relationship with you throughout the viva. That is their personal style of doctoral examining.

Protecting your research boundaries is so important. Occasionally, a question is asked in goodwill, quite intentionally and properly that is on the boundary of your research. In this case, the examiner may simply hope to hear you expand on the potential significance of your work or findings. You have to judge why the examiner asked that question. You may decide to answer a question of this sort. If so, then you could open your response by explaining that it was on the boundary, or outside your research, but in this way you have signalled very clearly how you perceive its relationship to your research. Then, you might close your reply by thanking the examiner for the interesting question and look at both examiners ready to resume the viva.

Examiners could ask a question that is beyond the scope of your research. If this happens, you should be able to refer to the page in your thesis where the boundaries are stated. Alternatively, you can gently remind examiners that the question is outside your boundaries. Example 12.9 shows how examiners and a candidate viewed these occurrences in different vivas.

Example 12.9 Respecting research boundaries

Examiner A   I recognised immediately how the candidate had defined the limit of the thesis and its particular contribution to knowledge. It was absolutely explicit. That was good.

Examiner B   The candidate deflected one or two difficult questions that I asked by explaining that they fell outside the remit she had chosen. She even invited my colleague to discuss the issue after the viva because it interested her!

Candidate A   The examiner's statement was so long that when he finished I was unsure what the question was or how to answer it. So, I asked him to say what he really meant. He did and I answered the question now knowing what it meant.

Candidate B   In retrospect, I enjoyed the experience because I did not need to fight over issues that were not part of my thesis. My examiners only asked about the work that I had done. I appreciated that.

These accounts show how examiners' questions sometimes stray outside the boundaries of the research and how candidates dealt with those situations. You can, of course, revert to themes in your research as precursors to answering such questions:

- My research only sought to . . .
- The components of my conceptual framework indicate that . . .
- My conclusions correspond with/differ from/extend the work of . . .
- The variables in my research model were based on the work of . . .
- My conclusions relate directly back to the origins for the research because . . .
- My evidence shows that . . .

Each of these opening gambits reinforces your position in explaining and defending your research. The final gambit is a neat way of reminding an examiner that your research had outcomes and then to explain what those outcomes were. They are verbal tactics to make sure that the examiners focus their attention on what you are at your viva to defend. However, if the research quality of a thesis is poor, then candidates could not really use such gambits. If they did, then it would further confirm to examiners that they did not understand the research process.

There is truth in the adage: *Don't try to defend the thesis that examiners would have written if they had written your thesis.* Tensions will rise if candidates suspect that an examiner is examining the thesis that they would have written, but didn't. Point out, by referring to page numbers in your thesis, precisely what you sought to investigate in your thesis. Concede, by all means, that you could have defined, designed and conducted your research differently if you had adopted another paradigm for the research topic and methodological approach.

Then explain – again if necessary – why you chose to undertake your doctoral research within the parameters and boundaries that are stated in your thesis. This may open further discussion on your choices, but you can use those boundaries to justify your choice and accompanying delimitation of the research. As a last resort, point out that you are defending what is in your thesis rather than what might have been in another thesis. Although it is a risky strategy, it emphasises your position regarding what you are defending at your viva. You may have to take it from there!

A defence is different from an argument. Defending is when you explain what your work means through drawing on all the Kipling questions (see Chapter 6). It involves raising your level of thinking to provide answers that justify a position or argument. Defending is also not the same as being defensive where you would be unwilling to entertain any critical perspective about your work. Draw on how you handled the 12 components in Figure 3.2 to justify your position. How you explained your use of these research features can then become central to your defence.

Similarly, using the audit instrument (see Figure 10.1) will have focused your attention on how to protect what you set out to do and did. Of course, this presumes that your research was coherently planned, has been appropriately conducted and is written up clearly. You could change the ideas in Figures 3.2 and 10.1 from being originally diagnostic tools for your research into ways that now frame your responses to justify your earlier research decisions.

An element of give and take may creep into the exchange of views since you too are entitled to question the assumptions behind examiners' questions. Avoid sliding into an argument where positions are polarised. This is a prelude to entering a win–lose arena that is not conducive to scholarly discussion. Escape from it by moving to a safe-ground topic of shared views that have already been established by your earlier responses to the examiners.

Oddly, some candidates depart from their usual manner of talking or thinking in their viva. They adopt unfamiliar ways of expressing familiar ideas in an unusual grammatical style. Also, they frequently assume a convoluted form of talking that only introduces confusion for their listeners. Not surprisingly, examiners see through this façade. It is much easier to be yourself – especially when the work that you are defending is your own.

Examiners may not ask you many directly factual questions requiring either yes or no answers. They are more interested in hearing your reflections on your research practice. Their open-ended questions let you explain how you reflected on your research actions at the time (Schön, 1983: 353). They also seek deeper meanings in your interpretation of your research experience as an adult learner (Johnson, 2001). Or, you can introduce personal evidence from a reflective diary that you maintained during your doctoral studies (Glaze, 2002; Leshem and Trafford, 2006). This perspective on how your viva may proceed is shown in Figure 12.5.

Figure 12.5 portrays how the dynamics of your viva is a layered process. The three factors of doctorateness, emotional resilience and the viva itself evolve into willingness to defend, personal enthusiasm for your research and confidence in the merits of your research. The presence of these characteristics can generate synergy where the whole – your contribution to your viva – is greater than the sum of its parts. In practice, this means that if you have prepared for your viva by taking the long view of it, then you should be confident that your thesis contains a substantial and defensible story. This will have taken your readers from understanding how you discovered a gap in knowledge through to you claiming, as a very experienced examiner/supervisor suggested *a modest contribution to knowledge that is plausible and which can be defended*. Your research story will therefore self-evidently display doctorateness.

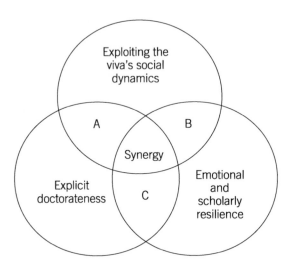

Legend for the overlapping areas

A   Enthusiasm and excitement about the research and the thesis and its contribution to knowledge.

B   Willingness and ability to defend the 'I believe' factor of doctorateness in the thesis.

C   Confidence in the architecture, design, conduct and conceptual conclusions of the research.

Figure 12.5   Domains of defence and location of synergy.

Looking back and ahead

This chapter has argued that the dynamics of your doctoral viva originated some time before the day of your viva. Taking this long view of how you can achieve doctorateness in your viva, coupled with seeking to influence what happens throughout the day of your viva, meld into the dynamics of your doctoral viva. This perspective allows you to plan how you would wish your day to proceed and then seek to control those features that are within your gift.

Our final chapter is an epilogue and an observation or two.

Epilogue: Arriving back at where we started

You have now almost reached the final page of this book. When we explained in the introduction why we wrote the book we hope that you were intrigued and have enjoyed the intervening chapters as your own stepping stones to doctorateness.

We have presented considerable evidence from the doctoral experiences of candidates and supervisors. However, the experience of examiners provides the theoretical underpinning for our writing. Without their comments on how they apply assessment criteria to judge the scholarly merit of doctoral theses, there would be no book. More than once, we have suggested that their comments form a template against which you can compare your progress and readiness to submit your thesis for examination.

A number of potential agendas have been presented for you to adapt and use. These items have included:

- exploiting the literature to support your research;
- raising the doctoral level quality of your research;
- emphasising conceptual aspects of the research process;
- taking the long view of preparing for your viva;
- managing the day of your viva;
- anticipating predictable questions that examiners ask in the viva;
- engaging positively in scholarly discussion with the examiners as you defend your doctoral research.

Supervisors and candidates can use such agendas as they seek to produce high-quality research that contains scholarly depth.

If you read this book as a candidate, then you have been one of our primary readers. You will recognise that, just like you, we sought to meet the needs of our own diverse readership. If you are a supervisor or examiner, then we hope that you found the chapters refreshing in how they packaged information that must have been familiar, at least in parts!

The notion of doctorateness infuses our text. It really represents what holders of doctorates demonstrate as personal capabilities and qualities when they engage in postdoctoral research. That is their hallmark of competence. It is generic since it transcends disciplines and fields of study or interest. As we saw in the examples, many examiners draw on their personal image of post-doctoral research scholarship as a yardstick to judge the merit of a thesis and a candidate. Their projection of such academic expectations into the viva room introduces a fascinating challenge to candidates and supervisors alike.

The various instruments and tasks that you met in the chapters were intended to raise your level of thinking about the doctoral process. For these reasons, we chose deliberately not to present examples of administrative practices concerned with the doctoral degree that were specific to any one university. Most of these procedures and practices are easily available now on university websites or by request if you want to see what they contain. Documents of this type are useful as they explain and describe how universities operate their doctoral processes. Unless you are registered, supervise or examine at a particular university, then such details are unlikely to be of immediate value to you. Certainly, they will acquaint you with the procedures of universities other than your own, but that was not our purpose in writing this book. Instead, we focused attention on those generic aspects of the doctoral process that are not proceduralised or open to public scrutiny.

By displaying the episteme of doctoral research you are thinking about the research process as a serious researcher. The ideas in the book have been presented to ensure that your thesis demonstrates doctorateness. We have argued that there is no one single feature of your thesis on which doctorateness depends. The notion of doctorateness contains multiple components. All have to be evident in your research and thesis for examiners to recognise the doctoral level quality of your research.

Our emphasis on conceptual aspects of the doctoral process, the thesis and the viva, was intentional. International evidence plus widespread professional experience shows that examiners devote considerable attention to the theoretical and conceptual aspects of doctoral theses. This stems directly from the intellectual tradition and corpus in which theses are set and to which contributions to knowledge are made. Thus, our focus has been on those critical features which, if present, will align a thesis with the conceptual expectations of examiners. If those features are missing from a submitted thesis, then the candidate who seeks to defend it will be at a major disadvantage.

Just as doctorateness has many components, so too do the research processes that lead to it. Accompanying this epilogue is a checklist of those familiar features that always receive attention by candidates who produce high-quality research. That is why it *is* high-quality research! None of the items that it contains is difficult or challenging for you to include in your thesis. Including them in your schedule as you undertake your research, write your text or defend your thesis should be easy. Having done it you will then have strengthened the foundations of your research. You should also have avoided responding 'oh dear' to a question about something that you have overlooked.

Two examiners conducted a viva entirely as an extended discussion. They were both satisfied with the scholarly quality of the thesis and so were more concerned to explore the ideas that the candidate had about this topic and its wider implications. The final question, when that discussion ended, was *What have you learned from your years of doctoral study?* The candidate's reply was: *I now appreciate the role and value of good theory*. Perhaps this is a subplot of this book that you have now finished reading!

In Chapter 2, we introduced a quotation from T.S. Eliot: *The end is where we start from*. Those few words capture the intentions of the approach that we have taken in this book. Now we close with some further lines from T.S. Eliot (1974: 209) that are equally appropriate for researchers to think about as they approach the end of their doctoral quest:

> *We shall not cease from exploration*
> *And the end of all our exploring*
> *Will be to arrive where we started*
> *And know the place for the first time.*

Something for doctoral candidates to think about

Compose a title for your doctoral research that is succinct, clearly expressed and not stated in the form of a question – then it will have the potential to attract and interest your readers.

Decide on the gap in knowledge that your research will fill, or the specific area of knowledge to which it will contribute. Explain how this guided your choice of research design, fieldwork and the method of analysing your evidence. Then, in the section of conceptual conclusions within your conclusion chapter, state quite unambiguously how this quest has been met.

Explain explicitly the paradigm(s) for your research topic and for your research approach.

State your research approach as assertions, followed by a full explanation of research choices.

Remember that you are writing for examiners to read. They are your primary audience. Ensure that they find evidence that you are displaying doctorateness in your thesis.

State your research boundaries, reminding readers in the design and conclusions chapters so that they do not expect you to deal with issues that are outside the remit of your research.

Offer explicit research questions in your introductory chapter, remind readers in the design chapter of them and then give the answers to these questions in the conclusions chapter!

Please do not have a chapter entitled 'literature review'. Instead, write a chapter/chapters of theoretical perspectives from which you can produce a clearly stated conceptual framework.

Show how doctorateness can be found by stating, in the both the introductory and the concluding chapters, what specific characteristics of doctorateness your thesis displays.

Accept that you are engaged in an academic marketing exercise. *You* are persuading readers – examiners – that your work is at the doctoral standard. *You* must ensure that you achieve that quest by checking academic and technical arguments which can support that claim.

Recognise that the content/subject part of your research must be accurate and relevant – so it must cite the primary and secondary sources that examiners expect to see in your thesis.

Note how your research might be improved and offer a critique of your own work. Be honest. Be fair to good work. Be open about other ways that it might have been undertaken. Be critical.

Help your readers. *Explain*. Guide them through the text. *Explain*. Introduce parts or/and chapters. *Explain*. Avoid surprises. *Explain*. Your thesis is *not* a mystery story. *EXPLAIN*.

Compose your text with care, recheck the grammar and proofread it again – so that the examiners are not distracted by typographical errors, grammatical mistakes or sloppy writing.

Always think how you will defend your doctoral thesis as you write your doctoral thesis.

Check that every reference in the text appears within a list of references, which follows your final chapter. *Do not include any reference in that list that is not included in the text of your thesis*. Thus, a bibliography of 'other sources' contributes *no* scholarship to a doctoral thesis.

Never forget that your thesis is going to be judged *more* on its conceptual foundations and rigorous analysis than on the factual findings. **Thus**, give yourself a conceptual framework to work with and then make sure that you explain how it has guided your research.

References

Andrews, R. (2003) *Research questions*. London: Continuum.

Baldacchino, G. (1995) Reflections on the status of doctoral defence. *Journal of Graduate Education*, 1, 71–76.

Barker, J.A. (1992) *Paradigms*. New York: HarperCollins.

Bell, J. (1987) *Doing your research project*. Milton Keynes: Open University Press.

Bell, J. (2005) *Doing your research project*, 4th edn. Maidenhead: Open University Press.

Bentley, P.J. (2006) *The PhD application handbook*. Maidenhead: Open University Press.

Berger, R.M. and Patchner, M.A. (1988) *Implementing the research plan*. Newbury Park, CA: Sage.

Bergquist, P. (2004) Advice from the examiners. In Burton, S. and Steane, P. (eds) *Surviving your thesis*. London: Routledge.

Bernstein, D. (1984) *Company image and reality*. Eastbourne: Holt, Rinehart & Winston.

Blaxter, L., Hughes, C. and Tight, M. (1996) *How to research*. Buckingham: Open University Press.

Blumer, H. (1969) *Symbolic interactionism: perspective and method*. Englewood Cliffs, NJ: Prentice-Hall.

Bouma, G.D. (1993) *The research process*. Oxford: Oxford University Press.

Boyer, E.L. (1990) The scholarship of engagement. *Journal of Public Service and Outreach*, 1, 11–20. In van der Ven, A. *Engaged scholarship*. Oxford: Oxford University Press.

Bryman, A. (1988) *Quantity and quality in social research*. London: Routledge.

Bryman, A. (2001) *Social research methods*. Oxford: Oxford University Press.

Bunton, D. (1998) Linguistic and textual problems in PhD and MPhil theses: an analysis of genre moves and metatext. Unpublished PhD thesis, University of Hong Kong. In Swales, J.M. (2004) *Research genres: exploration and applications*. Cambridge: Cambridge University Press.

Burgess, A. (1973) The art of fiction. *The Paris Review*, 56, 121–125. In Zerubavel, E. (1999) *The clockwork muse*. Harvard: Harvard University Press.

Burnham, P. (1994) Surviving the viva: unravelling the mystery of the PhD oral. *Journal of Graduate Education*, 1, 30–34.

Burnham, P. (1997) *Surviving the research process in politics*. London: Pinter.

Burrell, G. and Morgan, G. (1979) *Sociological paradigms and organisational analysis*. Aldershot: Gower.

Burton, S. and Steane, P. (eds) (2005) *Surviving your thesis*. London: Routledge.

Buzan, T. (2005) *Mind map*. London: Thorsons.

Caffarella, R.S. and Barnett, B.G. (2000) Teaching doctoral students to become scholarly writers: the importance of giving and receiving critiques. *Studies in Higher Education*, 25, 1, 39–51.

Cheney, T.A.R. (2005) *Getting the words right*, 2nd edn. Cincinnati, OH: F+W Publications.

Cohen, L., Manion, L. and Morrison, K. (2000) *Research methods in education*, 5th edn. London: Routledge Falmer.

Covey, R. (1989) *The habits of highly effective people*. New York: Fireside.

Creswell, J.W. (1998) *Qualitative inquiry and research design: choosing among five traditions*. London: Sage.

Czikszentmihalyi, M. (1990) *The art of seeing: an interpretation of the aesthetic encounter*. Los Angeles: Getty.

Czikszentmihalyi, M. (2000) *Beyond boredom and anxiety*. San Francisco: Jossey-Bass.

Davis, J.M. (2007) Rethinking the architecture. *Action Research*, 5, 2, 181–198.

Denicolo, P. (2003) Assessing the PhD: a constructive view of criteria. *Quality Assurance in Education*, 11, 3, 84–91.

Denicolo, P. and Boulter, C. (2002) Assessing the PhD: a constructive view of criteria. UK Council for Graduate Education Research Degree Examining Symposium, London. April.

Dissanayake, E. (2002) *What is art for?* Seattle, WA: University of Washington Press.

Dunleavy, P. (2003) *Authoring a PhD*. Basingstoke: Palgrave Macmillan.

Dunton, R. (2004) Developing a research proposal. In Burton, S. and Steane, P. *Surviving your thesis*. London: Routledge.

Eliot, T.S. (1974) *The four quartets: collected poems, 1909–1962*. London: Faber & Faber.

Evans, D. and Gruba, P. (2002) *How to write a better thesis*, 2nd edn. Carlton: Melbourne University Press.

Finn, J.A. (2005) *Getting a PhD*. London: Routledge.

Fuller, S. (2006) *Kuhn v Popper*. Cambridge: Icon Books.

Gaardner, J. (1997) *Hello. Is anybody there?* London: Orion. In Winter, R., Griffiths, M. and Green, K. (2000) The 'academic' qualities of practice: what are the criteria for a practice-based PhD? *Studies in Higher Education*, 25, 1, 25–37.

Gladwell, M. (2005) *Blink*. London: Penguin.

Glaser, B. and Strauss, A. (1967) *The discovery of grounded theory*. Chicago: Aldine.

Glaze, J. (2002) PhD study and the use of a reflective diary: a dialogue with self. *Reflective Practice*, 2, 2, 153–166.

Grabbe, L.L. (2003) The trials of being an external examiner. *Quality Assurance in Education*, 11, 2, 128–133.

Hart, C. (1998) *Doing a literature review: releasing the social science research imagination*. London: Sage.

Hart, C. (2001) *Doing a literature search*. London: Sage.

Hart, C. (2005) *Doing your master's dissertation*. London: Sage.

Hartley, J. (1997) Writing the thesis. In Graves, N. and Varma, V. (eds) *Working for a doctorate*. London: Routledge.

Hartley, J. and Fox, C. (2002) The viva experience: examining the examiners. *Higher Education Review*, 35, 1, 24–30.

Hartley, J. and Jory, S. (2000) Lifting the veil on the viva: the experiences of psychology candidates in the viva. *Psychology Teaching Review*, 9, 2, 76–90.

Herbert, M. (1990) *Planning a research project*. London: Cassell.

Higgins, G.O. (1994) *Resilient adults: overcoming a cruel past*. San Francisco: Jossey-Bass.

Hills, J. and Gibson, C. (1992) A conceptual framework for thinking about conceptual frameworks: bridging the theory–practice gap. *Journal of Educational Administration*, 30, 4, 4–24.

Holbrook, A., Bourke, S., Fairbairn, H. and Lovat, T. (2007) Examiner comment on the literature review in PhD. theses. *Studies in Higher Education*, 32, 3, 337–356.

Hughes, J. (1976) *Sociological analysis: methods of discovery*. London: Nelson.
In Rose, G. (1982) *Deciphering sociological research*. London: Macmillan.
Hussey, J. and Hussey, R. (1997) *Business research*. Basingstoke: Macmillan.
Hutton, G. (1972) *Thinking about organization*, 2nd edn. Bath: Bath University Press/ Tavistock Publications.
Jackson, C. and Tinkler, P. (2000) The PhD examination: an exercise in community-building and gate-keeping? In McNay, I. (ed.) *Higher education and its communities*. Buckingham: SRHE/Open University Press.
Johnson, H. (2001) The PhD student as an adult learner: using reflective practice to find and speak in her own voice. *Reflective Practice*, 2, 1, 54–63.
Joyner, R.W. (2003) The selection of external examiners for research degrees. *Quality Assurance in Education*, 11, 2, 123–127.
Kamler, B. and Thomson, P. (2006) *Helping doctoral students write: pedagogies for supervision*. Abingdon: Routledge.
Kane, E. (1985) *Doing your own research*. London: Marion Boyars Publishers.
Kipling, R. (2004) *Just so stories*. London: CRW Publishing Limited.
Koch, T. (2004) Expert researchers and audit trails. *Journal of Advanced Nursing*, 45, 2, 134–135.
Kuhn, T.S. (1996) *The structure of scientific revolutions*, 3rd edn. Chicago: University of Chicago Press.
Lawton, D. (1997) How to succeed in postgraduate study. In Graves, N. and Varma, V. (eds) *Working for a doctorate*. London: Routledge.
Leshem, S. (2007) Thinking about conceptual frameworks in a research community of practice: a case of a doctoral programme. *Innovations in Education and Teaching International*, 44, 3, 287–299.
Leshem, S. and Trafford, V.N. (2006) Stories as mirrors: reflective practice in teaching and learning. *Reflective Practice*, 7, 1, 9–27.
Leshem, S. and Trafford, V.N. (2007) Overlooking the conceptual framework. *Innovations in Education and Teaching International*, 44, 1, 93–105.
Lewin, K. (1952) *Field theory in social science: selected theoretical papers* (D. Cartwright, ed.). London: Tavistock.
Major, L.E. (1994) A very British stew. *The Times Higher Educational Supplement*. 8 July.
Mason, J. (1996) *Qualitative researching*. London: Sage.
May, T. (1993) *Social theory: issues methods and process*. Buckingham: Open University Press.
Miles, M.B. and Huberman, A.M. (1984) *Qualitative data analysis: a sourcebook of new methods*. London: Sage.
Mulgan, G. (1997) *Connexity*. Harvard: Harvard Business School Press.
Mullins, G. and Kiley, M. (2002) 'It's a PhD, not a Nobel Prize': how experienced examiners assess research theses. *Studies in Higher Education*, 27, 4, 369–386.
Murphy, G.L. and Medin, D.L. (1999) The role of theories in conceptual coherence. In Margolis, E. and Laurence, S. (eds) *Concepts*. Cambridge, MA: MIT Press.
Murray, R. (2002) *How to write a thesis*. Buckingham: Open University Press.
Murray, R. (2003) *How to survive your viva*. Maidenhead: Open University Press.
Murray, R. (2005) *Writing for academic journals*. Maidenhead: Open University Press.
Murray, R. and Moore, S. (2006) *The handbook of academic writing: a fresh approach*. Maidenhead: Open University Press.
Neumann, R. (2004) Resource issues in undertaking postgraduate research. In Burton, S. and Steane, P. (eds) *Surviving your thesis*. London: Routledge.
Oliver, P. (2004) *Writing your thesis*. London: Sage.

Oppenheim, A.N. (1992) *Questionnaire design, interviewing and attitude measurement.* London: Pinter.

Packard, V. (1957) *The hidden persuaders.* Brooklyn, NJ: Ig Publishing.

Parahoo, K. (2006) *Nursing research: principles, process and issues.* Basingstoke: Palgrave Macmillan.

Park, C. (2003) Levelling the playing field: towards best practice in the doctoral viva. *Higher Education Review*, 36, 1, 47–67.

Parry, G. (2007) Mists of time. *Making history: antiquities in Britain 1707–2007.* The Royal Academy, London: Thames & Hudson.

Parsons, T. and Shills, E.A. (eds) (1951) *Toward a general theory of action.* Cambridge: Cambridge University Press.

Pearce, L. (2005) *How to examine a thesis.* Maidenhead: Society for Research into Higher Education/Open University Press.

Pennac, D. (2006) *The rights of the reader* (S. Adams, trans). London: Walker Books. [Original title *Comme un roman.* Paris: Galliard Jeunesse, 1992.]

Perkins, D. (2003) Making thinking visible. New Horizons for Learning. http://127.0.0.1:4664/cache?event_id=52032&schema_id=8&q=David+Perkins&s=RI (accessed 1 May 2006).

Perkins, D. (2006) Constructivism and troublesome knowledge. In Meyer, J.H.F. and Land, R. (eds) *Overcoming barriers to student understanding: threshold concepts and troublesome knowledge.* London: Routledge.

Phillips, E.M. and Pugh, D.S. (2000) *How to get a PhD* (3rd edn). Buckingham: Open University Press.

Prose, F. (2006) *Reading like a writer.* New York: HarperCollins.

Punch, K.F. (2000) *Developing effective research proposals.* London: Sage.

Quality Assurance Agency (2007) UK Descriptor for qualifications at doctoral (D) level. http://www.grad.ac.uk/cms/ShowPage/Home_page/Policy/National_policy/QAA_code_of_practice/p!eLaeXjl#UK%20Descriptor%20for%20qualifications%20at%20Doctoral%20(D)%20level (accessed 31 October 2007).

Richardson, G.E., Neiger, B.L., Jensen, S. and Kumpfer, K.L. (1990) The resiliency model. *Health Education*, 21, 6, 33–39.

Robson, C. (1993) *Real world research.* Oxford: Blackwell.

Robson, C. (2002) *Real world research*, 2nd edn. Oxford: Blackwell.

Rose, G. (1982) *Deciphering sociological research.* London: Macmillan.

Rotter, J.B. (1966) General expectations for internal versus external control of reinforcement. *Psychological Monograph*, No. 609, 1–28.

Rudestam, K.E. and Newton, R.R. (1992) *Surviving your dissertation: a comprehensive guide to content and process.* London: Sage.

Rugg, G. and Petre, M. (2004) *The unwritten rules of PhD research.* Maidenhead: Open University Press.

Salmon, P. (1992) *Achieving a PhD: ten students' experience.* Stoke-on-Trent: Trentham Books.

Sardar, Z. (2000) *Thomas Kuhn and the science wars.* Cambridge: Icon Books.

Schein, E.H. (1965) *Organizational psychology.* Englewood Cliffs, NJ: Prentice-Hall.

Schön, D.A. (1983) *The reflective practitioner.* London: Maurice Temple Smith.

Sillitoe, J. and Webb, J. (2007) Facilitating the active interplay between the conceptual and methodological aspects of a higher degree research project – Gowin's *Vee heuristic.* In Enhancing Higher Education, Theory and Scholarship, Proceedings of the 30th HERDSA Annual Conference, Adelaide. 8–11 July.

Taylor, S. and Beasley, N. (2005) *A handbook for doctoral supervisors*. London: Routledge.

Tietze, S., Cohen, L. and Musson, G. (2003) *Understanding organizations through language*. London: Sage.

Tinkler, P. and Jackson, C. (2000) Examining the doctorate: institutional policy and the PhD examination process in Britain. *Studies in Higher Education*, 25, 2, 167–180.

Tinkler, P. and Jackson, C. (2004) *The doctoral examination process*. Maidenhead: Open University Press.

Trafford, V.N. (2003a) *Views from inside doctoral vivas*. Richmond College, London: UK Council for Graduate Education Conference.

Trafford, V.N. (2003b) Questions in doctoral vivas: views from the inside. *Quality Assurance in Education*, 11, 2, 114–122.

Trafford, V.N. (2008) Conceptual thresholds as a threshold concept in doctorateness. In Land, R., Meyer, J.F.H. and Smith, J. (eds) *Threshold concepts within the disciplines*. Rotterdam: Sense Publications.

Trafford, V.N. and Leshem, S. (2002a) Anatomy of a doctoral viva. *Journal of Graduate Education*, 3, 2, 33–40.

Trafford, V.N. and Leshem, S. (2002b) Starting at the end to undertake doctoral research: predictable questions as stepping stones. *Higher Education Review*, 35, 1, 31–49.

Trafford, V.N. and Woolliams, P. (2002) Wisdom development through stealth landscapes in two professional doctoral programmes. In Kroath F. and Trafford, V.N. (eds) *A conference tells its story*. Chelmsford: Earlybrave.

Trompenaars, F. and Hampden-Turner, C. (1997) *Riding the waves of culture*. London: Nicholas Beasley Publishing.

van der Ven, A.H. (1989) Nothing is quite so practical as a good theory. *Academy of Management Review*, 14, 4, 486–495.

von Bertalanffy, L. (1969) *General system theory: foundations, development, applications*. New York: George Brazillier.

Vygotsky, L.S. (1978) *Mind in society: the development of higher psychological processes*. Cambridge, MA: Harvard University Press.

Wallace, S. and Marsh, C. (2001) Trial by ordeal or the chummy game? Six case studies in the conduct of the British PhD viva examination. *Higher Education Review*, 34, 1, 35–59.

Walliman, N. (2005) *Your research project*, 2nd edn. London: Sage.

Weaver-Hart, A. (1988) Framing an innocent concept and getting away with it. *UCEA Review*, 24, 2, 11–12.

Wellington, J., Bathmaker, A.-M., Hunt, C., McCullough, G. and Sikes, P. (2005) *Succeeding with your doctorate*. London: Sage.

Wenger, E. (1998) *Communities of practice: learning, meaning and identity*. Cambridge: Cambridge University Press.

Whetten, D.A. (1989) What constitutes a theoretical contribution? *Academy of Management Review*, 14, 4, 490–495.

White, B. (2000) *Dissertation skills for business and management students*. London: Continuum.

Wilmoth, S. (2006) Personal communication.

Winter, R., Griffiths, M. and Green, K. (2000) The 'academic' qualities of practice: what are the criteria for practice-based PhD? *Studies in Higher Education*, 25, 1, 25–37.

Wisker, G. (2001) *The postgraduate research handbook: succeed with your MA, MPhil, EdD and PhD*. Basingstoke: Palgrave Macmillan.

Wisker, G. (2005) *The good supervisor*. Basingstoke: Palgrave.

Wisker, G., Robinson, G., Trafford, V., Creighton, E. and Warnes, M. (2003a) Recognising and overcoming dissonance in postgraduate research. *Studies in Higher Education*, 28, 1, 92–105.

Wisker, G., Robinson, G. Trafford, V., Warnes, M. and Creighton, E. (2003b) From supervisory dialogues to successful PhDs: strategies supporting and enabling the learning conversations of staff and students at postgraduate level. *Teaching in Higher Education*, 8, 3, 383–397.

Woolliams, P. (2005) Personal correspondence.

Zerubavel, E. (1999) *The clockwork muse: a practical guide to writing theses, dissertations and books*. Cambridge, MA: Harvard University Press.

Index

Author Name Index

Related books from Open University Press
Purchase from www.openup.co.uk or order through your local bookseller

---

HOW TO FIND INFORMATION 2e
A GUIDE FOR RESEARCHERS
Sally Rumsey

- How do I find relevant information for my thesis, dissertation or report?
- How do I evaluate the relevance and quality of the information I find?
- How do I find the most up to date information in my subject area?

Anyone setting out to research a topic, whether at undergraduate or postgraduate level, needs to find information to inform their work and support their arguments. This book enables researchers to become expert in finding, accessing and evaluating information for dissertations, projects or reports.

The book works systematically through the information-seeking process, from planning the search to evaluating and managing the end results. It suggests how to do this efficiently and effectively whilst using a range of sources including online bibliographic databases and the internet.

This edition has been thoroughly updated to reflect the use of new technologies in research by offering the most contemporary information on:

- Online research
- Critical evaluation of resources
- Intellectual property rights
- Research communities
- The changing landscape of research information
- Subject-specific resources

Written by an academic librarian, this book provides key reading, not only for academic researchers, but for anyone working for commercial, public or government bodies who has to contribute to research projects.

Contents
List of figures – List of tables – List of abbreviations – Foreword to the first edition – Preface – Acknowledgements – The information gathering process – Making the most of a library – Finding information about existing research – The type and detail of information required – Discovering relevant materials – The online searching process – Citation searching – Obtaining the full text – Using the World Wide Web for research – Accessing materials – Evaluation of resources – Citing references – Keeping records – Intellectual property and plagiarism – The research community and keeping up to date – The changing landscape of research – Summary checklist – Appendix 1: Using a library – Appendix 2: Formats of information sources – Glossary – References and bibliography – Web addresses – Index.

2007   248pp
978–0–335–22631–3 (Paperback)